S0-AGD-355

[MIS]MANAGING THE SYSTEM

[MIS]MANAGING THE SYSTEM

HOW TO CHANGE THE SYSTEM

§§§

You can help change The System.

Wesley G. Matthei

Wesley G. Matthei

Copyright © 1997 Wesley G. Matthei

All rights reserved under International and Pan American Copyright
Conventions. No part of this book may be reproduced or transmitted in any
form, by any means, electronic or mechanical, including photocopying,
recording, or any information storage retrieval system, without permission in
writing from the author, except by a reviewer, who may quote brief
passages in a review.

Page 326 constitutes an extension of this copyright page.

Cover design by BizArt
Printed in The United States of America
Published by:
NUSYSTEMS, P.O.Box 14040, Sarasota, FL, 34278

Publisher's Cataloging-in-Publication
(Provided by Quality Books, Inc.)

Matthei, Wesley G.
    (Mis)managing the system : how to change the system/ Wesley G.
    Matthei. -- 1st ed.
    p. cm.
    Includes bibliographical references and index.
    Preassigned LCCN: 94-73196
    ISBN: 0-9658493-0-9

    1. Organizational effectiveness.   2. Organizational change.
    I. Title

HD58.8.M38 1997   658'.001
              QBI97-807

CONTENTS

PART 1: HOW IT IS

PART 2: HOW IT SHOULD BE

TABLES

FIGURES

To those within The System
who are waiting for
real change.

§§§

WARNING—DISCLAIMER

[Mis]Managing The System is intended to provide information regarding how The System influences people in organizations, institutions and in their personal lives. It is sold with the understanding that the publisher and author are not engaged in rendering legal, accounting or other professional services.

It is not the purpose of this book to discuss and document all the information that may be otherwise available to the author or publisher. Its purpose is to educate and entertain: The System is shown to be the active force in an organization. Every effort has been made to present information that is complete and accurate as possible. However, there may be mistakes both typographical and in content. The examples given are indicative of a valid basic concept—how The System works.

The author and publisher shall have neither liability nor responsibility to any person or entity with respect to any loss or damage caused, or alleged to be caused, directly or indirectly by the information contained in this book.

If you do not wish to be bound by the above, you may return the book to the publisher for a full refund upon presentation of the actual receipt of purchase payment.

PREFACE

The purpose of this book is to help people understand how and why organizations and institutions work the way they do. New ideas or concepts that can profoundly affect the performance of organizations are rare, to say the least, and their implementation is even rarer. Most new ideas or concepts that can improve daily work activities are marginal in nature and result in modest improvements at best. Occasionally, however, a new concept is proposed that if implemented could cause major, fundamental changes that significantly improve the performance of any organization or institution. I propose such a new concept in this book. I do so by introducing and developing the concept of The System and how it controls the organization or institution, and by describing a "new" concept of how it can be changed.

While establishing the concept of The System as a valid and extremely critical management tool, *[Mis]Managing The System* proposes means to change The System that if carried out will eliminate the problems normally associated with it. The problems discussed in the book are self-evident and I have not tried to justify my choice of the examples. Although my approach is nonpolitical, I sometimes propose policies or solutions which could have political ramifications. As an example, I suggest an unprecedented way to change the United States Congress in order to make it more efficient and effective.

No other management book treats The System as a valid concept or presents a comprehensive approach to changing The System in a fundamental manner. This book presents a unique method for solving problems that have plagued organizations and institutions for years. Significant fundamental changes in any organization or process can be realized only if top management replaces The System with a New System.

This book is a result of the many lessons that I learned in my career as an individual contributor and manager. My operations management experiences have been both theoretical and practical. During the years I worked in a federal government engineering laboratory, I served as a research solid state physicist, a microwave engineer, a section chief, and a deputy branch chief. While in private industry, I worked as a director of research, an engineering manager, a plant operations manager, a business center manager, a program manager of a classified military program, an acting-director of human resources, a quality control manager, and a government relations manager. I served on many corporate committees and wrote many of the policies and procedures that were generated and implemented by those committees. My management experience extends into many other aspects of my life. I served in the U.S. Navy for approximately one year and for two years in the U.S. Army. I also served, and continue to serve, as an officer or leader in many educational, social, political, and religious organizations.

The genesis of this book was an analysis that I made at work in answer to my question, "How can so many intelligent and outstanding people continue to work so inefficiently and ineffec-tively over long periods?" I was sorely bothered and frustrated over my inability to attract top management's attention to the need for real change. Most of my attempts to have top management address the concept of The System and its implications for the company's long-term future were rejected. Apparently the cor-porate managers had more pressing problems that they felt needed their immediate attention, and their focus were mainly on the quarterly profit and loss (P&L) status.

After years of observing, querying, probing, and analyzing, I finally understood the nature of the problem. The System is the problem. Understanding how it controls an organization and the organization's performance and long-term future is the key to initiating change.

ACKNOWLEDGMENTS

This book is the culmination of values, concepts, ideals, and visions endowed to me by my parents, teachers, pastors, friends and co-workers, and especially my wife and sons. The concept of this book was formulated as a direct result of the experience I received over forty-five years as a volunteer, contributor, and manager.

My "discovery" of The System and how it works led me to propose and promote fundamental changes in the company where I was employed. My mentors and friends, Dr. Frank A. Brand, Dr. Joseph Saloom, Thomas C. Leonard, and Harry Wells, were protective of my efforts to introduce the concept of changing The System into the company. Tom Leonard in particular was especially helpful; he arranged for me to help him introduce basic changes into the division of the company in which he served as president and general manager.

The book reflects the contributions of many people. I should like to extend my appreciation to Mrs. Nancy D. Howland, Librarian of the Jesup Memorial Library, Bar Harbor, Maine, who was extremely helpful in obtaining books and reprints used for background information and references used in the book. I am also grateful to the research staffs of the Selby Public Library, Sarasota, Florida and the University of Maine, Raymond H. Fogler Library, Orono, Maine who assisted me in the acquisition of needed materials.

I am blessed with and indebted to the following friends who read, critiqued, corrected, and counseled me about many initial drafts of the chapters: Howard Ellowitz, Donald Gecks, Vincent Higgins, Marjorie Hults, Raymond Matthei, Charles Skirven, and Edmundas Vambutas. Over the past twenty years my very good friend Dr. Henry Miranda has guided and expanded my thinking about most of the topics dealt with in the book. Without his unrelenting support and specific suggestions I would not have had the confidence to publish this book. So many other people contributed directly or indirectly to this book that I cannot possibly name them, but I should like to thank them for their comments, ideas, and support. The final choice of examples and especially the proposed solutions to changing The Systems are solely mine and do not necessarily reflect the approval of those who gave me their advice on these matters. Clearly, any errors of commission and omission are mine alone.

Special thanks are given to the editor, Karen L. Jacob who has done an excellent job of editing the draft of the manuscript. She has shown me why a professional is needed to edit a book of this type. I should like to thank the editor Sushila Blackman, who suggested many helpful revisions to the text, thus making it more reader friendly and useful.

Most of all, this book would not have been written or published without the constant encouragement and help of my best friend and wife, Marie. She took my hieroglyphics and translated them using a word processor that allowed the generation of many revised drafts of each chapter. She read and criticized all the drafts and contributed to much of the clarity and meaning of the book.

INTRODUCTION

The System controls, manages, and influences everyone in an organized activity. It is indigenous to every organization and institution and affects each one uniquely. Most problems in organizations and institutions are due to The System. This concept bears repeating: People are not the cause of most problems that organizations and institutions have—The System is!

[Mis]Managing The System is not about general systems theory (as it is called today) nor organizational or operations theory. Rather it identifies a broad new concept of The System, and shows how it replaces the management of such organizations. It addresses the need to understand The System first, so as to understand how to address the need to change, and how to carry out change.

The term "The System," as I use it, may be defined as the formal and informal management process and operation of the way things actually work, and the rationale for social or other transactions that occur or do not occur in an organization or institution. The general but limited concept of a System continues to be discussed in the literature. In *Thriving on Chaos*, Tom Peters states that "Systems are more important than ever, principally because today's systems cause real harm."[1] *[Mis]Managing The System* suggests, among other things, that this is correct.

This book identifies the major reason many organizations are not significantly changing and improving their performances on a continuing basis: The System and not top management controls the organization, and its basic objective is to maintain itself by promoting the status quo. The book explains how most organizations operate, and how difficult it is to initiate significant change, that is, improvements that enhance an organization's products and services. A new concept of how The System must be changed is presented: A second-order change, i.e., a change function, is required to implement fundamental changes to The System, resulting in a New System. Changing management attitudes, changing The System, and maintaining a continuous renewal to the concept of total quality management throughout the organization are discussed in detail in the following chapters.

Chapter 1 introduces the concept of The System, and its historical basis. The role of the organization and how it operates and how The System is created and nourished are discussed. Examples are used in order to establish the concept that the general but limited characteristics of The System were well known many years ago, but the concept of The System as an independent, operational entity was apparently never conceived of until now.

Chapter 2 characterizes the symptoms that indicate that The System is in control in an organization. The System's attributes and laws are disclosed for the first time. How the organization is managed and operated by The System is explained in detail.

Chapter 3 discusses the need to change The System and provides quotations about the need to change The System in particular organizations. Representative symptoms of problems that The System controls are discussed in detail.

Chapter 4 gives detailed examples of The System for a representative sample of various organizations and institutions. These Systems are in place today and will continue to control their respective organizations or institutions until fundamental changes are made to The System.

Chapter 5 discusses how to change The System. The significance of the types of change are noted. Various types of approaches for changing The System are identified, and evaluated. Seven steps for changing The System are presented and justified.

Chapter 6 explains the difference between cosmetic changes and fundamental changes to The System and provides a theoretical basis for making structural or fundamental changes. The new concept of a change function is introduced and examples given. The process for changing The System is provided in detail.

Chapter 7 offers examples of my proposed specific change functions that would change The System if top management applied such change functions to their respective organizations or institutions.

Chapter 8 outlines the actions that should be taken in order to apply and maintain a new change function in an organization.

Chapter 9 summarizes the basic concepts that have been presented and also discusses an individual's personal System. To change one's personal System, the same steps that are required to change The System of an organization need to be followed: Understand that The System exists. Have a vision of a New System, with new (personal) goals. Find a change function that will destroy the old and establish a New System. Apply the change function in a timely fashion. Measure and monitor the results of the changes. Maintain renewal of personal empowerment.

The failures of various change functions are analyzed.

The general characteristics of The New System that replaces The System are outlined. The New System follows eleven new laws.

The book shows that the proposition that The System is in de facto control of almost every organization is true. *[Mis]Managing The System* establishes that top management usually has abdicated its leadership function in running the organization and that The System manages and leads the organization. A drastic change function (a second-order change) must be applied to destroy The System and replace it with a New System. It concludes that only top management is able to change The System and therefore top management must either initiate such changes or it must be replaced with a more enlightened System-wise management.

PART 1

§§§

HOW IT IS

CHAPTER 1

The Concept of The System

"It must be considered that there is nothing more difficult to carry out, nor more doubtful of success, nor more dangerous to handle, than to initiate a new order of things."
— Niccolo Machiavelli (1469-1527)[2]

This chapter introduces a new concept of The System. The System as an entity is established naturally but inadvertently by the top management of an organization. The System is greater than the sum of the formal and the informal management controls upon the operations of the organization. Most books and articles on the subject of management use the term "system" in two contexts: the narrow context of a particular process in the organization, and the broader context of an organizational-wide process such as the financial, manufacturing or shipping systems. The term "The System" usually means the ways in which an organization or institution operates. This book establishes the principle that The System exists in every organization and controls its activities and operations. In a few organizations it is actually controlled by the top management. However, except for these few cases, The System itself is the de facto controlling management of the organization. The System is established slowly during the growth of an organization and eventually becomes the protector of the organization's members since it allows them to perform their functions without the close supervision and control of top management. The members of the organization rely on The System to justify their continuing satisfactory performance according to The System's standards. Others have discussed the organization's human nature, mind, life cycles and laws. These issues are covered in this chapter as part of the justification for the concept of The System as the controlling management in most organizations.

1

INTRODUCTION

Management of an organization or institution in today's world is a demanding task. Successful managers have to satisfy their customers, the owners of the organization, their suppliers, their employees or associates, and government laws and regulations. However, most organizations are not performing in a superior manner, and therefore their customers or potential customers may eventually patronize their competition.

This book discusses the way most top managers perform their functions. The book introduces the new concept of The System. The System controls each organization uniquely, and in most organizations The System assumes the role of top management. Top management maintains its methods and operations, but the organization marches to the drum of The System.

This chapter discusses how the organization works and how The System is created and nourished. It establishes the foundation for the concept that The System manages the organization.

People in an organization respond to management based on the response they receive from The System. The importance of how management interacts with The System and the people has been highlighted in the past. Douglas McGregor[3] notes in *The Professional Manager* that under the veneer of formal organizations lie informal organizations in which people "are violating the conventional principles of organization constantly, and in a great many ways." He states in his book that Melville Dalton presents evidence, in *Men Who Manage*, "of the informal ways in which cooperative relationships are established to *circumvent* the formal organizational requirements. Many, but not all, of these are ways of getting the job done *in spite of* what [middle] managers perceive is hampering formal requirements."

McGregor points out that because of the nature of information feedback control Systems:

a human being's perception of information about his own performance involves selection and either acceptance or rejection in varying degrees. [He notes that] the process of responding to feedback of information involves both intellectual and emotional reactions that are largely inseparable [and,] as a result, the human being exercises self-control in his responses. . . . Noncompliance tends to appear in the presence of perceived threat. This noncompliance takes the form of defensive, protective, resistant, aggressive behavior. [To compensate for noncompliance, management usually] introduces administrative procedures into the information feedback loop. These consist in standards of acceptable performance, in objectives, in extrinsic rewards for compliance and punishments for noncompliance.

McGregor lists the unintended consequences of such control Systems. Besides yielding compliance to some degree, they in addition yield:

1.   Widespread antagonism to the controls and to those who
     administer them.
2.   Successful resistance and noncompliance . . . [throughout the
     organization.]
3.   Unreliable performance information. . . .
4.   The necessity for close surveillance. . . .
5.   High administrative costs.

He predicts the following four forms of noncompliance in response to real or perceived threats [my paraphrasing]:

1.   Failure to comply with demands for change.
2.   Ingenuity to defeat the purpose of the control system.
3.   Justification and rationalization for dishonest behavior.
4.   Playing a numbers game in relation to the performance criteria,
     such as ignoring pertinent data, choosing select data, or
     interpreting the data in a prejudicial manner.

[McGregor states that] there is a common and mistaken tendency to attribute a dishonest act by an individual to a characteristic of his personality. . . . A dishonest act by the average man, however, tends to be specific to certain circumstances and is not the manifestation of a general character trait. . . . The error is to seek the cause in the dishonesty of human beings rather than in the pressures to which they were subjected. Just as individuals try to 'beat the system,' organizations try to 'beat the rascals'.

A typical example of bending the rules today is a person using an out-of-tolerance part in a subassembly, because the total assembly would probably meet The System's specifications tolerances.

Bennis and Slater[4] have noted that the social territory of an organization encompasses groups, organizational and cultural norms, and traditions. They state that:

another aspect of the social-territory that has key significance for leadership is the idea of system. For at least two decades, research has been making this point unsuccessfully. . . . The fact that this evidence is so often cited and so rarely acted upon leads one to infer that there is something naturally preferable (on the order of an involuntary reflex) in locating the source of problems in the individual and diagnosing situations as functions of faulty individuals rather than a system of malfunctioning social systems. . . . [In] any case, as one gets entrapped by inertia and impotence, it is easier to blame heros and villains than the system. For if the problems are embroidered into the fabric of the social system, complex as they are, the system can be changed. The effect of locating problems in people rather than systems frequently tends to organizational paralysis because changing human nature often appears to be and frequently is more difficult than changing systems.

The management of a task or project usually involves optimizing input and output of people. The following sections summarize the history of management and are given as background for the basis of The System. Organizational behavior, stages of management, and the natural laws of organizations are shown to lead to the development of The System as a substitute for management or, more rarely, as a tool for management.

MANAGEMENT AND THE SYSTEM

From earliest times, individuals and families practiced management in dealing with each other. Rulers, builders, warriors, hunters, farmers, priests, and tradesmen exercised considerable management skills. One of the early records of organizational management by man is given in the eighteenth chapter of Exodus: "So Moses harkened to the voice of his father-in-law, and did all that he had said. And Moses chose able men out of all Israel, and made them heads over the people, rulers of thousands, rulers of hundreds, rulers of fifties, and rulers of tens. And they judged the people at all seasons: the hard causes they brought into Moses, but every small matter they judged themselves."[5]

In his classic book, *Management*, Drucker[6] points out that management was discovered before there was any management to speak of. He notes that the great English economists Adam Smith, David Ricardo, and John Stuart Mill along with Karl Marx "knew no management. To them business activity was impersonal and objective." Business dealt with commodities, and the behavior of men was thought to be inconsequential. The Frenchman J. B. Say articulated the new concept that "the pivot is not the factors of production. It is the entrepreneur—a word Say coined—who diverts resources from less productive into more productive investments and who thereby creates wealth."

Say was followed by Fourier and Saint-Simon who:

'discussed' management before it actually came into being. Saint-Simon, in particular, saw the emergence of organization. And he saw the task of making resources productive and of building social structures. He saw managerial tasks.

The Scotsman Robert Owen, according to Drucker, became the first manager on record when in the 1820s he "first tackled the problems of productivity and motivation, of the relationship of worker to work, of worker to enterprise, and of worker to management—to this day key questions in management."

So it appeared that management of people therefore required constant communication and interaction *with* people. As the span of supervision became too large for the initiator of the group, other people were delegated authority and responsibility for particular areas. Thus the group became organized with a chain of command structured on the lines of a two-dimensional pyramid.[*] Bennis[7] describes bureaucracy as an organization with the following definitive components:

a well-defined chain of command, a system of procedures and rules for dealing with all contingencies relating to work activities, a division of labor based on specialization, promotion and selection based on technical competence, impersonality in human relations.

Cleland and King[8] state that bureaucracy is:

characterized by a number of fixed jurisdictional areas, each with official duties and with individuals who have authority regarding the discharge of these duties. The "system" operates according to fixed rules of superior and subordinate. Individuals are appointed to official positions by superiors, and their status with respect to subordinates is guaranteed by rules of rank.

Cleland and King note that the bureaucracy's primary advantages have been argued by Max Weber:

"Bureaucratization offers above all the optimum possibility for carrying through the principle of specializing administrative functions according to purely objective considerations. . . . The objective discharge of business primarily means a discharge of business according to *calculable rules* and without regard for persons." . . . The bureaucratic view is that the "passions" of humans must be strictly controlled by their organization in order to effectively direct their energies toward the accomplishment of the organization.

They explain that once management determines the direction the organization should take:

the process of the day-to-day accomplishment of the objectives becomes a matter of organizational routine. . . . Of course, it is just not that simple. Rigid authority patterns do not assure the accomplishment of goals. . . . People are indeed important, and their motivations must be accounted for if goals are to be accomplished efficiently.

---

[*] Today's large conglomerates are actually 3-D pyramids.

Using the basic assumptions of Theory X* articulated by McGregor, most managements probably unconsciously have created centralized organizations that are accompanied by centralized policies, procedures, rules, processes, controls, and environments. Under such conditions, people tend to optimize their behavior in order to maximize their own best interests. This dichotomy between management regulation and people's responsiveness forms The System. The System becomes the controlling entity since it is used by people to shield themselves from the consequences of their mistakes or deficiencies and to further their basic objectives, some of which may coincide with management's goals.

McGregor[9] indicates in *The Human Side of Enterprise* that: progress in any profession is associated with the ability to predict and control. . . . One of the major tasks of management is to organize human effort in the service of the economic objectives of the enterprise. As organizations increase in size, the management of people is increasingly important. Every managerial decision has behavioral consequences. Successful management depends not alone, but significantly, on the ability to predict and control human behavior. . . . Many managers would agree that the effectiveness of their organizations would be at least doubled if they could discover how to tap the unrealized potential present in their human resources.

When management insists upon regulations that people perceive are not in their best interests, then people behave, McGregor says: in ways which tend to defeat organizational objectives. [They can become] resistant, antagonistic, uncooperative. . . . People, deprived of

---

* Theory X assumes that:
  1. The average human being has an inherent dislike of work and will avoid it if possible.
  2. Because of this human characteristic of dislike of work, most people must be coerced, controlled, directed, and threatened with punishment in order to get them to put forth adequate effort toward the achievement of organizational objectives.
  3. The average human being prefers to be directed, wishes to avoid responsibility, has relatively little ambition and wants security above all.

opportunities to satisfy at work the needs that are important to them, behave exactly as we might predict—with indolence, passivity, unwillingness to accept responsibility, resistant to change, willingness to follow the demagogical, unreasonable demands for economic benefits.

People thus use The System to isolate themselves from management. The System functions as management, and the people and top management become passively content with the organization's operation. In most instances, management does not perceive that it has lost control to The System because The System appears to respond to management's overall direction and objectives. The System is like a giant bowl of gelatin dessert: it can be molded into various shapes and moved in response to management's stimulus (pushing) but then it relaxes back to its original shape as management's initiative wanes.

When discussing the merits of positive reinforcement, Peters and Waterman[10] note:

attribution theory attempts to explain the way we assign cause for success or failure. Was it skill? Did we do good? Were we defeated by the system? . . . We typically treat any success as our own and any failure as the system's. If anything goes well, it is quite clear that "I made it happen, I am talented," and so on. If anything bad is happening, "It.'s them, it's the system." Once again, the implications for organization are clear. People tune out if they feel they are failing, because "the system" is to blame. They tune in when the system leads them to believe they are successful.

Most failures or problems are the fault of The System that top management has unfortunately established. In most cases, The System has generated informal policies, procedures, and controls that are inadequate for outstanding performance. Since The System maintains or optimizes the status quo whenever possible, there is little opportunity for individuals to make significant and lasting improvements to The System. Nevertheless, individuals who understand how The System works can bypass and overcome The System's controls and thus improve their personal condition and welfare, and sometimes the organization's well-being. In Peru, for example, overcoming the official economic system is considered pseudo-legal. Black markets are another example of how The System can be surmounted.

ORGANIZATIONAL BEHAVIOR

Organizations are made up of groups of people who generally share a culture of similar aspirations, common goals, and personal values. By definition, the organization creates, maintains, changes, or limits the modes of operation and behavior of its members. The organizational groups thus generate norms through which the organization lives and thrives. In *Productivity: The Human Side,* Blake and Mouton[11] show how norms affect the organization and its ability to perform its function in an outstanding manner. They define a norm as "any uniformity of attitude, opinion, feeling, or action shared by two or more people" and describe how norms are important in organizations.

Groups are characterized by the norms their members share. For all practical purposes, a group could not be a group if it lacked norms to regulate and coordinate interactions among members. The reason is that there would be no basis for coordination or cooperation. If norms were absent, we might refer to the individuals who are physically assembled in the same place as an *aggregate*, but not as a group.

Group norms are used in different contexts. Blake and Mouton state:

A "tradition," for example, is a norm established in the remote past that continues to influence our current behavior. A "precedent" is some action taken at a prior time that served to model a solution to a problem. . . . A "habit" is a typical way of dealing with something almost automatically. . . . A "rule" is an explicit statement of how something should be done. When people accept it as sound and okay, a rule takes on the status of a norm and also governs our attitudes towards specific behavior. The same is true of "regulations." . . . "Policy" also refers to desired uniformities of behavior that define strategic considerations of action. When behavior is consistent with policy, policy has become a norm. The term "standard operating procedure," or SOP, also describes ways in which organization members are expected to act in carrying out their assigned job activities. A "ritual" is a sequence of activities that unfold more or less in a fixed way, and since everyone knows the ritual, the norm for how to implement it is widely shared. A "rite" is the same. . . . A "custom" describes what group members are expected to do, while a "taboo" is a norm that describes what people are expected *not* to do.

These various norms are important to The System; they are reinforced by their de facto acceptance by management. These norms become part of The System and are used by people to explain and justify their output.

They define The System in the following way:

The phrase, "informal system" has been used to characterize the unwritten rules—regulations, policies, traditions, precedents, standard operating procedures that are not formalized in a documented sense but do govern how people act. The informal System is a normative one to which organization members are expected by other organization members to conform.

Thus The System becomes the real management of the organization whenever top management fails to understand The System's existence and function. Blake and Mouton go on to note:

The existence of a norm—and the attitudes that follow from it—is therefore highly significant. It can lead to promoting productivity or restricting output, to making decisions promptly or in a tortuously slow way, to exploiting opportunities or letting them pass almost unnoticed, to stifling or stimulating creativity, and so on.

It is obvious that organizations are groups of people who are formally associated with activities that involve common objectives or goals. Brown[12] points out:

science and technology have not altered the persistent and controlling attribute of human organization—namely, whatever the organization's size or form, it continues to be subject to the complex and unpredictable initiatives and responses of the individual human beings who make it up. [He indicates that] the organization, because of its mass and its internal cohesion, appears to attain a personality and momentum of its own. It becomes easy to think of the organization in monolithic terms, as if it were no longer a combination of human beings but rather a separate entity following self-determined, pseudo physical principles. The subtle shift appears not only in common speech such as in discussing "General Motors," "The Department of Defense," or the "Catholic Church" as if they were monolithic structures, but also in the sophisticated studies of the social scientist.

But Brown is adamant that such a metaphor is not valid. He writes that "the initiating forces which control the behavior of an organization remain human and disparate even under the greatest pressures for cohesion and conformity. Human organizations persist in being human."

The concept of a corporate conscience itself is specious according to Brown.

The community of organization itself possesses no conscience apart from the individuals within it, even though the predisposition of many individuals, reinforced by *their* sense of tradition, *their* total background, or *their* innate character, might create the impression that the community or organization had itself gained an introspective conscience, a corporate soul. Regardless of any legal fiction, an organization is not a person. Nor can it have a soul. [He points out that large organizations tend to submerge the individual.] As the individual becomes more and more overwhelmed by mass, an organization takes on a quality of impersonality, as if it were a great machine subject to physical laws rather than human initiative. The whole seems to become greater than the sum of its parts, not merely in economic and engineering terms, but in spiritual, ethical, and moral terms as well. This impersonality is reinforced by momentum, an assumption that any direction in which the organization moves has become more than that determined by any individual. Conformity to the direction of movement or to the current ethical climate affords the individual of security which dulls anxiety, blunts the questioning mind, and assuages the individual conscience.

Thus Brown inadvertently touches on the basic concept of The System, which he states is basically generated by the largeness of the organization. In spite of his questionable assertion that large size is the cause of the problem, he correctly identifies the root cause of the problem as the leader of the organization. It is the leader who must:

prevent the influences of size, impersonality, momentum, and conformity . . . from restricting human dignity and fulfillment. . . . It is he who must encourage others to respond to their conscience—with conviction and consistency—in the functioning of the organization he leads whether it is a government, a corporation, a church, or a university.

Brown ignores or understates the concept that although people make up an organization, most people do not control the organization and thus cannot change it, but they can maintain it. Management without leadership is the reason why The System controls the organization. Thus The System also may be described as a monolithic entity that follows "self-determined, pseudo physical principles."

Heirs and Pehrson[13] assert that the key to:

improving the quality of life, whether in economic, ecological, environmental or peace-seeking terms [is] the decision-thinking processes of the human mind and those of the organizations.

They clearly identify the need for an improved problem solving thought process and decision making within organizations:

Individuals and organizations both function through a combination of thought and action. Therefore, we believe it is accurate and practical to recognize that an organization possesses a "mind" of its own, that is, a *collective* mind that includes but transcends the combined individual minds of the executives and employees who work and think together to make an organization function. . . . The important decision-making thought process of the mind can be identified, and . . . since an organization also has a mind that follows the same thought process decision-makers will be better equipped to guide their organizations successfully into the future if they both clearly identify this process and deliberately encourage the mind of their organization to follow it.

Thus unlike Brown, they attribute a synergistic concept of management to The System.

Heirs and Pehrson present an analysis of the decision-making process (see Chapter 8) that should help:

decision makers derive practical benefit from [their arguments. They] also propose that recognition and use of the theory of the *mind the organization* offers managements a new and meaningful frame of reference and therefore a new and practical tool—that can be directly applied to help them improve the quality of thinking, planning, and decision-making in their organizations as well as improve the ultimate effectiveness of decisions taken.

They suggest that an organization may have a threat or inclination of its own and that "in neglecting the individual human minds managements neglect the cooperative processes and requirements of the *collective* mind of the organization."

They and Brown have, in effect, established a rationale for the existence of The System, which could be summarized as follows. They declare that the organization as a whole behaves as if it was an "individual" that controls the entity. In other words, the organization behaves as if it was controlled by The System, which is another name for that "individual." The following pages discuss how management's neglect of its duties and responsibilities manifests itself in the establishment of The System, which eventually controls and maintains the operation of the organization. However, in some cases management and other special interest groups use The System to further their group's and thus their personal welfare.

The type of organization and its structure obviously can have a major influence on the performance of the organization's members. An organization can be structured as a pyramid, matrix, comb, or as a combination of these structures. A small organization can be unstructured, wherein the members share the tasks to be performed.

Cribbin[14] suggests that:

there are at least six kinds of organizations. Some are innovative and risk taking, while others strive merely to avoid failure. Some are concerned primarily with maintaining the status quo, while still others are ultraconservative and tradition-bound. Some firms focus on improvement and management by objectives. And some are erratic and impulsive. Each of these kinds of organizations has quite a different administrative system and a radically different value orientation.

The informal or nonformal organization that exists within the formal organization is part of The System. As top management changes the formal organizational structures or as the kind of organization changes with time and leadership, The System reacts accordingly. If The System perceives that the changes are for the betterment of the people, it modifies its behavior accordingly. But if The System believes that the proposed organizational changes are detrimental to the welfare of the people or merely cosmetic, it tries to optimize the status quo consistent with the new organizational structure. After all, if only the names are changed, the work still must go on.

As organizations change, grow, and decay, they pass through a series of stages or life cycles. Each of these stages affects the behavior of the organization by affecting how the norms are utilized or changed and how The System reacts to the new cycle or stage. As the organization passes through each stage, The System adjusts to the new environment in order to optimize its existence. The following section outlines the seven stages of an organization's life cycle.

ORGANIZATIONAL LIFE CYCLES

Organizations are created to fulfill the needs of individuals. Entrepreneurs create businesses to bring products or services to the marketplace. Political, business, social, religious, and charitable organizations are generated by people who wish to improve particular human conditions or in some cases just their own. All institutions may be considered to have a life of their own: they are created and grow, sometimes give birth to other organizations, wane, and die. Some institutions repeat certain phases over a period of years.

Miller[15] observes in *Barbarians to Bureaucrats* that:

all living things, whether plants, animals, people or groups of people, exhibit patterns or cycles of development, moving from periods of vitality and growth, to periods of decay and disintegration. The pattern of business growth and decline—and the behavior of leaders—follow this same course.

He presents a theory of corporate life characterized by the following leadership styles:

1. **The Prophet**: The visionary who creates the breakthrough and the human energy to propel the company forward.
2. **The Barbarian**: The leader of crisis and conquest who commands the corporation on the march of rapid growth.
3. **The Builder and Explorer**: The developer of specialized skills and structures required for growth, who shift from command to collaboration.
4. **The Administrator**: The creator of the integrating system and structure, who shifts the focus from expansion to security.
5. **The Bureaucrat**: The imposer of a tight grip of control, who crucifies and exiles new prophets and barbarians, assuring the loss of creativity and expansion.
6. **The Aristocrat**: The inheritor of wealth, alienated from those who do productive work, who is the cause of rebellion and disintegration.
7. **The Synergist**: The leader who maintains the balance, who continues the forward motion of a large and complex structure by unifying and appreciating the diverse contribution of the Prophet, Barbarian, Builder, Explorer, and Administrator.

The Prophet and Barbarian leaders are in tight control of the organization, and the organizational structure and controls are simple, direct, and personal. The System is slowly created during the age of the Builder and Explorer as the organizational structure becomes more complicated and areas of specialization and internal competition form. With the Administrator, the operations expand and become more complex, as more levels of management control are added. The System is informally recognized, and people use it to minimize the uncertainty and new controls being imposed by management.

Under the Bureaucrat, professional management is emphasized; this would include tight controls, financial and otherwise, and multiyear plans that are essential to maintaining the financial stability and slow growth of the organization. The organizational structure becomes top heavy with additional layers of management, and vertical communications along with normal communications are often impaired or ignored. The System expands to encompass the operation of the excessive bureaucracy. The System maintains itself by going along with the cyclic cost savings programs, human resource programs, and cosmetic organizational changes. Almost everyone in the organization realizes that The System will not change significantly and thus acquiesces to the apparent changes and the alleged new controls imposed by top management.

With the Aristocrat, the primary business of the organization declines because The System has replaced top management in running the organization. During this phase, there is a lack of effective new investment and creativity, and the quality of products and services remains constant. The previous and present leaders have spent much of their resources on acquiring new businesses that, being outside of the core understanding of the original organization's goals, become poorly managed and a burden on the organization. Miller indicates that now:

> the organization is characterized by excessive layers of management, poor communication from top to bottom, little clarity of mission, and poor motivation. Various sorts of internal warfare, and competition among fiefdoms, are likely to be rampant. There is a clear formal organization, but that is not how things get accomplished. There is an informal organization used by those managers who are still genuinely interested in getting something done.

The Synergist is required if an organization is to reverse its decline. Miller defines a Synergist as a "leader who has escaped his or her own conditioned tendencies toward one style and has incorporated the different styles of leadership that are needed as the corporation goes through its life cycle." He then formulates nine axioms that the successful Synergist will use in preventing the decline of the institution (see a review of these axioms in Chapter 8) along with other prescriptions that are required for the organization to become a world class institution.

Miller summarizes the problem as follows:

If there is one lesson . . . let it be that the decline in corporate culture precedes—and is the primary causal factor in—the decline of a business, and that decline is the result of the behavior and spirit of its leaders. Similarly corporations and societies are regenerated by creative leaders recognizing and responding to challenge.

A Synergist must recognize The System's control over the organization and thus initiate programs to change the existing System into one that supports the people in the organization and the organization's long-term goals. The key to initiating effective change is to recognize and understand The System's control over management and people.

NATURAL LAWS OF ORGANIZATIONS

Allen Weiss in *The Organization Guerrilla*[16] has analyzed the dynamics of individuals within organizations and the tensions that are intrinsic to their interactions. He discusses eight Natural Laws of Organizations that he recommends as "a starting point for a study of the political strategies that will help individuals survive and prosper in an organizational framework."

These Natural Laws of Organizations reflect, in part, how The System takes root in an organization. With a laissez-faire type of management, people follow these laws of their own accord. The net result is that The System is created and becomes the entity that controls the organization. Weiss' eight laws, which concern control and power, are found in Table 1-1.

In examining Weiss' Natural Laws of Organizations we see that some laws are indicative of The System being in control. Laws two through six, concerning group survival, rationalization, self-interest, constraints, and influence are part of the System's modus operandi.

Table 1-1 Weiss' Natural Laws of Organizations

1. Law of Aggrandizement	Whenever people join together in any activity, some will seek to take advantage of others and of the group's power.
2. Law of Group Survival	The continued existence of the organization must never be imperiled from within.
3. Law of Rationalization	No one can be counted on to reveal the real reasons for what he [or she] does.
4. Law of Self-Interest	Only egotists favor the reasons they like best, rather than the arguments that convince others and are least vulnerable to counter attack.
5. Law of Constraints	No one in any organization has absolute control over any activity or any group.
6. Law of Influence	Everyone . . . has a capability for exerting pressure on others to a greater or lesser extent.
7. Law of Fugling	Success in management ranks depends in large measure on fugling with grace.
8. Law of Power	Power follows money.

The Law of Group survival seeks to maintain and promote the status quo so that the jobs of employees not in top management are protected. This law is fundamental to understanding The System and how it works. Although top management initially created The System as a means of managing efficiently, the rest of the employees eventually learn to work The System as a means of individual and group survival. After all, performing one's job in accordance with The System's procedures and policies is all that is usually required and is blessed by the default management.

The Law of Rationalization is taught to employees early in their careers. The System's rules must be followed, and those who try to change them soon learn that is futile. Thus employees learn to play the game and follow The System and outwardly maintain a demeanor that has been shown to be acceptable over long periods of time by The System.

The Law of Self-Interest is learned after many failed attempts to introduce significant change in The System. Since it usually wins in the long run, employees eventually use The System in order to minimize their exposure to attack by management.

The Law of Constraints is normally obvious to everyone except top management. The rest of the employees (or members) know that significant changes in The System cannot be made by anyone since top management, which is captured by The System, is oblivious to the need for real change.

The Law of Influence is learned by the members of the organization in order to make sure everyone understands that The System should not be modified lest adverse effects occur that could lead inadvertently to survival problems. Therefore, in general, the law is used only to preserve The System, since The System usually is the only real protection the members have within the organization.

From among the three other laws that Weiss discusses, The Law of Aggrandizement may be used locally in subgroups, but never to the extent that it disturbs The System. The Law of Fugling and The Law of Power are top management prerogatives that have little to do with The System and the organization's effectiveness.

As Weiss points out, people in organizations act according to his natural laws. These actions, when taken as a whole help to form the foundation of The System, which eventually becomes the controlling function in the organization with management's de facto abdication of its responsibilities. The System's Laws, which are discussed in Chapter Two, are complementary in that they are the laws which govern how The System controls the organization. Thus the members of the organization do their work based on their collective understanding of how The System works.

DEVELOPMENT OF THE SYSTEM

Three interlinked reasons exist for the creation and development of The System. It provides the social system within the organization, the functional system that is necessary for the organization to operate effectively, and a vehicle for management to focus on its short-term results.

In every organization, people are required to work with other people. Either because of the organizational structure or in spite of it, formal or informal groups are established. It is human nature that people communicate and interact with others in the group since they support each other in a social manner. The more cohesive the group, the greater the degree and frequency of interaction. An increase in social interaction reinforces behavior that is pleasing and rewarding to the group members.[17] The increase in social activity also reinforces the work activities since the group generates norms that affect the work output and efficiency of the group members.[18] The group often "protects"[19-20] its members from unwanted stimuli from top management or outsiders. Hampton et al.[21] note that "once social structure develops, however, it takes on a life of its own. A group pursues objectives which may contribute to individual goals but which may also limit the individual."

Every organization has a formal organizational structure in which management, control, and work is distributed in accordance with a preconceived plan. Hampton et al.[22] establish that:

when the organization is animated with people carrying out the prescribed activities and interactions, a social system, or what some authors call a sociotechnical system, comes into being. The problem of management can be conceived as one of coordinating the elements of the system, of making sure the organization moves in the desired direction and is not an anarchy.

Barnard[23] acknowledges that informal organizations are created by personal contacts and interactions and that "informal organizations are necessary to the operations of formal organizations as a means of communication, of cohesion, and of protecting the integrity of the individual."

Katz[24] confirms this concept and states:

(1) Workers have considerable autonomy within the confines of the organization. Even when their work is prescribed in exact detail, the work role tends to be defined narrowly. This leaves a considerable portion of the worker's life within the work organization *undefined*; (2) Workers tend to use this autonomy to bring their working-class culture into the organization, even though this is alien to the bureaucratic ethos of the higher echelons of the organization. . . . Indirect delegation of autonomy results from the absence of rules; in a sphere were no rules exist, autonomy exists by default. . . . The limited bases for the worker's *allegiance* to the work organization are given tacit recognition not only in the worker being excluded from administrative decision making. but also in his being allowed to bring into the work setting working-class culture patterns and to fashion them into relatively autonomous subcultures.

Katz goes on to declare that there are many "well-documented studies . . . which show production control and worker collusion against management by informal groups of workers."

Having initially established a basic organization with its associated policies, procedures, and controls, top management then manages in order to meet its growth and profit or budget objectives. In time, however, the formal policies, procedures, and controls become outdated, ineffective, and inefficient. Brown[25] observes that in their place, tradition, which is:

the time dimension in human organization(s) . . . [is established as] an evolving, pervasive system of assumptions, habits of mind, customary behavior, and attitudes which stamps an organization with a distinct personality by predisposing its members to think and act in a way generally favorable to the survival of the organization.

Brown's definition of the term "tradition" corresponds to what may be called "The System." Brown goes on to expose the root cause of the problem:

But the fundamental importance of tradition in human organization does not assure its beneficial effect if it is not continuously influenced by the interaction of leadership and communication. . . . . Traditions have sometimes held back progress by their controlling influence upon the minds of all levels of management as well as of the rank and file. . . . The trouble is not that traditions exist, but that they get out of hand. It is interesting to note that corrective measures are seldom initiated at the bottom. Fundamentally, only revitalized leadership can save the organization from hardening of the arteries and death.

When management is mainly concerned with short-term results and becomes content with cosmetic changes to The System and with its personal rewards and satisfactions, the organization's performance declines. This is evidenced by the shrinking market shares, excessive costs, reduced profits or missed budgets, and the loss of outstanding employees. When management's approach to controls is oblivious to The System's way of control, the organization's performance suffers.

Drucker[26] identifies the ultimate control of organizations:

There is a fundamental, incurable, basic limitation to controls in a social institution. This lies in the fact that a social institution is both a true entity and a fiction. As an entity it has purposes of its own, a performance of its own, results of its own—and survival and death of its own. . . . But a social institution is composed of persons, each with his own purpose, his own ambitions, his own ideas, his own needs. No matter how authoritarian the institution, it has to satisfy the ambitions and needs of its members, and do so in their capacity as individuals but through *institutional* rewards and punishments, incentives, and deterrents. The expression of this may be quantifiable—such as a raise in salary. But the reward system itself is not quantitative in character and cannot be quantified.

Yet here is the real control of the institution, that is, the ground of behavior and the cause of action. People act as they are being rewarded or punished. For this, to them, rightly . . . is the true expression of the values of the institution and of its true, as against its professed, purpose and role.

A system of controls which is not in conformity with this true, this only effective, this ultimate control of the organization which lies in its people decisions will therefore at best be ineffectual. At worse it will cause never-ending conflict and will push the organization out of control.

Thus Drucker has identified a problem that is indicative of The System being in control of an organization. The reward and punishment system (a process) is not tightly coupled to top management's objectives because The System is the de facto management of the organization.

SUMMARY AND CONCLUSIONS

This chapter, which has introduced the concept of The System, suggests that The System has particular characteristics, follows rules and in fact controls—instead of top management—the actions taken in an organization. The System acts like a buffer layer of management in a large organization; it is invisible to top management but evident to the rest of the organization's members.

McGregor was attuned to the problem of control by The System. Brown emphasizes the humanity of the organization and that people control the organization and are constrained to conform to the momentum of The System. Heirs and Pehrson prefer to look at the overall scope of an organization and find it to possess a mind of its own, like The System.

Miller and others write about life cycles and leadership types in organizations. They show that The System evolves through the life cycles and eventually controls the organization unless a leader (the Synergist) takes charge of the organization and The System.

Weiss analyzes the dynamics of individuals and identifies eight natural laws of organizations. People in organizations interact with and support each other and the groups to which they belong. Informal procedures generated for people to perform their jobs result in social interactions. Management's control is attenuated because of misguided priorities, and The System eventually assumes control. In effect, The System establishes its own culture, to which most of the people other than top management subscribe. Thus the organization's culture is that of The System. People act in accordance with the de facto standards, incentives, rewards, and punishments that they experience, not those promulgated by management.

This chapter has presented the theoretical and historical background information to justify the concept that The System is in charge of an organization. It has established the premise that The System is the problem to be overcome if significant change is to be accomplished.

In the next three chapters [which complete PART 1: HOW IT IS] The System's characteristics are analyzed and the need for changing The System explained. Representative examples of The System are given in the fourth chapter. How to change The System is discussed in PART 2: HOW IT SHOULD BE. Only fundamental, structural changes that are properly applied have a chance of changing The System. The usual cosmetic type changes merely strengthen The System's status quo.

CHAPTER 2

Characteristics of The System

In any organization the permanent officials will gradually obtain such influence that its day-to-day program will increasingly reflect their interests rather than its own stated philosophy.
— Roberto Michels[1]

This chapter examines how The System works in an organization. The System exemplifies The Law of the Vacuum: Action Expands to Fill the Void Created by Human Failure. Gall's axioms, theorems, laws, and corollaries about The System are presented. General symptoms of The System in operation are listed. Examples are given which are indicative of a System problem. The System is characterized by a discussion of its various attributes. The laws that govern how The System performs are identified for the first time. Three laws are critical to the understanding of how and why The System works: The Law of Oligarchy divulges the fact that The System gradually gains control over the entire organization. The Law of Bureaucratic Displacement discloses that in a bureaucratic system an increase in expenditure will be matched by a decrease in output. The Law of The Iron Triangle reveals that The System controls (but responds to) the members of the Iron Triangle. The seventeen laws when taken together define why and how The System works, and why it remains so powerful over a long time. An example is given about the operation of The System in a typical organization.

INTRODUCTION

In his delightful book, *Parkinson: The Law,* Parkinson[2] generalizes his law to read as follows: "Action Expands to Fill the Void Created by Human Failure." This "Law of the Vacuum" can be applied to The System, which expands to fill the void created by management.

Every organization has an informal organization, an informal way of doing things, and an informal value system.[3] People acquire experience and habits that replace knowledge and understanding if they are not continually trained, educated, or expected to expand their capabilities. Overhead functions become frictional by impeding the thrust of the job and thus hindering the potential superior performance by the organization.

To ease the throughput around the organization's obstacles and bottlenecks, management creates assistants, coordinators, expediters, and committees to solve the problem. Usually none of these "solvers" can get to the root cause of the problem, and therefore the problem is maintained and institutionalized.

As top management perpetuates the problems, marginal performances, and emphasis on short-term results, The System takes control. Top management is tolerated but soon ignored, since The System has long demonstrated that this is the best way to operate in such an environment.

Gall[4] notes that:

the fundamental problem does not lie in any particular system but rather in *systems as such.* Salvation, if it is attainable at all, even partially, is to be sought in a deeper understanding of the ways of systems, not simply in a criticism of the errors of a particular system. . . . No one can afford not to understand the basic principles of *How Systems Work.* Ignorance of these basic laws is bound to lead to unrealistic expectations.

In his book *Systematics: How Systems Work and Especially How They Fail,* Gall offers, among others, the following axioms, theorems, laws, or corollaries about systems:

- Systems in general work poorly or not at all.
- Failure to function as expected . . . is an *intrinsic* feature of systems.
- People in systems do not do what the system says they are doing.
- To those within a system, the outside reality tends to pale and disappear.
- Big systems either work on their own or they don't. If they don't, you can't make them. . . . Pushing on the system doesn't help.
- If a system is working, leave it alone. Don't change anything.
- Systems develop goals of their own the instant they come into being.
- The system has a blind, instinctive urge to maintain itself.
- The work of change agents is made enormously more delicate and uncertain by the fact that the mere presence of a change agent (recognizable as such) . . . promptly induces bizarre and unpredictable alterations in the behavior of the system. . . . Changes will certainly occur as a result, but they are not likely to be the changes desired.
- What is clear is that the remedy must strike deeply at the roots of the system itself in order to produce any significant effect.

GENERAL SYMPTOMS OF A SYSTEM PROBLEM

The easiest way to understand that a problem is due to The System is to determine if the problem has been around for some time. If a problem exists after repeated attempts to solve it, it is due to The System that management created. This type of problem cannot be solved within The System, since The System constraints prevent solutions.

Table 2-1 lists comments heard in various organizations indicating symptoms of The System in operation.

Table 2-1   Indications of a Top Management Problem

- We've tried, but no one listens. **They** don't care.
- No one seems able to change things around here.
- You can't beat The System.
- **They** don't know we exist.
- It's the nature of our business (or technology).
- We cannot do it — our people are too busy shipping.
- Why doesn't somebody solve this problem?
- We have always done it this way.
- We lost the recipe.
- Ship it — we'll worry about it later.
- Whose problem is this? It's not my job.
- We've had this problem for years.
- **They** don't pay us enough to solve those problems.
- The customer really doesn't know what he wants.
- It's not my problem. That's corporate's problem.
- That's good enough.
- It's against company policy.
- My supervisor is only interested in meeting the schedule.
- I don't know—it's regulations or policy I guess.
- "It's so tough to convince top management. . . ."[5]
- "They never give us accurate data."[6]
- "You have to recognize that our business is different."[6]
- "People just don't do good work."[6]
- "Our competition can buy cheaper than we can."[6]
- "Oh, business would be fine if only we didn't have to make the stuff."[7]
- "Nobody ever tells me anything."[8]
- "You're way ahead of your time."[9]
- "Why change? We're doing O.K."[9]
- "We're too small (or too big) for it."[9]
- "We don't have the time. . . . It isn't in the budget."[9]
- "It won't work in our department."[9]
- "You need written approval from above."[10]
- "It's no use trying to be imaginative around here."[11]
- [You'd think] "they didn't want anything to happen."[11]

George Box[12] points out that "nothing is perfect and Murphy's Law says that the day-to-day operation of a system itself can help tell us what's wrong with it. The catch is that it will only tell us *if we listen.*" Often the key word revealing problems in The System is the impersonal *they.* It is used when explaining that something is wrong and indicates that The System is in charge. People recognize that The System is faulty but believe that the responsibility to change or solve the problem is not theirs but rather the *they* who are in charge of the situation.

The System overcomes an individual's ability to affect significant change and therefore is in control of the situation. The individual may introduce superficial changes that do not affect The System's ability to maintain its operational control.

Table 2-2 lists some examples indicative of System problems found in organizations. All of these problems are due to management's lack of leadership, direction, and control. If management perceives that there is a problem, it usually looks to see who is causing it. The fact that the problem has existed for months or years is lost on management. Unless management discovers that The System is controlling the problem, it usually tries to solve the problem by assigning someone to find and implement the solution.

The person or group involved immediately recognizes that the problem is controlled by The System. Playing the game accordingly, they institute the classical get-well procedures that are tailored for the situation and moderately successful. They subsequently declare the problem solved and resume their normal work. The System responds by accepting the procedures that are easy to accomplish and perceived as supportive by those who are affected by the changes. The procedures that are thought to be threatening or not in the best interests of those affected are relaxed or ignored, and the root cause of the problem remains undetected. The problem eventually resurfaces, albeit sometimes with different characteristics or a different name.

Table 2-2   Examples of a System Problem

1. Chronic failures to meet objectives.
2. Manufacturing yields less than 99.9999998 percent.
3. A process periodically loses its recipe.
4. Late deliveries from suppliers.
5. Excessive throughput times for an operation.
6. Long lead times for processes.
7. Consistently late deliveries to customers.
8. Excessive setup times for an operation.
9. Poor quality of output.
10. Excessive manpower turnover.
11. Excessive absenteeism.
12. Persistent customer dissatisfaction.
13. Poor customer service.
14. Excessive inventories.
15. Customer apathy.
16. Poor morale.
17. Corporate management changes every 3-5 years.
18. Annual plans never met.
19. Management cover-up of problems.
20. Ideological behavior by employees instead of satisfying their customers.
21. Unions: the need for; and interference with The System.
22. Insular behavior by departments or parts of the organization.
23. Job descriptions based on restricted tasks and responsibilities.
24. Merit reviews which ignore the existence of The System, or which are based on faulty statistics.
25. Lack of a dynamic, fearless feedback system.
26. Excessive prerogatives and rewards of management.
27. Rubber stamp board of directors.
28. Environmental problems.
29. Poor relations with local communities.
30. Illegal behavior by the organization or institution.
31. A pervasive environment of fear.
32. A lack of basic freedoms.

ATTRIBUTES OF THE SYSTEM

The following list of attributes can be observed in most Systems:

Pervasive: The System encompasses everyone in the organization and invades and tailors itself to every operation.

Self-consistent: The System automatically adjusts to all perturbations, optimizing its ability to maintain its status quo.

Self-regulating: The System rebuffs, discards, or finesses all attempts at real change by anyone other than top management. Management-induced changes are tested over time to determine if they are cosmetic. If management is not concerned about the long term application of the change, The System will gradually modify the change to satisfy its norms and modus operandi.

Learnable: Most people can master The System within three to six months of joining the organization. Nevertheless, the more experience a person has the harder it is to understand The System in a new organization. Thus, newly hired experienced people or senior managers could take up to three years to master it, if ever.

Deeply Rooted: The System starts to grow with the formation of the organization. As the organization becomes fixed and top management mainly becomes concerned with short term results, The System matures into an operation that is perpetuated throughout the organization. The System remembers and acts on things that top management once knew but has forgotten.

Periodic: The System also follows the organization's beat—the monthly, quarterly, and yearly actions and exercises that the organization generates.

Maximizing: The System maximizes its efforts in order to meet the apparent periodic objectives of the organization.   This maximization is consistent with The System's norms but not necessarily with the organization's objectives and goals.

Reproducible: The System is transferred naturally from an organization to a new organization as people leave to start-up a competing organization. Thus, The System becomes linked with the competitor's System if that organization is also limited by its top management's capabilities.

Competitive: The System will do whatever is necessary to satisfy management's short term objectives. It will bend any procedure, cut any corner, and maximize output while ignoring any long term consequences such as reliability and costs.

Self-Protecting: The System protects itself by never directly challenging top management. Instead, The System acquiesces or finesses top management's requirements.

Self-Sufficient: It grows sufficient resources and procedures to perpetuate its character and existence over a period of time.

Compartmentalized: The System differentiates between work areas in an organization. Some of its norms and operations may be insular.

Responsible: It is mainly responsive to those in the organization who are not in the upper management levels. People can depend on The System to help them cope with the poor support they receive from management.

Sovereign: The System is the de facto management of the organization. In fact, The System could maintain most organizations even if the top management took a long term sabbatical.

Stable: The System only slowly changes itself as a response to an overall thrust by its members for a change. In order for real change to occur, people must believe that it is in their best interest, and that the organization will be better as a consequence.

Yesterday's Culture: The System maintains the previous culture, norms, and standards. It resists new ideas, technologies, and procedures unless it perceives that its members will benefit because of their assimilation into The System.

Tenacious: The System resists changes introduced by upper management because it has learned that most of the proposed changes are fads which will wither away within the year or two. Thus, The System will "go along" with such changes at the same time using its methods to neutralize their impact.

Methodical: It maintains its methods over many years, and is unrelenting in its application to the work of the organization.

Mandatory: In order to be able to work effectively and efficiently, one must use and understand The System. Ignoring The System invites disagreements, disunity, and difficulties in doing one's job in the organization.

Monolithic: There is only one System within an organization, such that all its members understand it, and also understand the subtle differences which occur in various parts of the organization.

Flexible: The System can change itself if need be in order to recognize real, i.e., fundamental, change being introduced into the organization. Real changes are absorbed and The System modifies its actions accordingly.

The above list, while not comprehensive, reveals the major characteristics of The System. The System is necessary for every organization. The problem is that if the organization's leadership and management is poor or marginal, The System will provide the necessary management needed to keep the organization running and surviving according to the previous standards upon which The System was generated. Moreover, if external conditions change which are not acted upon by management, The System also will not change and thus the organization will fail to respond to the opportunities that arise or are at hand. The System cannot prevent management's failure to build, nurture, and grow a successful, profitable or useful organization.

LAWS OF THE SYSTEM

Since The System pervades the entire organization and has more longevity than most if not all of management, it operates and controls the organization with a set of unwritten laws. These laws, listed in Table 2-3, are fundamental to understanding how The System works.

Table 2-3   The Laws of The System

1. Hierarchy of Policies	10. Hidden Factory Rule
2. Don't Fix it if it Ain't Broke	11. Law of Profits
3. Gamesmanship Rule	12. Law of Growth
4. Management by Exception	13. Dèjá Vu Law
5. Law of Superiority	14. Law of Squeaky Wheel Assets
6. Law of Invisibility	15. Law of Oligarchy
7. Rule of Alternate Efficiency	16. Law of Bureaucratic
8. Law of Priority	Displacement
9. Technical Law of Inertia	17. Law of the Iron Triangle

1. Hierarchy of Policies: *Unwritten System policies and procedures take precedence over the organization's new written policies and procedures.* The System transforms new policies into procedures that are optimum to those affected by the new policies. The procedures are continually modified in response to management's degree of control over the new policy. If the new policy is contrary to the best interests of the people, then those who must implement the new policy institute countervailing procedures to offset or regain the threatened previous prerogatives. The System always tries to win the competition and is willing to lose a few battles in order to maintain its primacy.

2. **Don't-Fix-It-If-It-Ain't-Broke Rule**: *Any proposed change will upset* The System *and make things worse!* This law is based on The System's belief that management does not understand the root causes of problems and thus proposes solutions that turn out to be nonsolutions. At best, the new solutions will accomplish marginal results at the expense of increased opportunity costs. Such solutions only reinforce the people's evaluation that management is captured by its own part of The System, which is foreign to the organization's long-term interests.

3. **Gamesmanship Rule**: *The introduction of a new policy or procedure is a game worth playing for a few months*. Most new policies or procedures introduced by management, if they are perceived by the people of the organization as antithetical to their best interests, are followed to the extent that management's interest is maintained. But The System's experience is that management usually relaxes its interest in how the new policy is being implemented. Therefore, The System either modifies or slowly starves the procedure such that it is replaced by The System's procedure, which might be a modified version of its previous procedure. A corollary to this law is Le Chatellier's Law: "If some stress is brought to bear on a system in equilibrium, the equilibrium is displaced in the direction which tends to undo the effect of the stress."[13]

4. **Management by Exception Law**: *Management of The System is by exception*. Since most middle managers live with The System and have learned not to try to change it, they seldom initiate any fundamental changes that would alter The System. Top management may introduce fundamental changes in policies and procedures that it believes are necessary and will result in

favorable consequences to them, the organization, or both; it will also make a sustained effort to ensure that the changes are incorporated into the organization's operations. Such actions are the exception to the law, however.

5. **Law of Superiority**: *Managers come and go but The System always remains in place.* As the organization gets older and presumably grows in size and output, top management personnel changes occur more frequently. In a short time, many upper managers do not understand or even know of the existence of The System. Eventually The System obtains greater longevity than the top managers, and thus the organization's and the System's existence becomes independent of top management. It is obvious that top management's decisions can lead to the destruction of the organization and consequently also of The System.

6. **Law of Invisibility**: *The System is invisible to top management.* Top management's main focus is on the organization's financial data and the managers who are responsible for those results. Because top management oversees the results of The System's operations, it perceives that it controls the organization's operations through the management hierarchy of the organization. The concept of a System problem is not considered since management perceives that all problems are caused by people's poor performance. Thus by virtue of its position and authority and its lack of understanding how The System works, top management maintains its basic philosophy of McGregor's Theory X.[14]

7. **Rule of Alternate Efficiency**: *Internal consistency is valued more highly than efficient service.* Having developed procedures that are or were optimum for the group that uses them, The System tends to maintain them even if the internal or external environment has changed. Since The System prevents or minimizes

change, present inefficient procedures (including poor quality) are continued to the detriment of the organization.

8. **Law of Priority**: *Look after the mountains and the molehills will look after themselves.* Once The System's procedures have been established and (unknowingly) accepted by management, The System ignores the results and maintains its status quo. Thus while top management is involved in such things as reviewing the profit and loss, the output, or the budget, and evaluating estimates of future performance, The System is sustaining itself by establishing new first-order changes while continuing or modifying the old procedures.

9. **Technical Law of Inertia**: *Established technology tends to persist in spite of new technology.* Since The System has developed many procedures with the old technology and usually opposes any radical changes, it maintains the old technology to hinder management from looking into new technology. Because there is no obvious benefit from new technology to those who use The System, many have an aversion to it being introduced into the organization. Some people also are afraid that new technology will either make their job harder to perform or potentially eliminate their job. Moreover, The System remembers that some previous new technologies were ineffective or too uncertain in their capability to improve the operation. Therefore, The System applies its Gamesmanship Rule (see law number three) to the introduction of new technology.

10. **Hidden Factory Rule**: *Every organization shall ignore the existence of its Hidden Factory.* Every organization has a hidden factory where various activities are not measured or evaluated, but are the result of inefficient, incorrect, or wasteful work. The System runs the hidden factory and sanctions all of its activities. The hidden factory is operated by middle managers and others

who have been taught that such work is required and is beneficial to The System and all members of the organization. Since top management usually is unaware of The System's existence, top management and the organization ignore the hidden factory's existence. Although the concept of the hidden factory has been published and discussed by management and others, most top managers are unaware of the concept.[15-18]

11. **Law of Profits**: *Increasing demand is the way to obtaining new revenues.* The System also extends into top management's level, without its awareness, where the Law of Profits is followed. In a business, management's desire is to increase new orders since increased sales usually means increased profits. For a nonprofit service organization, management's desire is to obtain more demand for its organization's service, since that leads to increased funding and security for management and organization. The System always operates from the demand side, because the supply side requires fundamental changes to occur in The System if quality and productivity are to be improved and the customers' needs anticipated and satisfied. The demand side requires more of what The System already provides.

12. **Law of Growth**: *Increase the organization's capacity to meet requirements by adding more people, more space, and more equipment.* This law is a corollary of the Law of Profits. Caught in The System, management usually promotes expansion and growth by incremental changes within the organization. Management rarely seriously tries to improve the productivity of the organization. In fact, bureaucracies have a negative incentive to improve productivity since their continued existence also depends on the Law of Growth.

13. **Déjà Vu Law**: *There's never time to do it right, but there's always time to do it over*! This law, known previously under the title

of   Meskimen's Law,[19] is usually ignored by management but is proven true by experience. Since The System is in place and resists change, operations proceed in accordance with The System. Because The System's procedures may not be adequate to accomplish the operation's objectives, the work is usually repeated after some System modifications are made. Invariably, the costs involved are more than double the initial estimate for the work.

14.   **Law of Squeaky Wheel Assets**: *Assets are assigned to the squeaky wheels of The System.* As Drucker has implied, managers, other employees, capital equipment, and all other assets are assigned according to the number of transactions required to perform an operation of The System rather than their importance and their potential contribution to the long-term profitability of the organization. Drucker observes that unless top management has an active, periodic inventory of who the "knowledge workers" are (the critical performers) and where they are assigned, they:

will be assigned by the demands of the organization. . . . In no time they will be misassigned. They will be where they cannot be productive, no matter how well-motivated, how highly qualified, how dedicated they are.[20]

15.   **Law of Oligarchy**: *In any organization The System will gradually obtain such influence that its day-to-day program will increasingly reflect The System's interests rather than the organization's stated philosophy.* The System's Law of Oligarchy supplements the Iron Law of Oligarchy in an organization, which is encapsulated in the quotation at the opening of this chapter. The Iron Law in such a case means that the organization's management prefers to look after the short-term concerns and is willing to acquiesce to The System's Law of Oligarchy, that is, to The System controlling the performance of the organization. (The System's Law of Oligarchy is a consequence of The System's Law of the Vacuum.)

16.   **Law of Bureaucratic Displacement**: *"In a bureaucratic system . . . increase in expenditure will be matched by fall in production. . . .* Such systems will act like 'black holes' in the economic universe, simultaneously sucking in resources, and shrinking in terms of 'emitted' production."[22] This law applies to The System as it appears in bureaucracies. In the U. S. Department of Health and Human Services, for example, continued increases in funding have resulted in a larger bureaucracy and a poorer result in the health care and human services of the recipients served by the bureaucracy. The U. S. Postal Service in June 1996 filed with the independent Postal Rate Commission its third rate increase in a year and a half. It has sought permission to raise base post office box rates by 20% to 100% for 17.5 million customers, to increase the cost of certified mail from $1.00 to $1.50, and to increase a pre-stamped postal card by an additional two cents. These proposed rate increases would be accompanied by a reduction in its present service—the elimination of special delivery service.

17.   **Law of the Iron Triangle**: *The System controls the iron triangle.* The System shall use, trade off, and balance out the influence of the three groups—the lawmakers and their staff, the bureaucracy, and the special interest groups served by the laws and regulations. In a business organization, the iron triangle consists of top management and the owners; research, development, operations, sales, marketing, and service departments; and the special interests such as the suppliers, governments and agencies, trade associations, and subcontractors. The System shall tailor its responses to each member of the iron triangle and reflect that member's desire for control of the output of The System.[22]

As these laws indicate, The System is the major component in the operation of an organization. To be successful the leader must understand that The System exists and that it probably must be changed. Failure to understand this will result in being at best a manager, or at worst a caretaker or undertaker of the organization.

THE SYSTEM IN OPERATION

After a period of benign neglect by management, The System gradually assumes control of the various operations within the organization. Top management usually is not aware of or has forgotten The System or its importance, while the other managers have learned to live with The System since it is easier for them to maintain The System's procedures rather than to change them.

The System is created by the vacuum left by management's initial establishment of the structure, objectives, and policies and procedures of the organization and by the value system and culture of the employees. Since it is impossible for top management to develop, establish, and write policies and procedures for every potential opportunity or problem, middle managers and other workers create informal policies and procedures when required. In addition, standard policies and procedures become outdated and redundant, incorrect, or misleading if not formally changed. Hence in most cases, they are changed informally by The System, which induces managers and nonmanagers to alter the procedures so as to obtain the desired better results. These System changes eventually become acceptable to top management, which inadvertently acquiesces because the end justifies the means.

By developing many policies and procedures that become the accepted way of operating and which greatly outnumber those created by management, The System assumes control. The employees understand, use and work within The System subconsciously. New employees are required to accept The System. Most of the work is completed in accordance with The System's dictates.

When The System is in control, monthly and quarterly shipments are The System's gods. Because The System has been created to facilitate short-term objectives, future potential profits are sacrificed to these gods. Decisions are made that maximize the desired quarterly profit and loss results and ignore long-term customer requirements and potential new orders. The hidden factory flourishes as the organization expands and new problems are generated. The hidden factory costs can be 35 percent or more of the sales revenues.[23-28] In nonprofit organizations, the periodic or yearly budget review and justification are The System's gods. Because The System has been created for these periodic justifications of worth, The System generally ignores the quality and quantity of the organization's output. The System's main duty is to protect and promote the organization's endurance and the jobs of its members. The hidden factory also flourishes in nonbusiness organizations. In them the percentage of hidden factory costs is probably greater than that of the average business, which is more cost conscious since it has profit objectives to meet.

The System works in the same manner for all members of any organization. For example, a worker who becomes aware of a problem related to a task has one of four choices. He or she may choose to: (1) ignore the problem and let The System worry about it; (2) attempt to alleviate the problem by covering it up, repairing it, or attempting to remove the cause; (3) notify the manager and wait for directions; or (4) discuss the problem with other group members and jointly decide on a course of action.

Options 2 and 3 usually are the most difficult to choose, since the consequences to the worker are potentially more severe. Option 2 opens the door for criticism if the operation is not completely successful, and option 3 could cause complications, especially if the worker's supervisor could blame the worker for causing the problem. Option 4 is more viable, since it tends to broaden the scope of the problem and its solution without severe risks to the worker. Option 1 is the easiest choice to follow, since in the past it has led to a minimum of risk to the worker and an optimization of satisfaction. Thus if someone from management inquires about the problem, the standard response is that the problem was always present under the present System.

In the case of a particular recurrent problem, management aperiodically attempts to change The System. The usual approach is that management decides what the problem and solution are and then communicates the action that is to be taken by the appropriate individuals or group.

A typical example would be a problem related to the profits and losses being generated by a group. Management usually decides that excessive costs are the cause of the problem and directs the group to reduce overhead, labor, or materials. Because management rarely understands the root cause of the problem, solutions are demanded that usually do not impact the root cause and may make the problem more extreme and critical.

For example, assume that management decides that the root cause of a problem is poor quality of a product or service. Therefore it directs the group to improve its quality, expecting significant positive results in the near future. The group then pays special attention to the procedures in all of the operations that are part of the product or service. At best, the net result is less variation from the previous norm (average), and at worst, increased variation from the mean. In this case, poor quality was merely a symptom and not the root cause. The root cause might have been that the operation was out of control due to faulty understanding, processes, or procedures. Faulty understanding includes poor or inadequate training, incorrect or inadequate objectives, and poor management. Faulty processes or procedures include The System's attempt to fill the management void in the entire operation. Thus in this example, management's idea that improving the quality of the operation would be beneficial backfires because the fundamental understanding of what is required to accomplish such an objective was missing. The net result of such a fiasco is that the entire process of quality improvement is delayed and The System barrier is again strengthened.

SUMMARY

The void created in the absence of top management's leadership leads to the establishment of The System. The System eventually assumes de facto control of the organization.

Most problems are System problems—that is, most problems are not caused by people but are inherent in the process that was initially established by management. The System problems remain or are cosmetically addressed and modified, because the root causes of such problems are usually never identified.

The characteristics of The System have been described in terms of its symptoms, attributes, and laws. Just by listening to people talk about their jobs one can identify that a System problem exists. Common examples of System problems are listed. Most of the attributes of The System are discussed, and the seventeen laws that determine how The System operates are identified.

The System in operation may be thought of as the operating layer of management, with top management isolated from the rest of the organization and The System. Since The System is the result of top management's creation, by definition it is not responsible for any System problems that the organization has. The sole responsibility for any System problems is top management, its creator. Thus The System is the personification of a buffer layer of management that is unseen but very supportive of the people in the organization. In fact, most people in the organization feel much more comfortable with The System's management than they do with top management's.

CHAPTER 3

The Need For Changing The System

There is nothing permanent except change.
— Heraclitus, 531 B.C.[1]

This chapter discusses the need for changing The System in an organization or institution since usually it has become ineffective, inefficient, and resistant to change. Sample quotations are provided which expressly discuss The System in various organizations or institutions. One can tell that The System is in control by the repetitive poor performance (output) of the organization. The poor results are symptoms of problems due to The System that top management initially created. Typical symptoms of problems due to The System are discussed for specific important organizations. As an organization matures, The System becomes entrenched along with the growth of the bureaucracy. The System becomes a mature, non-threatening environment within which most processes and operations maintain their status quo. Deming has suggested that many such companies have become infected with many management-caused "diseases," i.e., with many poor policies and practices that limit the welfare of the company and its people. The tendency of top management in most organizations is to make cosmetic changes that strengthen The System. Thus the problems that many companies have are being compounded while their competition is getting stronger.

45

INTRODUCTION

The System that top management originally created eventually overwhelms poor management with its omnipresence, utility, and comprehensive and continuous interactions with members of the organization. The System starts as a valid crutch for management and eventually becomes the substitute for impotent management. The System may be very useful, efficient, and effective in its infancy but because of top management's neglect, over the long run it becomes ineffective, inefficient, and impervious to significant change in spite of economic and political changes.

The System is endemic to every organization, and generic systemic problems occur in every part of the organization. No two Systems are identical in their policies, procedures, and operations, and a large organization may have multiple sub-Systems. Each System's relationship to the management of its organization is also different.

Examples of the need to change The System appear almost daily in newspapers, magazine articles, and books. The need to change The System is explicitly stated in some cases but couched in indirect terms in most cases, such as in descriptions of the struggle against government laws and policies or bureaucratic controls and regulations. The extracts and quotations that follow describe the need to change The System.

Our systems are the scar tissues of past mistakes. . . . And each layer of that scar tissue—the initial system that was developed—made perfectly rational sense when created. Yes, each layer is rational, or micro-rational. Every line on every form makes sense—taken alone. It's the thousands of lines taken together that, unintentionally, add up to a micro-illogic.[2]

The Systems come to take on a life of their own. The Systems end up having little to do with what we are trying to accomplish. Tiny distortions are added by each person who holds the job. . . . Systems, after all, are supposed to mirror and abet the way things are done, are supposed to make things easier. Yet The Systems, so often, don't look like the creature that we are attempting to build.[3]

The fault is not in the character of the particular individuals who serve as bureaucrats. On the whole, they are a fair and representative sample of the citizenry. Many public servants are dedicated to pursuing the purposes for which they have been hired. Like some of the rest of us, some are lazy, incompetent, and inefficient. The problem is not the people as individuals; the problem is the system.[4]

A Hungarian scholar[5] in the early 1980s reported:
No, you no longer find the kind of brutality in Hungary we experienced in the Stalinist era of Rakosi and immediately following the 1956 revolution. But why? Partly because it is no longer necessary—people have accepted the system and have come to learn how to live around it. . . . But the system does not work in a more profound sense: one cannot govern a society in terms of it. . . . Planning a society is literally impossible, and we now know this. Marx, Lenin, Stalin, and the rest did not know this, nor did their idolized supporters. Among Hungarian intellectuals no one believes in the possibility of a genuine socialist society. . . . To allocate resources to generate creative energys [sic] to prepare for future needs, wants, and contingencies of actual people . . . one requires a free marketplace, period. We know this, the Poles know it, and I know some of the Russians are coming to realize it too.

Karel van Wolferan[6] discusses what he calls the power that "systematically suppresses individualism in Japan . . . [and] the fiction of responsible central government." He goes on to say that:
the frustration of many a foreign negotiator, meeting the umpteenth mediator sent his way, can be summed up in a single cry "Take me to your leader." Japan does not have one. It is pushed, or pulled, or kept afloat, not actually led, by many power-holders in what I call the System. . . . It denotes little more than the existence of a set of relationships, with reasonably predictable efforts, between those engaged in socio-political pursuits. The term "system" is also frequently used to suggest an arrangement of inescapable forces against which the individual

is helpless without resort to violence.[7]

The preservation of its own power is the first priority of every System component. This is achieved by ceaseless restraint, mutual scrutiny and interference among the components, preventing any one of them from growing strong enough to dominate the rest. . . . The System presents a variety of apparent paradoxes. . . . It exists without most of its participants being consciously aware of it; and it has no shape or form, let alone any justification, in law.[8]

The systematic deprivation of choice in practically all realms of life bearing on the political organization of Japan is essential for keeping the system on an even keel.[9]

In the following extract, Mario Vargas Llosa reviews the basis for Hernando de Soto's[10] analysis of the economic and political systems of Peru.

The state, in our world, has never been the expression of the people. The state is whatever government happens to be in power—liberal or conservative, democratic or tyrannical—and the government usually acts in accordance with the mercantilist model. That is, it enacts laws that favor small special-interest groups . . . and discriminates against the interests of the majority, which has marginal power or token legality. The names of the favored individuals or consortia change with each new government, but the system is always the same: not only does it concentrate the nation's wealth in a small minority but it also concedes to that minority the *right* to that wealth. . . . Within it, success does not depend on inventiveness and hard work but on the entrepreneur's ability to gain the sympathy of presidents, ministers and other public functionaries (which usually means his ability to corrupt them). . . . At the same time that the mercantilist system condemns a society to economic impotence and stagnation, it imposes relations between citizens and between citizens and the state that reduce or eradicate the possibility of democratic politics. Mercantilism . . . is based on laws that mock the most elementary democratic practices.

Deming[12] discusses in his first chapter how The System is the cause of problems, "The aim of this chapter is to illustrate a stable system of trouble in a manufacturing plant, and to explain that because the system is stable, improvement of quality is the responsibility of the management." He goes on to declare:

The fact is that most troubles with service and production lie in the system. . . . We shall speak of faults of the system as common causes of trouble, and faults from fleeting events as special causes. . . . I should estimate that in my experience most troubles and most possibilities for improvement add up to proportions something like this: 94 percent belong to the system (responsibility of management), 6 percent special. . . . No amount of care of skill in workmanship can overcome fundamental faults in the system. . . . To the production worker, the system is all but him.[13]

Christiansen[14] states,

The Challenger accident was not the first time the U. S. Space Agency had suffered a setback and in retrospect found wanting. In 1967 three astronauts were killed by a flash fire in the crew cabin while the Apollo Command and Service Module sat on the launch pad at Kennedy Space Center. . . . In May 1973, about one minute into the flight of Sky Lab 1, a meteoroid shield around the orbital workshop was ripped away by unanticipated aerodynamic forces, causing the subsequent loss of one of the workshop's two solar array systems.

What did the three accidents have in common? . . . The investigative board appointed by the NASA administrator, James Fletcher, acknowledges that:

the management system developed by NASA for manned space flight places large emphasis on rigor, detail, and thoroughness. In hand with this emphasis comes formalism, extensive documentation, and visibility in detail to senior management. While nearly perfect, such a system can submerge the *concerned individual* and depress the role of the intuitive engineer or analyst. . . . An emphasis on management systems can, in itself, serve to separate the people engaged in the program from the real world of hardware.

Any organization as large and complex as NASA must systematize and formalize its management procedures. Bureaucratization of this sort is necessary, but with time the system may overshadow the real organization objectives.

The engineers worked within the system to try to get action. Could they have done more? Post accident critics have blamed them for not being vocal enough to shut down the shuttle program. Yet engineers are conditioned to work "within the system," not to be strident when making a point and not to resign from the job on principle.

If one assumes that deterioration in the behavior of an aging bureaucracy is inevitable, then what happened at NASA . . . may not be completely surprising.

Brookes notes that when Nobel economist Milton Friedman was asked:

why it was, given the appalling and obvious failures in the world contrasted to the stunning successes of market capitalism, that most American students still graduated from high school with such a surprising socialist perspective, his answer was characteristically clear: "Because they are products of a socialist system—namely public education. How can you expect such a system to inculcate the values of free enterprise and individual entrepreneurship and competition when it is based on monopoly state ownership, abhors competition, and survives only through compulsion and taxation?"

Brookes himself points out that:

if we want to be genuinely candid about it, the American public education system today is not that much more effective than the Polish economic system that Lech Walesa reluctantly inherited, and the challenge facing would-be education reformers in the United States is no less daunting.

Unless they, like Walesa, first understand why the system has been failing, they cannot hope to succeed. If they follow his example and merely tinker at the margins, and "reform" with the present system, their efforts could well be as Myron Lieberman[15] warned in his new book on education privatization, entirely, "futilitarian."[16]

Newt Gingrich, in *Policy Review,* emphasizes that:

the education crisis in America is an even greater crisis than the crisis of drugs and violent crime. It undermines our most fundamental values. Government cannot be truly representative without widespread public knowledge of the issues elected officials are debating. It is impossible to compete in the world market when many of our citizens lack basic math, science, and work skills. This is a crisis of the first order. Yet, Republicans haven't used the language of crisis; we haven't talked with a sense of urgency: we haven't held the system accountable.[17]

Sven Rydenfelt[18] has studied sixteen socialist economies, all of which have a similar pattern of failure:

Soviet governments since Khrushchev have tried to cure the chronic ills of socialist agriculture with larger investments—more fertilizers, more machines, and so on—but despite these efforts, agriculture has steadily deteriorated. . . . The ills of socialist agriculture seem to be immune to materialistic remedies applied so far. The only logical conclusion is that the roots of the trouble must lie deeper, within the socialist system itself.

The same conclusion is drawn by Lester R. Brown:[19]

Soviet leaders may not yet have studied agricultural modernization elsewhere enough to see the inherent conflict between a centrally-planned agriculture and a highly productive agriculture. So far they have only attempted to improve the existing system, rather than turn away from centralized planning and control. But the problem is not that Soviet planners are unintelligent or that the Soviet farm labor force is lazy and inept. It is the faulty design of the system itself. It does not work effectively and cannot be expected to. Fixing the ills of Soviet agriculture without reforming the system will be like treating the symptoms of an illness rather than the cause. In agriculture, as in medicine, the risk in such an approach is that the patient's condition may worsen.

Henry Grunwald[20] writes:

We now know that the failure of communism is one of the great events of out time. Marx based much of his intellectual system on the forces of economics, yet he did not really understand economics. Neither did most other communist theorists. . . . Economic forces to them meant tribute, taxes and trade. If one needed more money, one raised taxes or borrowed.

But the most serious misconception of communism has to do with psychology—the failure to understand what motivates people. Property was seen as a form of theft rather than the object of a seemingly universal instinct. Profit was seen merely as capitalist greed, not a necessary incentive. Equality was seen as a universal ideal, not an ambiguous value—ambiguous because, while most people want equality in certain respects, they resent the enforced equality that downgrades individual merit, effort, or luck. And individual freedom was seen as a bourgeois vice, not a deep human need. In the classic Communist trade-off, freedom was exchanged for equality—except that in communist practice equality proved to be a sham.

We are all fascinated by reformers' attempts to mix communism with enough economic and political freedom to make the system work. Some reformers now speak in praise of private property, profit, incentives, and market forces as if they were compatible with communism. In effect, they reject the system's moral and intellectual legitimacy.

But it is increasingly clear . . . that political freedom is essential to an efficient economy. Some of the more daring reformers want a new order that would look remarkably like social democracy. In effect they are seeking a peaceful dismantling of the system—what might be called The Cold Counter-Revolution.

Paul Craig Roberts[21] also has commented on the decline of the Soviet System:

It wasn't so long ago that central planning was the "in" thing. People who believed in the free market were labeled unrealistic ideologues. . . . Today the Kremlin cannot compete in the world arena unless it creates incentives within the economy. The desperate need for better performance from human and physical resources has forced Gorbachev to take on the trenched bureaucracy and its perverse system of perks. In the end, the system may be too powerful for him.

The book *The System* provides "basic facts about how the government works."[22] One of the five chapters is entitled *Congress and The Realities of Life on Capitol Hill*.[23] The following extract is taken from that chapter.

When one approaches Congress one comes upon an actual and separate village, set down in the midst of Washington, D.C., the national seat of power, yet as isolated in the interests of its inhabitants, and in its purposes, customs and history, as if it were established in the midst of some remote and disassociate section of the country . . . for the purpose of preserving and perpetuating its own particular customs and culture from the encroachments of the outside world. It is a closed community containing not just the 535 representatives, but more than 17,000 souls, sharing their working lives in five office buildings connected by underground passageways, all of it beneath the postcard image of the Capitol Building itself.

The institution of Congress, as it really exists, confronts the new member with a profound and dismaying cultural shock for which he is seldom prepared, and from which he may never recover.

. . . He is quickly advised by custom and colleagues as to the role he will be expected and permitted to play—which, with rare exceptions, is none. . . . Yet perhaps the most troubling perception is the discovery that this legislative impotence and obscurity are not results of his freshman status, but are conditions that afflict most members of Congress. . . . There remains the shock of knowing that the institution itself is obscure and ineffective and not organized in any fashion which might permit it to function meaningfully.

At the same time, he will perceive that this ineffective institution is feverish with work and activity, bursting with energy. . . . However irrelevant they be, bills and resolutions will stream forth. . . . Much of this feverish application of energy, including his own, has to do with members getting reelected. That prospect, the new members discern, will depend not on what Congress or the individual members are doing, but on what they *seem* to be doing.

. . . The new member of Congress thus enters not so much into the realm of rational discourse and decisive action but into a world of illusions. In embarking on his legislative career, the new member finds himself drawn, inexorably and perhaps unwittingly, into a conspiracy by members of Congress to cover up the institution's flaws and failures—and their own. To reveal the true condition of the institution, and their role in it, would be to jeopardize their reelection.

Congressman Henry J. Hyde[24] identifies the moral foundation of capitalism:

"Democratic capitalism" is a complex system composed of three interlocking subsystems: a democratic political system in which legitimacy is conferred by popular consent; a market-oriented economic system for the creation and distribution of wealth; and a pluralistic moral-cultural system in which it is yet understood that rights involve obligations. There is no inherent contradiction, in other words, in being "for" capitalism and democracy, and being "for" classic Judaeo-Christian values and moral norms.

. . . We may well be at the beginning of the argument over morality and culture: that is, the argument over the relationship between free markets and the cultural glue which holds the tripartite system of democratic capitalism together. . . . Markets offer us a vast number of choices, to be sure: and some of those choices are, by any decent ethical measure, morally inferior to others. But it is individual human beings, not some abstraction called "the market," who make those choices. . . . Choice . . . is still a function of human will and intelligence, not of economic systems. Blaming "the system" for moral failures of individual Americans is a cop-out.

The market system is not a machine that can run by itself, to be sure. Rather, capitalism requires certain habits—"virtues," in theological parlance—if it is to function successfully. Honesty, creativity, openness to others' ideas, cooperativeness, a commitment to providing customer satisfaction, a willingness to defer gratification in order to achieve a long-term goal; today's philosophers of democratic capitalism are emphasizing, correctly, that without these virtues, capitalism will fail.

. . . Let no one say, however, that our democratic-capitalist System is devoid of moral/cultural problems. We need to foster a new conversation about the common good and its relationship to individual liberty. Rights have got to be reconnected to responsibilities in philosophy, religion, law, and politics.

. . . Most particularly, we need to reflect, and precisely as democrats and advocates of the free market, right on the true meaning of freedom. Lord Acton got it right in the nineteenth century: Freedom is not the power to do what we like, but rather the right to do what we ought. Acton's postulate is an essential moral component of a culture capable of sustaining economically and politically free societies.

SYMPTOMS OF SYSTEM PROBLEMS

Whenever an organization's performance is unsatisfactory or degrading, it is probably because The System is maintaining the status quo to the eventual detriment of the organization. An iron triangle of politicians, bureaucrats, and special interest groups runs most countries by using The System of the government in question to control and maintain the status quo for its benefit. In most organizations, The System largely controls the performance of the organization's members and the output of the organization.

A System problem in an organization is a problem that has persisted over a long period of time and has resisted all attempts at resolution.

Examples of the symptoms of these System problems as they occur in various organizations are given in the pages that follow. Each example directly or indirectly affects the quality of life of most people who interact with the problem.

System Problems in the
U.S. Federal Government

1.   Spending

Total federal, state, and local spending now absorb over 50% of GNP. Table 3-1 shows the increase in spending by major programs over the past forty years. Adjusted for inflation, the federal government's spending for 1995 was about four times its spending in 1955. During these four decades the country's population increased about 1.86 times, or about 86%.

The government's spending on health care programs has increased almost 16,000 percent over the past 40 years. Total federal spending (outlays) over this period has gone from $ 388.9 billion to $ 1,550.9 billion, which is an increase of about 300%.

Table 3-1 Federal Spending in Billions of 1995 Dollars

	1955	1995	% Growth 1955-95
Social Security	$ 25.2	336.1	1,234
Health	1.7	272.4	15,924
National Defense	242.8	271.6	12
Interest	27.6	234.2	749
Welfare	28.8	223.0	674
Education & Social Service	2.5	56.1	2,144
Transportation	7.1	39.2	452
Veterans' Benefits	26.6	38.4	44
Justice/General Gov't.	5.2	32.1	517
Energy/Natural Resources	7.2	26.5	268
International Affairs	12.6	18.7	48
Science & Technology	0.4	17.0	4,150
Agriculture	20.0	14.4	-28
Community Development	0.7	12.6	1,700
Offsetting Receipts	-19.8	-41.4	109
TOTAL OUTLAYS	**$ 388.6**	**$ 1,550.9**	**299%**

Source: Budget of the United States Government, Fiscal Year 1995, Historical Tables

Some specific examples of excessive federal spending are:

• The Comptroller General of the General Accounting Office states that fraud, waste, and mismanagement in the federal budget will total $120 to $200 billion a year.

• The Dept. of Agriculture employs one full-time bureaucrat for every 3 American farms. In 1989 it spent $1.2 billion on research to increase crop yields, and spent another $4.2 billion to keep almost 60 million acres idle in 1991. Congressmen benefited in the 1988 elections from the $2 million campaign contributions by the dairy lobby, while mandating $1.2 billion in payments to dairy farmers to quit dairy farming, creating 144 millionaires. The subsidy for each cow is up to $700 a year. The supply of peanuts is restricted in order to double their price. The honeybee lobby gets $100 million a year which is spread among 2,100 American beekeepers. ($47,000/year welfare checks!) The 1993 per-capita federal benefits for farmers was $21,724.

• Out a total of $184 billion in non-institutional welfare spending in 1990, the U.S. Census Bureau counted only $32.5 billion as income. It excludes food, housing medical assistance, and undercounts cash aid. It ignores that 40% of all "poor" households owned their own homes, including one million poor people owning homes valued at more than $80,000, and 75,000 poor owning homes valued at more than $300,000.[25]

• Congress paid for studies to determine the median nose length of stewardesses ($66,000) and the sexual habits of Japanese quail ($107,000), and to find out how long it takes to cook an egg ($46,000).[26]

• The Environmental Protection Agency, in the past 3 years, has expanded its budget by 31%, and its staff by 23%. These regulators have issued rules which have exorbitant consequences:

Since 1986, the average cost per cancer risk averted by EPA rules has escalated from $440 million to more than $2 billion, with recent regulations under the Resources Conservation and Recovery Act reaching the astonishing level of $204 billion per single cancer risk.[27]

• The Balanced Budget and Emergency Deficit Reduction Act, referred to as the Gramm-Rudman-Hollings Law was a cosmetic charade played on the public. The idea was to cut the 1985 budget deficit of about $200 billion by $36 billion per year until it reached zero in 1991. What actually happened was that over this six-year period the yearly average budget deficit was $206 billion. As a result of the continuing federal budget deficits, the national debt continues to increase. The interest on the debt in 1995 was about $234 billion or about 15% of the annual budget. The total federal debt in 1995 officially was $4.9 trillion. But this did not include other potential liabilities (social security, Medicare, civil service and military pensions, etc.) for an estimated 27 trillion in unfunded obligations.   Increased spending by Congress over revenues has caused the budget deficit, which keeps growing every year because Congress continues to create new entitlements and subsidies for the special interest groups. Since 1970, in spite of federal revenues increasing each year, every dollar of tax revenue has been accompanied by $1.20 in higher spending by the government.

•   The budget deficits are funded, in part, by the federal Reserve Bank which creates (i.e., prints) money to buy government securities, thereby inflating the money supply. Since its establishment in 1914, prices have risen at a 3.28% annual rate through 1991. (Since 1946 the rate is 4.07%.) However, when the U.S. was under the gold standard (1879 to 1914), prices rose at an annual rate of 0.42%.

•   The U. S. Department of Agriculture's Food and Nutrition Service reported that they lost by mistakes, checks lost in the mail, and fraud in the food stamp program, 1 billion dollars in 1989 and also in 1990. By March 1992, a record 25.7 million people were receiving food stamps.

•   In 1991, 713 bills to increase spending and 108 bills to cut spending were introduced by Congressmen. If every bill in 1991 that was submitted by House Representatives became law, U.S. spending would have risen by $783 billion per year! Passage of every pending bill submitted by Senators would have cost an additional $443 billion per year.

2.   **Taxation**

According to the Congressional Research Service and the Office of Management from 1982 to 1993 the government passed nineteen separate tax bills that increased our tax burden during this period by $934 billion. The federal tax code has become so increasingly complicated that no one knows completely what it contains. By 1996 it had expanded to 9,451 pages and is used for other purposes than to raise revenue for the federal government.

Justice Learned Hand[28] said in a dissent that "taxes are enforced exactions, not voluntary contributions." What the government does would be a crime if an individual did it. It extorts money from its owners and gives it to others who have no legal or moral right to it. It uses the money to subsidize special interest groups, such as farmers, dairymen, the sugar industry, research groups, social engineering (via redistribution of wealth by entitlements), food stamps, and other programs.

The tax code is used to restrict, inhibit and control free (investor owned) enterprises. The government taxes the profits of businesses in addition to taxing the income of the owners of business. It permits nonprofit, non-taxpaying companies and agencies to compete with the taxpaying companies. It permits dividends to be taxed twice, first by the company that generates them and second by the person who earns them. It selects different depreciation deductions and investment credits for different businesses, thus enhancing the cash flow and profit of certain businesses. It allows deductions for state and local taxes that "encourages people to get some of their economic services through state and local governments, rather than in the private marketplace."[29] An example of this last statement would be the use of city or town garbage collectors rather than private collection services.

Our tax laws encourage individuals and companies to borrow money, while taxing income from savings. The net U.S. savings rate dropped from 9.8 percent of gross domestic product in the 1960s to 2.0 percent in 1993.

The U.S. Treasury Department estimated that the public spent 5.1 billion hours in 1995 filling out some 260 different tax forms.

Moreover, the total costs in 1990 of complying with the tax code in terms of man-hours, paperwork, and other activities such as increased enforcement, litigation, and the like was estimated to be about $618 billion.

The regulatory burden on businesses and individuals caused by the federal government is increasing yearly. The total federal regulatory costs for 1990 were $312 billion. "The total federal regulatory and tax compliance cost to the economy in 1990 was at least $600 billion."[30] This estimate clearly understates the burden. According to Hall and Rabushka:

> [these] numbers, for example, don't include some further estimates . . . concerning productivity loss and other costs that would double the tax compliance figure, nor do they include the burden of state and local regulations; nor the massive further costs impending from the Clean Air Act, Americans With Disabilities Act, etc.

3.   Social Security

The Social Security program was initiated in 1937 to be a partial replacement of earnings to supplement one's retirement starting at age 65. In 1940, the employer and employee tax rate was one percent on the maximum earnings of $3,000. The maximum monthly retirement benefit at age 65 for men was $41. In 1991, the employer and employee tax rate was 7.65 percent each on the maximum earnings of $53,400. The maximum monthly retirement benefit in 1989 was $1,541, which is an increase of 3,659 percent since 1937. During the same period, inflation increased by about 520 percent. It now is a Ponzi scheme where by the year 2023 the Social Security system will be bankrupt. At that time, the government is going to have to find "the money for all of the trillions of dollars in IOUs it has written itself. To keep The System solvent, Congress will then have the same four choices it had before the 1983 mandated tax hikes: it can raise taxes, reduce Social Security benefits, cut other programs, or borrow huge sums of money."[31] In addition to the Social Security trust fund problem, the Medicare trust fund will be depleted by the year 2001.

4.   Constitutional and Judicial Issues

The Constitution of the United States of America is the supreme law of the country, having been ratified by 11 states and made operable on April 30, 1789. The judicial power of the United States was "vested in one supreme Court, and in such inferior Courts as the Congress may feel free to ordain and establish. The judges . . . shall hold their offices during good Behavior. . . ."[32]

James Wilson,[33] signer and principal framer of the Constitution, signer of the Declaration of Independence, author of the Pennsylvania State Constitution, and member of the first Supreme Court from 1789 to 1798, wrote that in settling cases of law, "the first and governing maxim in the interpretation of a statute is, to discover the meaning of those, who made it." Alexander Hamilton[34] earlier wrote the following:

> The interpretation of the laws is the proper and peculiar providence of the courts. A constitution is, in fact, and must be regarded by the judges, as a fundamental law. It therefore belongs to them to ascertain its meaning, as well as the meaning of any particular act proceeding from the legislative body. If there should happen to be an irreconcilable variance between the two, . . . the Constitution ought to be preferred to the statute, the intention of the people to the intention of their agents.

However, in the past sixty years the Supreme Court has had a tendency to write new laws by ignoring the Constitution and by ruling that laws that had no foundation in the Constitution were constitutional anyway!

The yearly civil case load of the federal courts has increased 200 percent from 1960 to 1987, while the actual court days have increased only 40 percent. "There are two reasons for the recent bureaucratization of the judicial system: an increase in legal activism (which encourages parties and lawyers to seek judicial redress of an ever-increasing list of judge-made legal 'wrongs') and the government's inability to respond to the courts' added work load."[35] Because of the excessive number of cases, the associated costs have skyrocketed.

More important, "The negative rights of protection against government," as guaranteed by the Constitution, "have given way to positive rights of access to government benefits—in effect, the right to use government against other citizens."[36] Justice, as guaranteed by our Constitution (and the state constitutions), is not now certain when in the hands of activist judges and a weak "Solicitor General, who manages the Administration's cases in the Supreme Court and formulates the arguments that are presented to the Justices."[37]

Berger[38] confirms that for the first 150 years of the government of the United States under the Constitution, the role of the Supreme Court was:

to police the boundaries of constitutional grants, not to interfere with the exercise of legislative or executive discretion *within* those boundaries. . . . At the adoption of the Constitution the notion that judges . . . could *make law* as an instrument of social change was altogether alien to colonial thinking. . . . There was first the fact that the common law rules—that is, judicially enunciated rules in the field of contracts and the like—were conceived of as *founded in principles, that are permanent,* uniform and universal. Consequently, judges conceived their role as merely that of discovering and applying preexisting legal rules and derived the rule of strict precedent from such preexisting standards discoverable by judges. It followed that judicial innovation was regarded as an impermissible exercise of will.

In the early years of Franklin D. Roosevelt's administration, "federal judges issued 1600 injunctions preventing federal officials from carrying out federal laws; numerous statutes enacted by the Roosevelt Congress were declared unconstitutional."[39] However, Roosevelt eventually succeeded in changing the constitutional direction of the Court after threatening:

to undermine their authority by "packing" the Court with new members of his choosing. . . . Thanks in large part to the Court's Fourteenth Amendment jurisprudence, the Constitution came to be seen not as the embodiment of fundamental and clearly articulated principles of government but as a collection of hopelessly vague and essentially meaningless words and phrases inviting judicial construction. In other words, it came to be understood as no more than an invitation to these insulated judges to make constitutional law and, when necessary, remake it. . . . The situation is confused today because the judges, and more precisely, The Supreme Court justices, have taken upon themselves the authority to *create* rights, and with every right created they have narrowed the range of the public or political area.[40]

The System has generated many laws that previously would have been deemed unconstitutional. Three such examples are given in the Appendix. The result of such decisions is that the Supreme Court continues to create new laws that expressly were not passed by Congress. Because of these kinds of unconstitutional laws there is a stigma attached to those who receive rewards based on their sex or race. There is also the connotation that the government is a big fraud wherein the iron triangle inmates perpetuate their preferred positions in our society.

On the other hand, Pilon[41] notes that if one is serious about liberty, then the judiciary must use the Bill of Rights' 9th and 10th Amendments, along with the enumerated powers to which Congress and the executive branch are limited, in order to "hold the acts of the other political branches up to the light of strict constitutional scrutiny." In other words, the people must get control of The System that controls the Supreme Court, Congress, and the executive branch of government.

5. Quasi-independent Government Monopolies

Bennett and DiLorenzo[42] discuss how government "competes unfairly with the private sector. . . . Governments in the U.S. produce literally thousands of goods and services in direct competition with the private businesses." Government enterprises are granted legislative and regulatory advantages over private businesses by being exempt from federal, state, and local income, sales, and property taxes and from minimum wage, securities, bankruptcy, antitrust, and myriad other regulations. They can exercise eminent domain, borrow at low interest rates, and have capital and spending costs subsidized by tax revenues and are often granted a monopoly status.

As of 1981, federal employees were operating over 11,000 commercial or industrial activities that the private sector also performs. As of October 31, 1985, over 418,000 federal employees were employed in fifteen categories of commercial occupations.

The government sponsors privately owned enterprises, such as the Federal Home Loan Banks, Federal Home Loan Mortgage Corporation, Federal National Mortgage Association, Student Loan Marketing Association, and Farm Credit System. These enterprises receive special benefits from the government that are not received by other private financial competitors. These special advantages have allowed government-sponsored enterprises to issue credit backed by the U.S. Treasury. From 1980 to 1985, the loans by these enterprises grew 142 percent (from $153 billion to $370 billion). Private business loans grew 45 percent over the same period. Thus, lending by these enterprises crowds out private business lending and makes the latter more expensive because less financing is available. Many of these loans are not part of the federal budget, and thus the potential debt of the government is much larger than the recognized debt.

The government is the largest printer in the United States, having over 6,200 employees and more than 300 printing plants in various government agencies. Private utilities compared with government-owned utilities, such as the TVA, have lower construction and operating costs, innovate more rapidly, offer more services, and pay taxes. In 1990 the Bonneville Power Administration, owned by the government, charged about 30 percent of the national average for its hydroelectric power, thus subsidizing its customers' use of electricity and requiring the taxpayers to fund the extra costs. The United Parcel Service (UPS) handles twice as many parcels as the U.S. Postal Service and is faster. UPS has cheaper rates, and their damage rate is one-fifth that of the U.S. Postal Service. The processing costs of the government's health insurance administration costs in 1990 were 35 percent greater than those of competing public firms. The government's debt collection is expensive and slow compared with that of commercial debt collectors. U.S. Navy ship repair costs generally are 17 times higher than commercial ship repair costs. Private sector weather forecasters' costs are only 28 percent of government costs. The monthly cost per child at government day-care centers in 1990 was $188 compared with $102 at comparable private centers. For military base support services, private contractors' costs generally are 15 percent less than government in-house costs.

State and local government services are also more costly than those of privately owned services. Refuse collection in the private sector is 29-37 percent less costly than local government services. Fire protection by the private sector costs 53 percent less than government fire departments. The government tax supported primary and secondary schools over the past 30 years generally have performed very poorly. Private schools spend about 50 percent less than public schools and usually provide much higher quality education. Public agencies that supply water have higher operating costs than private firms. Local law enforcement costs have been reduced by contracting out to private firms vehicle regulation enforcement, accident investigation, and non crime calls for assistance.

6.   Growth of Bureaucracy

The federal bureaucracy has been growing at an exponential rate. In 1816, the government employed 4,837 civilians; by 1871 there were 51,020 employees, by 1916 there were 399,381, and by 1966 the number of civilian employees had increased to 2,759,019.

During the same period, the U.S. population grew to over 196.5 million—22.7 times the 8,659,000 figure of 1916. Thus the growth rate of the bureaucracy was about 25 times higher than the growth rate of the population.

From 1966 to 1995, the rapid growth of the bureaucracy continued but at a reduced rate. The civilian government employment had increased to 2,918,674, while the total population grew to 263,034,000. During those 29 years, the bureaucracy increased about 1.06 times compared with the general population increase of about 1.34 times.

System Problems in the United States

Illicit Drugs

- Within a year after the passage of the nation's first drug law, the Harrison Narcotic Act (1914), which was interpreted to prohibit supplying narcotics to addicts even on a physician's prescription, the costs of such drugs increased along with an increase in violence and crime.[43]
- From 1982 to 1988, the federal government alone has "spent $21.5 billion to control the drug trade. The result? The supply of cocaine, the latest drug of choice, more than doubled."[44] From 1989 to 1991, federal spending exceeded an additional $25 billion, which had not reduced violent crime, according to the director of the office of National Drug Control Policy.[45]
- The government estimated in 1991 that 12.9 million Americans used illicit drugs and 5.7 million were addicts.
- In 1987, about 6,000 deaths were attributed to cocaine, heroin, and marijuana. The National Institute for Drug Abuse estimated that 158,400 cocaine babies were born in this country in 1990, which added $504 million to U.S. health care costs. By June 1991, there were "about 375,000 drug-exposed babies in the U.S. The treatment of these infants is $63,000

per baby for just the first five years—or about $25 billion."[46]
- According to the Department of Health and Human Services 1994 report, the rate of current illicit drug use increased for youth 12-17 years old between 1993 and 1994 (from 6.6% to 9.5%), after declining from 18.5% in 1979 to 6.1% in 1992. An estimated 508,900 drug-related episodes in 1994 were reported as hospital emergencies, a 10% increase from 1993.

System Problems in Other Countries

Canada

- Canada's new Liberal Party government in 1994 increased annual taxes by C$1.4 billion ($1.9 billion), resulting in a projected deficit totaling C$39.7 billion ($54.8 billion) for fiscal year 1995. The forecast deficit amounts to 4.2 percent of the gross domestic product, compared with the parallel projected United States ratio of 3.5 percent for fiscal 1995. The Canadian government's deficit rose in 1995 to a net C$551 billion ($760 billion). Thirty-three cents of every tax dollar was spent on the public debt interest in 1995, compared with 14 cents of every tax dollar in the United States.
- The average household debt in May 1991 was 78 percent of annual disposable income, the highest percentage recorded to date.
- In the 1991 budget, federal payments to provinces totaled C$36.5 billion ($49 billion): 37 percent of Nova Scotia's budget and 50 percent of Prince Edward Island's budget was funded by the government. The average province received 20 percent of its budget from the government. The average payment per Canadian was C$1,365, from a high of C$16,832 per capita in the Northwest Territories to a low of C$1,015 per capita in Ontario.

- Canada's seasonally adjusted unemployment rate hit 10.5 percent in March 1991, while in May 1990, New Brunswick had 12 percent, Prince Edward Island 14 percent, and Newfoundland nearly 15 percent.
- About 90 percent of Ontario citizens think of themselves as Canadians first and Ontarians second. Only 74 percent of Albertans, 61 percent of Nova Scotians, and 44 percent of Quebeckers think of themselves that way.
- The government work force in 1991 numbered 215,000 people. The average Public Service Alliance of Canada government union member earned $29,000 a year.
- There is considerable duplication in many of the provinces with the federal government. For example, five provinces send trade missions abroad; environmental regulations are set by both the government and the provinces.
- A large percentage of the French Canadians, who make up about a quarter of Canada's population, favor sovereignty for Quebec, while 70 percent of English Canadians oppose an economic union between a sovereign Quebec and the rest of Canada.
- "In Ontario, which is 5 percent French-speaking, drivers' licenses and other official documents are printed in French and English; in Quebec, which is 20 percent English-speaking, such documents were printed in French only."[47] In 1991, Quebec lifted the ban on English because of condemnation by the United Nations and Canada's Supreme Court for violating the Canadian Charter of Rights and Freedoms.
- In March 1988, 48 percent of the 31,263 government employees in the top 29 government agencies were Francophones.
- The Consumer Tax Index relative to the Consumer Price Index increased 1,005 percent from 1961 to 1990.
- Private charitable giving from 1976 to 1991 was down 25 percent individually and more than 60 percent corporately.

- In 1988, the federal expenditures on various social programs totaled almost C$60 billion ($82 billion), about 72 percent of which went to middle and higher income Canadians.
- Canada lost 7.1 million work days in 1987, about 6 times as much is the United States when normalized for the population differences.
- "Of the 25,309,330 people living in Canada in 1986, only 69,065 declared themselves to be Canadians in the last census."[48]

Peru

Except where noted otherwise, this section paraphrases or quotes Hernando de Soto.[49]

- Peru's economy never recovered from the policies of left authoritarian and military dictator, Juan Velasco Alarato (who governed from 1968-75), that disrupted and distorted modernization of Peru. The statest strategies of subsequent governments encouraged stagnation and hyperinflation, and discouraged growth, producing the current economic crisis. Meanwhile an incredibly violent, proudly-Maoist guerrilla movement, the Shining Path, terrorized peasants and politicians and threatened to undermine all order.[50]
- To set up a typical new factory in Peru, an entrepreneur must battle a bureaucratic maze and pay bribes whenever the process is threatened. In the summer of 1982, to register a typical factory required 289 days, the full time labor of a group assigned to the task, and $1,231. That amount at that time was equivalent to the minimum monthly wages for thirty-two people!
- If a group of low income families in 1985 petitioned the state for a vacant lot on which to build, it required interfacing with various ministries and municipal offices for six years and eleven months to get the desired approvals. In addition, it

would cost the equivalent of fifty-six times the minimum monthly wage per person. It should be noted that those who acquire state land receive a defective title that allows them to sell or encumber the land only with the express consent of the provincial government.

- It takes forty-three days to get a license to sell as a street vendor; cost of the license is equivalent to fifteen times the minimum monthly wage.

- In Peru, as elsewhere in Latin America, the poor have fled from the countryside to the cities in search of a better life. In 1940, two of every three Peruvians lived in the countryside, but by 1981 two of every three lived in the city. . . . In Lima alone, the black market (excluding manufacture) employed 439,000 people. Of the 331 markets in the city, 274 have been built by the black-marketeers (83 percent). The black marketeers have invested more than $1 billion in vehicles and maintenance, and 95 percent of the public transportation belongs to them.

- The number of laws and executive orders in Peru exceeds half a million. Of these, only about one percent emanate from the body created to make them: the Parliament. The other 99 percent derive from bureaucrats who run the executive departments. From 1947 to 1985, the legislature passed an annual average of 358 laws, while the executive branch issued an annual average of 26,822 laws and decisions.

- The migrants discovered that their numbers were considerable, that the system was not prepared to accept them, that more barriers were being erected against them, that they had to fight to extract every right from an unwilling establishment, that they were excluded from the facilities and benefits offered by the law, and that, ultimately the only guarantee of their freedom and prosperity lay in their own hands. In short, they discovered that they must compete not only against people but also against the system.

- In defiance of laws, people have acquired, developed, and built their neighborhoods. State or private land is occupied illegally, and settlements are constructed rapidly with great planning (known as "the contract") by the group doing the settlement. This execution of the (invasion) contract among the group has an effect of establishing extralegal rights to the land, which are called expectative property rights. Such rights are similar to the squatter's rights of the developing west in the United States.

- Between 1960 and 1984 the state constructed low income housing at a cost of $173.6 million. During the same period, the black-marketeers (otherwise know as the "informals") managed to construct housing in Lima valued at the incredible figure of $8,319.8 million. . . . As of June 1984—the average value of an informal dwelling was $22,038.

- Informal organizations spring up as a result of the invasion contracts. These organizations provide a whole range of functions; they negotiate with authorities to obtain *ex post facto* approval, preserve the informal law and order, provide services and public works, administer justice within the association, keep a register of the land in the settlement, and conduct censuses.

- A major cost of informal businesses is the ten to fifteen percent of their gross income that they pay in bribes and commissions, compared with the one percent that owners of formal small businesses pay to authorities.

- Individuals are not " all equal before the law, because no two people pay the same tax, no two imports are taxed in the same way, no two exports are subsidized in the same way, and no two individuals have the same right to credit."

- Former President Alan Garcia (1985-1990), who nationalized the country's banks in 1987, deposited the country's bank reserves under his wife's name in a Panamanian bank and a Luxembourg-based bank, Bank of Credit and Commerce International. By February 1991, Garcia's deposits in BCCI amounted to $250 million, in addition to Peru's gold reserves. [51]

- In January 1991, Peru eliminated the 10 percent tax on imports and reduced the value-added tax. The government also announced a crop substitution program to combat Peru's $1 billion annual cocaine trade and the privatization of twenty-three state companies. In March 1991, Peru dropped all restrictions on the use of foreign currency.
- Terrorism and kidnappings are a major factor in reducing the economy. Violence destroyed $18 billion of property between 1980 and 1990 and claimed 3,384 lives in 1990. Security costs are a major ongoing investment for all formal companies.
- Cholera has become an epidemic in Peru. In the first three months of 1991, there were 65,000 cases and 363 deaths.
- Villamonte[52] observes that independent opinion polls in Peru show that more than 70 percent of Peruvians agreed with the coup d'etat of elected President Alberto Fujimori in April 1992:

  The COUP'S announced goal was the alleviation of the pressing problems of Peru: terrorism, violence, corruption, and economic disarray. Everyone in Peru agrees that something has to be done. . . . Mr. Fujimori has done three shocking things. He has closed Congress; he has suspended the constitution; and he again involved the military in politics. It is not hard to understand why many Peruvians are unperturbed by these acts.

  Closing Congress: Peru's Congress is elected every five years in a system of proportional representation. . . . Senators are elected from the country at large; members of the House of Representatives are supposed to represent a province. Congressmen do not represent and are not really accountable to their districts and the nation. . . . Mr. Fujimori is correct when he blames the Peruvian Congress for blocking necessary legislation to spur economic growth and stop terrorism.

  Suspending the Constitution: Peruvians associate the constitution with excesses like parliamentary immunity and special protection for big figures and terrorists. The Peruvian constitution is a highly ambiguous and technical document, and many Peruvians feel that it is understood by only the ruling elite and the politicians.

Calling on the military: Much of the police force and the judiciary is notoriously corrupt. . . . The confidence of Peruvians in the legal system is zero.

Fujimori's efforts have been effective: between 1990 and 1994, inflation has shrunk from 7,650 percent to 15 percent, the GDP grew from $34 billion to $50 billion, and annual per capita income has grown from about $1,000 to $1,250.

Japan

The cost of living, measured against average income, is exorbitantly high. Urban housing is cramped, confined and extraordinarily costly. Only about one-third of Japanese homes are connected with sewers.[53] Japan, with 846 people per square mile, is less density populated than New Jersey (986 people per square mile).[54] However, the supply of residential properties is artificially limited by government rules and tax preference, thus pushing prices to astronomical levels.

- The commuter trains are extremely overcrowded and transport many people very long distances to and from work each day. The roads are inadequate, and the parking facilities in major cities are grossly insufficient for both the inhabitants and commuters. "Urban congestion increases annual commuting hours by nearly eight billion hours, or 30 percent."[55]

- According to Japan's labor ministry, the average Japanese white-collar worker worked 2,044 hours in 1990, or 200 to 400 more hours than a U.S. or European worker. Japanese workers spend an average of twelve hours a day working and commuting, about one-and-a-half hours more than workers in the United States, Germany, Great Britain, and France.[56] Forty percent of the work force, including part-timers, are women, but only one percent of them hold managerial positions.[57] Japanese workers at private companies in 1990 were paid an average of average of 4,250,000 yen ($32,644) a year.[58]

- The government restricts large chain stores from growing, thus limiting the choice that Japanese consumers have and correspondingly increasing the price of goods. Thus Japan has three retail establishments for every 141 people, compared with one retail establishment for every 126 people in the United States.

- Political power in Japan is shared by semiautonomous groups, including government, industry, and major service institution officials. This power structure consists of a complex of overlapping hierarchies, which has no peak. Van Wolferen[59] notes that "there is no supreme institution with ultimate policy-making jurisdiction. [This means that the] prime minister and other powerholders are incapable of delivering on political promises they may make concerning commercial or other matters requiring important adjustments by one of the components of the System."

- The Japanese basis for commercial transactions with foreigners is unlike the basis that foreigners have experienced since trade in the West began. "For the past four centuries the Japanese people have been told to consider socio-political loyalty as the supreme virtue. The result, as one anthropologist has put it, is that truth is socially constituted." Therefore, Japanese traders fundamentally and inherently use multiple and contradictory truths in dealing with foreigners. "It is the near absence of any idea that there can be truths, rules, principles or morals that always apply, no matter what the circumstances."

- Japanese companies are immune from antitrust laws and have been able to boost profits by keeping prices high in the domestic market while subsidizing (dumping) products overseas. Such practices by many industries have combined to lower the standard of living for the average Japanese.

OPERATIONS BECOME OSSIFIED

The growth of The System coincides with the growth of the bureaucracy in an organization. The System expands its scope into every group within the organization, while the bureaucracy flourishes by using The System to expand and maintain its prerogatives, status quo, and longevity and security.

As The System becomes mature, all operations maintain their status quo because it is comfortable, nonthreatening, and easier to perform and sustain their work habits and actions. The operations gradually lose whatever remaining dynamism they have, and sustentation becomes the underlying mode of action.

Deming[60] suggests that deadly diseases and obstacles afflict most companies in the Western world and stand in the way of transforming the Western style of management. (Deming's Western style of management includes much of McGregor's Theory X type of management.) Deming states that curing some of the diseases and obstacles requires a complete shakeup of the Western style of management.

The list below of nine deadly diseases and obstacles are discussed in detail in the section that follows. Quotes and extracts are Deming's unless otherwise noted.

1. Lack of constancy of purpose
2. Emphasis on short-term profits
3. Misevaluation of performance
4. Excessive mobility of management
5. Management by the use of standard, financial data
6. Excessive medical costs
7. Excessive liability costs
8. An environment of fear
9. Resistance to knowledge

1. **Lack of Constancy of Purpose:** Management lacks the resolve to lead the organization into long-term planning for products and services that will ensure access to profitable markets which will keep the company in business and provide secure jobs for its employees. Deming states:

> It is better to protect investment by working continually toward improvement of processes and of product and service that will bring the customer back again.
>
> There are two problems: (1) problems of today; (2) problems of tomorrow, for the company that hopes to stay in business. . . .It is easy to stay bound up in the tangled knot of the problems of today, becoming ever more and more efficient in them. . . . Problems of the future command first and foremost constancy of purpose and dedication to improvement of competitive position to keep the company alive and to provide jobs for their employees. . . . Establishment of constancy of purpose means acceptance of obligations like the following: [innovation, increased resources in research and education, and continuous improvement in the design and production of the product and service].[61]

2. **Emphasis on Short-Term Profits:** "Pursuit of the quarterly dividend and short-term profit defeat constancy of purpose." Deming offers the following quotation from an article by Yoshi Tsurumi:

> Part of America's industrial problems is the aim of its corporate managers. Most American executives think they are in the business to make money, rather than products and service. . . . The Japanese corporate credo, on the other hand, is that a company should become the world's most efficient provider of whatever product and service it offers. Once it becomes the world leader and continues to offer good products, profits follow.
>
> Fear of unfriendly takeover may be the single most important obstacle to constancy of purpose. There is also . . . the equally devastating leveraged buyout. Either way the conqueror demands dividends, with vicious consequences on the vanquished.[62]

3. Misevaluation of Performance: Merit ratings or annual reviews can lead to devastating results. In discussing these, Deming notes the following about this process:

It nourishes short term performance, annihilates long-term planning, builds fear, demolishes team work, nourishes rivalry and politics. . . . It is unfair, as it ascribes to the people in a group differences that may be caused totally by the system that they work in. . . . Merit ratings rewards people that do well in the system. . . . It does not reward attempts to improve the system. . . . Moreover, a merit rating is meaningless as a predictor of performance, except for someone that falls outside the limits of differences attributable to the system that the people work in[63]. . . . These evaluation ratings or reviews can stifle cooperation, teamwork, and impair possible long-term changes or solutions that could benefit the entire organization. Such positive actions may not be recognized in the rating or review and could even cause a reduced rating since the department or group probably could be adversely affected by such altruistic actions.

4. Excessive Mobility of Management:

The job of management is inseparable from the welfare of the company. Mobility from one company to another creates prima donnas for quick results. Mobility annihilates teamwork, so vital for continual existence.

It is doubtful that any manager with an expected tenure of a maximum of five years would introduce or nurture long-term programs for quality and productivity improvements. Such a manager's goal would be to optimize his performance during his tenure so that his remuneration is optimized accordingly. Such an optimization most likely would not be in the long-term interests of the organization and its other members.

5. Management by the Use of Standard Financial Data:

Most managers run the organization using only standard financial data gathered for the company's controller and treasurer by the company's financial information system. "Actually, the most important figures that one needs for management are unknown or unknowable, but successful management must nevertheless take account of them."[64]

The following examples of unknown data should be important for management:

- Synergistic effect on sales from a happy or unhappy customer
- Improvement in quality and productivity along the line due to upstream improvements
- Improvement in performance due to the long-term commitment to stay in businesses suited to the market
- Improvement in quality and productivity from the continual improvement of the processes
- Improvement in performance of new products because of a team approach, including suppliers and customers
- Improvement in performance throughout the organization due to teamwork
- Losses due to annual performance ratings of people
- Losses due to The System
- Losses due to the loss of experienced people
- Losses due to improper or untimely maintenance
- Losses due to excessively long total cycle times

Johnson and Kaplan[65] note that:

today's management accounting information, driven by the procedures and cycle of the organization's financial reporting system, is too late, too aggregated, and too distorted to be relevant for managers' planning and control decisions. . . . Despite the considerable resources devoted to computing a monthly or quarterly income figure, the figure does not measure the actual increase or decrease in economic value that has occurred during the period.

They have documented the need to develop two new systems for process control costing and product costing. Johnson and Kaplan also provide the following examples of nonfinancial indicators that could be measured by companies, if the indicators are applicable to their products or services:

- Internal quality indicators: scrap, rework, part per million defect rates, and unscheduled machine downtime.
- External quality indicators: customer complaints, warranty expenses, and service calls.
- Low-cost producers: productivity measures.
- Improved manufacturing procedure indicators: just-in-time (JIT) production and delivery, average setup times, through-put times, lead times, average number of production days in inventory, average distance traveled by products in the factory, and percentage of delivery commitments met each period.
- Improved design and process flexibility indicators: total number of parts per product, percentage of common versus unique parts in products, and number of subassembly or bill of materials levels.
- Product innovation indicators: total launch time for new products, achievement of product and process development milestones, key characteristics of new products, and customer satisfaction with the features and characteristics of newly developed products.
- Enhancing employee value: absenteeism, turnover, recruiting success, morale, skills, promotability, and number of successful days without an injury or accident.[66]

6. **Excessive Medical Costs:** The organization's medical benefits are expanding at a higher rate than inflation. The largest supplier for some organizations is the health care organization. This growing cost is a self-limiting factor in the selling of a product or service. As costs get out of line, prices tend to increase, thereby causing decreased sales and profits.

7. **Excessive Liability Costs:** The potential increased liability costs, especially in the environmental, safety, and discrimination areas, are in some cases prohibitive and a potential cause for bankruptcy or dissolution of the organization. With the liberal

courts permitting third-party liability, no company is free of the potential of an excessive liability award to the detriment of the company's long-term viability.

8. **An Environment of Fear:** Deming does not list this as one of the diseases but includes it as a major problem in most companies.

> No one can put in his best performance unless he feels secure. . . . *Secure* means without fear, not afraid to express ideas, not afraid to ask questions. Fear takes on many faces. A common denominator of fear in any form, anywhere, is loss from impaired performance and padded figures.

Fear of layoffs affects almost everyone in an organization. People wonder if it can happen to them and consequently rigorously follow The System.

9. **Resistance to Knowledge:**

> Advances of the kind needed in western industry require knowledge, yet people are afraid of knowledge. . . . Another loss from fear is inability to serve the best interests of the company through necessity to satisfy specified rules, or the necessity to satisfy, at all costs, a quota of production.[67]

With these diseases simultaneously infecting most American companies, it is no wonder that their operations become ossified. The thrust to maintain the status quo eventually leads to decay. Some competitors, having conquered The System in their organizations, are cured from or are treating these diseases and thus are creating or winning new customers.

COSMETIC CHANGES REINFORCE THE SYSTEM

Most organizations do not understand the root cause of a problem and therefore propose solutions that reinforce the status quo and eventually worsen or extend the problem. Cosmetic changes address superficial aspects of the problem and are The System's way of maintaining itself, even to the detriment of the people in the organization. These changes do not solve or usually even address the fundamental problem. In fact, many of the same cosmetic changes are applied periodically. A few examples of the many cosmetic changes that abound around the globe are discussed below.

Companies and Organizations

Companies periodically initiate cost-cutting by downsizing usually only in non top management positions. Companies and organizations with similar excuses for poor performance also reduce spending for research, development, education, training, and marketing. Businesses introduce new models or programs that are only marginally different from previous ones. Companies initiate buyouts, install superficial quality control programs, establish offshore manufacturing or sourcing, buy market share through low price only, buy "cash cows," and create non independent new business start-ups. Organizations conduct excessive planning programs, and precipitously introduce ad hoc teams into the workplace.

Some companies institute wholesale reduction-in-force or offer "voluntary" early retirement programs with the latent threat of future layoffs a possibility. Such changes usually are cosmetic because they do not necessarily address the root causes of the problem nor do they generate solutions to the problem. In fact, many companies by their loss of many very experienced employees lose their ability to expeditiously protect their potential long term growth and profitability.

Governments

United States. The government continually makes cosmetic changes such as yearly changes in income tax rules, the Federal

Reserve Board controlling the money supply, the Treasury Department controlling the dollar exchange rates, Congress' ethics policies, the courts controlling the crime and punishment system, the Department of Education's programs, and the post office's productivity improvements. Perhaps the biggest charade is Congress' yearly federal budget exercise. In the name of cutting the deficit, Congress actually increases the deficit as it increases taxes and spending. While claiming over and over again to have agreed to nearly $500 billion in deficit-reducing savings and harsh cuts in spending, politicians actually increased domestic spending by 12 percent in October 1990 and set in place policies and programs that will cause "the nation's $3-trillion debt . . . to mushroom by another three-quarters of a trillion dollars by 1995."[68] One might say that Congress had its own version of a socialist five-year plan. In fact, by 1996 the official debt was over $4.9 trillion.

Soviet Union. Gorbachev's reforms of the Communist system were mostly cosmetic and self-defeating in the long run. Gorbachev proposed a new union treaty to replace the one that established the Union of Soviet Socialist Republics in December 1922. The treaty established a voluntary Union of Sovereign Soviet Republics (U.S.S.R.), which included the following cosmetic change: a new central government that would have even greater presidential control, while the heads of the republics could be part of the Federation Council that coordinated and determined major internal and external policies. Unlike the new constitution of the Russian Federation, which specifically includes the supremacy of individuals' right, such as the right to private property, the new union treaty was silent on these freedoms. Thus the new U.S.S.R. constitution lacked a Bill of Rights to guarantee individuals' rights and limit the government's rights. The new union was The System's way of maintaining the status quo while making cosmetic changes that did not threaten The System's existence.

Japan. Japan's response to the mutual lowering of trade barriers is clearly cosmetic from its trading partners' viewpoint. Japan's approach to the lowering of barriers is merely a propaganda effort to cover up maintaining the status quo of The System.

The Japanese System, moreover, continues to be structurally protectionist, shielding Japanese manufacturers and banks from the type of competition with which the System's corporations have diminished Western firms. The last-mentioned factor seems certain to keep the trade imbalance between Japan and the world permanent.[69]

Religions

Many of the mainline religions in the United States have relinquished their operations to The System. The gospel and the Ten Commandments are ignored or downgraded and secular themes, such as socialism, antinuclear power, abortion on demand, and situation ethics are promoted. These institutions have gradually abdicated their moral authority based on the Bible. Cosmetic pronouncements, such as the Catholic bishop's "Pastoral Letter on Catholic Social Teaching and The U-S. Economy"[70] or the liberation theology espousing communism as the wave of the future,[71] have confused, angered, and repulsed churchgoers. "Church membership declined to 65 percent in 1988 from 73 percent in 1965, and church attendance has similarly fallen."[72]

COMPETITION IS GROWING

The economy of every nation is now greatly affected by the global economy. In spite of government trade barriers erected to protect select industries at the expense of the general welfare of their people, the global economy is forcing nations to acknowledge that the concept of comparative advantage will eventually cause nations to trade more effectively. Therefore, increased competition on a global scale will improve the standard of living in those countries that participate.

The United States has suffered a decline in some of its manufacturing competitiveness in the 1970s and early 1980s. "Entire segments of industry have been decimated or no longer exist in this country." Items such as cameras, copiers, video recorders, auto equipment, machine tools are no longer manufactured on a large scale in the U.S.; the many large steel industries are also gone.

Of major concern, from a manufacturing viewpoint, is the American motor vehicle industry. In 1960 the U.S. produced 48 percent of the world's total supply of new motor vehicles. In 1980 U.S. manufacturers supplied 10 percent of the total production of motor vehicles for the world. For Japan these numbers were 3 percent and 28 percent, respectively. . . . Today, Japanese motor vehicle manufacturers produce over one-third of the world's motor vehicles.[73]

According to a 1985 Fortune 500 study, the return on sales by U.S. manufacturers was only 3.9 percent. For the same group, the return on total assets was only 4.6 percent in 1985 and has been less than 7 percent since 1970. This noncompetitive nature of many American industries has been due to many things, but the lack of responsibility by top management is clearly the major cause.

Many manufacturing companies find themselves burdened with obsolete plants and equipment, with distribution facilities that are totally outmoded, with work environments for human workers that need substantial improvement, and with manufacturing plants that are no longer close to America's desirable locations for work and education. . . . On a global basis, Americans have unwittingly encouraged the growth of manufacturing in foreign companies, particularly in the Far East. This has come about from two practices:[74]

(1) licensing technology to foreign competitors that substitutes short-term revenues for potential long-term revenues, and (2) moving manufacturing abroad in search of lower labor costs. These practices gave foreign competitors experience on the learning curve at the cost of creating future competitors for the U.S. manufacturers.

American management also has sanctioned many noncompetitive practices: high overhead expenses, excessive management layers, direct labor improperly burdened by allocation of excessive overhead costs, poor quality, outmoded manufacturing techniques and policies, excessive inventory, long setup times, inflexible manufacturing lines, excessive new product development and introduction times, limited research and development, and reduced capital investments.

Suzuki[75] analyzes the Toyota Motor Corporation production system, which is typical of most world-class Japanese manufacturers. The Japanese have emphasized the following good manufacturing practices: teamwork, continuous quality improvement, statistical process controls, Just-in-time (JIT) suppliers, *Kanban* (production control procedures), elimination of waste (from overproduction, waiting time, excess transportation, processing, inventory, product defects, and wasted motion, energy, or time), *Poka-Yoke* (foolproof mechanisms), setup time reduction, *Jidoka* (autonomation: machines with the autonomous capability to use judgment), and flexible, mixed production lines. Suzaki shows how these concepts can lead to improved production, lower costs, higher quality, increased customer satisfaction, and improved human relations throughout the organization.

Many of the Japanese manufacturers have radically changed their old manufacturing System into a new, world class manufacturing System. The System in these companies is a joint partnership among the management, the rest of the workers, and the organization. The System is controlled by everyone in the organization, and thus fundamental changes can be introduced and maintained to the benefit of The System and its customers. Many American companies have finally recognized the threat to their well being and existence, and have taken steps to counter the increased competition from foreign and domestic companies. Peters, et al.[76] have documented this responsive resurgence in many U. S. companies. Warren Brookes observes that:

at the end of the . . . Reagan decade of the 80's, manufacturing productivity—the measure of output hours per hours worked climbed to a record level in 1990. [A] report by the Bureau of Labor Statistics showed that manufacturing productivity grew at an average annual rate of 3.6% during the 1980's, almost three times as fast as in the 1970's. In addition, the manufacturing share of GNP hit a record level of 23.3% in 1990.[77]

However, most American companies either are applying cosmetic changes to The System that controls their companies, or are still ignoring the threat of increased competition. Many companies that supply original equipment manufacturers are being told that their quality must improve and they will have to meet the international quality standard, ISO 9000, and that they will have to start supplying their products on a JIT basis. Many of these companies will gradually decline because their management is incapable of changing The System.

SUMMARY

Many people are concerned about the organization and the need to change it, but most do not understand the new notion of The System as a generic concept of management and control. Therefore, usually they believe that it is just a general way of describing the total problems that they encounter.

Often The System is identified in the literature as the problem, but usually only its symptoms are discussed in detail. Sometimes a cosmetic solution is proposed as the way to change The System. What is needed, however, is a comprehensive analysis of The System that clearly identifies the fundamental aspects which need to be changed, because cosmetic changes if implemented only serve to strengthen The System. What is required, then, is a method of developing the optimum way of completely and fundamentally changing The System.

CHAPTER 4

Examples of The System

*The People under our system, like the king in a monarchy,
never dies.*
—*Martin Van Buren*[1]

This chapter presents examples of The System as it exists in the governments of four countries and the management of seven U. S. institutions. The System in the world's most powerful socialist country, Russia (the remnants of the Soviet Union), is an outstanding example of its leaders' lack of understanding of The System. Japan is reviewed because it is the United States' largest competitor in many business areas and its System is not understood by most Americans, including our government leaders. Peru is described because it is a typical third world country that has had a System controlled by a very small but powerful iron triangle. Canada, which is becoming more socialist, is discussed because of its importance to the North American cultural and trade environment. Five U.S. institutions are discussed in detail: Congress, public (i.e., government) education, health care, the Postal Service, and the Supreme Court. The Systems that control these five institutions comprise the major part of the overall System under which the U. S. is governed. Two private U. S. institutions are reviewed briefly. The System in a typical manufacturing business is presented, and The System of illicit drugs is outlined because it is a major problem that worsens each year.

INTRODUCTION

The System abides in every organization and is unique in its specific characteristics, its interaction with top management, and how it follows or uses its laws. In governments and bureaucracies, The Systems are used by politicians and bureaucrats to further their own aims. The System is used by people in an organization to isolate them from management's control.

From its inception, The System grows in usefulness and importance to the organization and its members. In conjunction with stimuli from management and the people, The System continually modifies its methods and its responses to new tasks. Thus, it attempts to maintain itself even while marginally changing. Over a prolonged period, however, The System can be changed fundamentally and its usefulness significantly increased.

This chapter discusses The System in various organizations or institutions. Similar organizations may have similar Systems, except for minor details of their operations. Organizations that differ in their activities and appearances also may have similar Systems. The System that ran the Soviet Union had similarities to the one that ran Peru, for example.

The Systems discussed in this chapter are indicative of the types of Systems in use today. They differ in their degree of authoritativeness, impact on their environments, and internal consistencies. The Systems that control governments are similar in that their respective iron triangle members are generically equivalent to other iron triangle members. The Systems that control businesses and other organizations have iron triangle member groups, but they differ according to their operations. The degree of control that each iron triangle member group has determines the basic thrust and operations of the government or organization.

GOVERNMENT EXAMPLES OF THE SYSTEM

Former Soviet Union: The System in the Soviet Union was created in 1917 by the Bolshevik revolution wherein the Communists seized control of the first Russian democracy. The institution of socialism became the foundation of The System. The Communist party became the core of the "new class"[2] of elitist political bureaucrats who controlled the government, military, courts, economy, press, and private lives of the people. The state became the owner of all property, and the individual became the servant of the state but the *de facto* servant of the Communist party leadership. The Communist party persecuted and outlawed every rival political party. The state controlled or regulated all economic transactions and social activities. The state discouraged such activities as religious services and used neighbors to spy on one another. Children were assumed to be wards of the state and were encouraged to spy on their parents and report any nonsocialist actions or expressions to the government.

The new class maximized its welfare by controlling and maintaining The System in order to use and dispose of nationalized property, set the wages and work rules for everyone, monopolize the distribution of goods and services throughout the country, and maintain the highest standard of living for itself.

The System was managed, protected, maintained, and enlarged by the top Communist party functionaries (*nomenklatura*), who were the top bureaucrats of all the organizations that made up the government. Since The System controlled the economy of the country, all improvements resulted in cosmetic changes to The System, which were always counterproductive. The System maintained a command economy in which the Government's centralized planners controlled all industrial output by issuing gross output orders and setting transfer prices for the products and services of the government-owned enterprises.

Roberts and LaFollette point out the disintegration of the Russian economy:[3]

The economy is plagued by shortages because The System forces an artificial disconnection between the producer and the consumer. Because producers work only to please planners, production output is largely unsuitable for the user's needs. . . . It is difficult for Western managers to contemplate the scale of waste that results from gross output targets. But if one considers that no enterprise director in the Soviet Union is constrained by a bottom line, that no director faces the specter of bankruptcy if the cost of production consistently exceeds the value of the final product, and that all directors can obtain subsidies from the state banking system to bail out their operations, then it becomes obvious that waste is built into The System. There is no incentive to conserve resources, because the factory manager is determined to meet gross output targets at whatever the cost.

Because the distribution system for supplies and materials did not work, theft and a market outside the law were unofficially condoned. "Everyone knows that the economy would come to a complete stop without the illegal supply system."[4]

The new class, when challenged by those outside the new class, typically promised to abolish the major problems of society by changing The System. Thus new cosmetic processes, such as liberalization, decentralization, *glasnost*,[*] and *perestroika*,[**] were introduced.

Forced to withdraw and surrender to individual strata, the new class aims at concealing this contradiction and strengthening its own position. Since ownership and authority continue intact, all measures taken by the new class—even those democratically inspired—show a tendency toward strengthening the management of the political bureaucracy. The system turns democratic measures into positive methods for consolidating the position of the ruling classes.[5]

---

[*] *Glasnost*: An official policy of openness concerning the problems and imperfections of Russian society.

[**] *Perestroika*: The official program of economic and political change in Russia.

To Soviet leaders, *glasnost* and *perestroika* are designed to save the system. To the people, they are a chance to change the system.[6]

The government of the Soviet Union (now Russia and the other republics) was the legal facade of The System. The government created and controlled the laws to maintain The System, which did not have to finesse proposed changes by the leaders of the country because the leaders of all of the organizations were trying to maintain the status quo of The System. The System encompassed every aspect of human activity and most people became resigned to its unyielding presence and consequences. Most people either became partners with The System and tried to grow within it or led dual lives. In one life, they were underground and illegal workers interested in optimizing their families' welfare and in the other, normal passive workers who minimized their time and efforts in government-mandated jobs for which they got wages that were insufficient to meet the minimum standard of living.

The System in the present independent republics incorporates all of the attributes of The System described in Chapter 2. The System's laws discussed in Chapter 2 are also applicable, in general. But The System's Law of Invisibility (The System is invisible to top management) is redundant since top management controls and uses The System to consolidate top management's welfare and security. In this case, the bureaucracy's top leaders understand the necessity for The System and its maintenance. The System's Hidden Factory Rule obviously applies to the republics if one understands that the hidden factory is the underground illegal activities and pseudo illegal black market upon which the entire economy depends. The party leaders understand and allow these illegal operations to exist because without them the economy would be in a complete shambles, which would result in chaos and active rebellions in all areas of the former Soviet Union.

The System's Law of Profits even holds in these socialist countries since, although the concept of profit "has no meaning for the Soviet Manager,"[7] it is replaced by a "gross output indicator," which is a target for the output of a supplier in terms of "goods measured by volume, surface area, weight, or number."[8] The System tries to maximize the gross outputs of each organization, and such concerns as the quality of the output, the usefulness of the output, the consumer demand for the output, and the efficiency and effectiveness of the output are nonessential because of the primacy of the overall state plan for the economy.

The System's Law of Oligarchy clearly has held for the Soviet Union. The Soviet constitution and laws were merely vehicles used to subvert the individual's freedom, such that all freedoms are sacrificed to promote the sanctity of the socialist state. The Communist Party leadership, the Politburo, used the lack of the rule of law in the Soviet Union as a cover for their activities and the activities of the *nomenklatura*, which promoted their own welfare, security, and power.[9]

The Systems in the republics have many problems, which can be identified by a variety of symptoms. Table 4-1 lists some of them.

In summary, The System in the former Soviet Union is the socialist (mercantilistic) philosophy of operation that requires and implements a dictatorship by the minority-run iron triangle—the politicians, bureaucracy, and special interests (the legal business managers, Communist Party members, and military organizations). This new class of people who occupy the positions in the iron triangle receives tremendous benefits from the government's laws, policies, and procedures by subjugating and reducing the welfare of the rest of the people. With the creation of independent republics, Russia has remained the dominant country. Boris Yeltsin has replaced Mikhail Gorbachev as the President of the country, but unlike Gorbachev and the previous dictators, he has limited powers and is constantly being weakened by the Russian Congress of Peoples' Deputies and the Supreme Soviet. These two legislative bodies were dominated by former Communist Party officials and politicians who were trying to maintain The System

Table 4-1   Consequences of a Communist System

1. Economic stagnation and degradation: a third-world standard.
2. Very low prices for basic foods: limited in type and kinds.
3. Empty food and other commodity shelves and stores everywhere.
4. Long queues for purchasing most commodities.
5. Poor quality of goods and services.
6. No rule of law: alleged violators are assumed guilty and must prove their innocence.
7. Unprotected citizens; police usually do not come to the aid of private people — only to the state and its minions.
8. Widespread breaking of the laws, many of which are conflicting; rampant (and usually accepted) theft from government property.[*]
9. Human resources are wasted on a huge scale.
10. Environmental pollution is excessive, rampant, and increasing.
11. Life expectancy is decreasing; infant mortality increasing.
12. Ubiquitous contaminated drinking water.
13. Medical care primitive for everyone except the *nomenklatura*.
14. Substandard housing is prevalent except for "the new class."
15. Private associations are being formed for protection from extortion and crime.
16. Widespread apathy, alcoholism, envy, and fear.
17. Preconditioned attitudes abound about socialism and private businesses. (Profit is thought to be theft, by many.)
18. Massive strikes throughout the country.
19. Government ownership and censorship of the press, radio, television, and book publishing.
20. Government controlled schools, curriculum, and attendance.
21. Internal passports are required in most cases.
22. *Perestroika* (i.e., restructuring) is continually changing the objectives, laws, controls, punishments, and the political organizations.
23. Individual freedoms are controlled and limited by the state.[**]
24. Over 20 million people have been deliberately starved or killed by government fiat.

---

[*]Bribery is the norm for most economic transactions. (This situation is typical in most non market societies. As noted in Chapter 1, McGregor's comment about The System causing dishonest acts is quite valid.)

[**]These are not an unalienable and inherent right of the individual. For example, the right to life, liberty, property, and the pursuit of happiness are subservient to the state and its supremacy in all matters.

and all its privileges for the ruling class. Yeltsin has tried by means of referenda and decrees to enact fundamental changes to The System. He disbanded the parliament and had a referendum on a new constitution and new elections to the parliament. The new constitution established a parliament of two new houses: the State Duma and the Federation Council. Under it, private property, andfreedom of trade, right of competition, privacy, freedom of movement, and freedom of the press would be guaranteed. However, new nationalistic parties have challenged Yeltsin's leadership. The System is trying to reassert itself with these new parties.

Since The System pervades every facet of life in the republics, other fundamental and structural changes will have to be made in all aspects of government and social behavior. Some of these suggested changes are outlined in Chapter 7.

Japan: The System that controls Japan has roots that began with the Meiji oligarchy, which took control in 1868. As a result of this oligarchy a new constitution was adopted in 1889. The imposition of a new constitution by the United States as a result of World War 11 never fundamentally changed The System. Although the constitution provides for a democracy with "more explicit safeguards protecting the citizen than those of Western Europe and the U.S.A., [it makes] the judiciary autonomous from the rest of government, [allowing the law purposely,] as much as possible, [to keep] out of the System."[10]

The System inherently suppresses individualism in Japan. The apparent Japanese acceptance of collective concerns is a result of a System that prevents individuals from having any significant choice in accepting arrangements that are still essentially political.

The System of ruling in Japan is controlled not by the central government but by a select, enigmatic, semi-informal network consisting of ministry officials, political cliques, clusters of bureaucrat-businessmen, agricultural cooperatives, police, the press, gangsters, Tokyo University's Department of Law, and others.

No one is ultimately in charge. These semi-autonomous components, each endowed with discretionary powers that undermine the authority of the state, are not represented by any central body that rules the roost.

The Japanese prime minister is not expected to show much leadership; labor unions organize strikes to be held during lunch breaks; the legislature does not in fact legislate; stockholders never demand dividends; consumer interest groups advocate protectionism; laws are enforced only if they don't conflict too much with the interests of the powerful; and the ruling Liberal Democratic Party (LDP) is, if anything, conservative and authoritarian, is not really a party and does not in fact rule.[11]

The LDP is actually a coalition of formally designated factions. Members are elected to the parliament from parliamentary districts in which as many as five representatives to the national Diet in Tokyo are chosen from a single district. Since the top vote-getters win the election and a party fields more than one candidate, the candidates in effect compete with their own party candidates. The System thus weakens and divides parties and politicians and consequently strengthens the bureaucrats who actually control The System.

The System also is a major factor in the economy of Japan. The business, financial, and government network of self interest groups gives special monopolistic control to key industries. In exchange for protection and special help from banks and the Justice Ministry, industries agree not to compete with each other, to pacify their employees and the consuming public, and to satisfy their international customers.

The Japanese economy may be described as a form of mercantilism.

Such economies are "rent-seeking societies," in which the government controls, described as "central planning," in reality provide monopoly profits for a privileged minority at the expense of consumers in general. The ideological claims made by the beneficiaries of such policies may play a significant role in maintaining the stability of The System, but do not necessarily reflect the actual economic motivations of those beneficiaries.[12]

The government bureaucracy in Japan is as powerful as the Communist party and *nomenklatura* of the Soviet Union, but more benign. The bureaucracy interacts with all of the private domains in the country to such an extent that it exerts considerable and almost absolute control over most public and private domains. For example:

> Japanese government bureaus have extraordinary powers of awarding licenses and other permissions for commercial pursuits, and of withholding advantages like subsidies, tax privileges or low-interest loans at their own discretion. Ministries can resort to "administrative guidance" to force organizations in their realm of endeavor to adopt "voluntary" measures. . . . The Ministry of Finance and The Bank of Japan also exercise powerful control. . . . By issuing binding instructions to the commercial banks, The Bank of Japan still maintains a very large voice in allocating the funds for all really big investments.
>
> The bureaucrats also preside over a proliferation of public and semi-public corporations serving all manner of economic and political purposes—including, incidentally, the provision of post retirement sinecures for the bureaucrats themselves.[13]

Because of General MacArthur's postwar administration, Japan has a Western style constitution that is very democratic but "in no way reflects Japanese political priorities."[14]

> A truly independent, nonpoliticized judiciary as provided for in the formal postwar rules, and a population gradually familiarized with the possibility of litigation, would have checked consolidation of the postwar System as we know it. [Adherence to the antitrust laws and] election laws would have checked it, as would consistent judicial investigation into the corrupt relationship between big business and the LDP, and the various other informal relations and practices that keep the System going. . . . The System, driven as it is by a myriad *jinmyaku* [the network of special personal connections], could not survive the political inspection made possible by consistent application of the legal process.
>
> The role of law in the System is most effectively minimized by keeping the number of lawyers and judges very small. The System

prefers conciliation, and makes sure that it remains the preferred alternative to litigation. . . . The judiciary and bar are kept artificially minuscule by strict controls over entry into the legal profession. The Ministry of Justice is gatekeeper to the Legal Training and Research Institute, through which all those aspiring to become judges, prosecutors or lawyers must pass.

The number of lawyers is restricted by keeping the entrance examination acceptance rate to about 2 percent annually. Van Wolferen goes on to comment that:

the number of judges has not even doubled since 1890, whereas the population has more than trebled. . . . Japanese courts are so overloaded with cases that even the simplest take between two and three years to resolve at the district court level. [The final resolution of big cases can take up to 25 years, and lawyers are difficult to find and very expensive.] The impartiality of judges is undermined by worry about promotion and postings, which come up for review [by the bureaucracy every three years. The bureaucracy uses a secret grading evaluation that is weighted in favor of the number of cases resolved or dropped during their three-year tenure of office.] The Japanese courts have no contempt powers. [The Japanese courts have been captured by The System, and therefore the Japanese people, knowing from long experience that The System cannot be changed,] cannot risk alienating themselves from their social environment by taking an individualistic stance.

The System is so ubiquitous and powerful that it has defused every attempt to change the ruling party in power, the LDP. Important pressure groups are assimilated into The System, leaving a small minority farmer-radical-activist coalition as its only real but ineffective opposition. "A well-tested ploy used by components of the System before they grow out of hand, or to expand control over an area which still eludes their grasp, is to establish their own 'opposition group'."[15] These opposition groups eventually become partners with the business or bureaucracy elements that are proponents of the System.

Internal friction in the LDP between the newer, younger members and the senior members controlled by the party's leadership has lead to the formation of various splinter parties. As a result, the LDP in July 1993 lost its majority in the lower house of the Diet. However, since The System is still in control, any changes that occur because of that election will be cosmetic.

"Rural Japan is most effectively made to serve the System –and the LDP in particular–through the agriculture cooperatives that were in fact inherited from the wartime System." A huge organization called the *Nokyo* virtually controls all aspects of the agricultural community and consists of the central confederation of agricultural cooperatives and most other agricultural organizations. Although Japanese agriculture is very heavily protected from foreign suppliers, the *Nokyo* provides a monopoly service to the System such that Japanese consumers pay exorbitant prices for most agricultural products while Japanese farmers receive prices that are too low to enable the average farmer to live without an extra job or a government subsidy. The bulk of the farm income goes to support the *Nokyo* bureaucracy and indirectly the LDP.

The *Nokyo* units, which are middlemen or distributors, buy the farm products (other than rice) and market them through the *Nokyo* trading companies. The *Nokyo* units sell the rural population practically everything that it needs for farming and many other products. The Nokyo units provide banking, health and welfare facilities, credit, storage and warehousing, insurance, and guidance and instruction, including voting guidance for the LDP. The farmers are trapped in The System deliberately in order to optimize The System and its proponents.

Van Wolferen notes that the labor union movement, having been captured by The System also, is relatively inactive.

The unionization rate has steadily declined, from 55.8 percent in 1949 to 28.2 percent in 1986. Except for seamen, teachers and groups of public workers whose nationwide unions could not so easily be tamed, there are today only management-supported company unions, which more often than not actively participate in campaigns to maximize production, at the cost of worker comfort. . . . There is no conflict between management and "organized" workers. . . .The System is well served by an established opposition. This institutionalized, impotent opposition absorbs potentially genuine opposition.

The best example of this is the Japanese Socialist Party (JSP), which allows intellectuals to promote Marxist doctrine in place of the alleged "injustices perpetrated by 'monopoly capitalism'." The JSP has become "so irresponsibly impractical and unattractive as to deprive the voter of a credible alternative to the LDP." The JSP is an ineffective opposition to the LDP because the realists among the Japanese left know that they cannot change The System and therefore do not try.

"There remain a few elements actively opposed to the System that are intransigent and unassimilable." A very small number of radical fringe groups periodically attempt terrorist activities. One major Japanese group, however, the Japan Teacher's Union, is actively opposed to The System. This union is dominated by moderate Marxists who oppose the Ministry of Education's nationalistic and Confucianist view of teaching as a "divine mission." The union has opposed the reintroduction of moral education and supported the usual left-wing causes, such as opposition to Japan's so-called Self-Defense Forces, U.S. Bases in Japan, etc. However, the rank and file's major concern has been for a truly independent educational program rather than Marxist ideology. "The forces of the System [are] gradually gaining ground, since the forces of the Japanese left as a whole are diminishing."

[Japanese schools, newspapers, and organized crime] are each highly politicized as servants of the System. . . . The aims of Japanese schools could hardly be further removed from original sense of the English word "education": to bring forth and develop the powers of the mind, rather than merely imparting factual information. Far from sharpening the reasoning ability of its charges, the Japanese education system, on the whole is hostile to such a purpose. . . . Instead, the emphasis is on rote memorization. . . . The overriding purpose of the Japanese educational system was summed up [by Rohlen[16]] as shaping generations of disciplined workers for a techno-meritocratic system that required highly socialized individuals capable of performing reliably in a rigorous, hierarchical, and finely tuned organizational environment.

In somewhat the same way as the old boy network of the English public (i.e., private) schools and universities, but in a more magnified and multiplied form, finely tuned elitists are dispersed throughout The System upon graduation, giving it cohesion and renewing its longevity. Graduates of the universities are hired by a quota System based on the hierarchical position of the university and the corresponding hierarchical position of the business-government entity.[17]

The press seldom takes a real adversarial role toward The System, being content to display a superficial anti-establishment attitude.

Most important, they make no attempt to analyze the System, to provide a critical frame of reference enabling readers to ask questions concerning the System's essential nature and the direction in which it is taking them. . . . Self-censorship continues to be a conspicuous characteristic of the Japanese press. Newspapers, agencies and broadcasting companies gather their news from government and business via *kisha* (reporter) clubs. . . .The *kisha* club represents the institutionalized symbiosis between journalists and the System's organizations they report on. They help the journalist . . . and they provide the power-holders with their main means of coordinating media self-censorship. . . . To gather genuine news from important organizations without going through the *kisha* clubs is difficult and sometimes virtually impossible. [Few editors] have faced up to the reality of a System which operates fundamentally at variance with the conventions and rules of parliamentary democracy. Those who have fall back on the worn-out cliché of monopoly capitalism to describe it. . . . In a country where laws exist for the administrative purposes of the bureaucracy rather than the protection of citizens, the press plays a critical sanctioning role. It can do this because Japanese strongly fear the consequences of having their reputation blemished. This concern with preserving their good names substitutes to a large extent for legal sanctions in keeping organizations and people in line.

Van Wolferen goes on to say:

The most startling example of how the System uses groups of presumed outsiders for its own ends is seen in the relationship between the police and criminal gangs. . . . In a traditional service that goes back centuries, the gangsters, who exert control over themselves within crime syndicates, help police keep nonsyndicate crime under control. [These syndicates] are accustomed to protection from people in high places. Both before and after the war they were used by the corporations to help break strikes. . . . It is an open secret that gangsters sometimes do the dirty work for politicians. . . . Considering how much can be accomplished in Japan by intimidation, it should be no surprise that some LDP politicians still consider good relations with highly placed *yukuza* [gangsters] to be useful. . . . The unwritten rules of the System hold that gangsters may run protection rackets, prostitution and related illegal businesses, but that they are forbidden to carry guns and deal in narcotics.

Japan has a clearly discernible ruling class. Its members—mainly bureaucrats, top businessmen and one section of the LDP—are all basically administrators; there is no room among them for the aspiring statesman. . . . Entry into Japan's relatively large administrator class is strictly via a very narrow ladder up the school hierarchy. . . . And since its survival depends on that of the System, its highest shared goal is to preserve the System. [This is accomplished by] keeping the criteria for membership, and the rules governing transactions among the administrators themselves, informal. The System is what it is by virtue of informal relations that have no basis in the constitution, in any other laws or in any formal rules of the ministries, the LDP, the corporations or any other of the administrator institutions.

The LDP politicians maintain themselves by extorting money from every part of The System. This is done in a myriad of ways, such as insider trading on the stock market, vote buying from the bureaucracy and businesses, illegal contributions from their constituencies, legal donations from commercial banks and other industries, and commissions charged (two percent of its value) for public projects paid for by the central government.

Corruption in Japan is in a sense legitimized by its systematic perpetration. It is so highly organized, and has become so much a part of the extralegal ways of the Japanese System on so many levels, that most citizens and foreign residents do not recognize it for what it is, but accept it as "part of the System." The press calls it "structural corruption," implicitly acknowledging that is a necessary aspect of the System in its present condition.[18]

However, recent television commentators have exposed repeated instances of political corruption, which have led to national and international scandals. They have highlighted the younger political reformers and their alleged programs and spotlighted the entrenched politicians and their self-serving actions and lack of performance.

Peru: Peru is considered a third world country, and The System that controls Peru is mercantilism.

"Mercantilism" means a bureaucratized and law-ridden state that regards the redistribution of national wealth as more important than the production of wealth. . . . Redistribution . . . means the concession of monopolies or favored status to a small elite that depends on the state itself is dependent.

The system includes . . . the state government [and] also entrepreneurs who work within the law. . . . This system is not only immoral but inefficient. . . . Instead of favoring the production of new wealth, the system, owned, in effect, by the closed circle of those who benefit from it, discourages any such effort and prefers merely to recirculate an ever-diminishing amount of capital. In that context, the only kinds of activity that proliferate are nonproductive, parasitic activities—the elephantine bureaucracies.[19]

The government of Peru consists of the executive, the Parliament, and the courts. Of the more than one million laws, decrees, ministerial resolutions, procedures, and other matters passed from 1947 to 1985, the Parliament only created about 1.3 percent. The rest were created by the bureaucracy. According to de Soto, "the system invents laws to frustrate the legitimate desires of the people to hold jobs and have a roof over their heads. Black-marketeering is the masses' response to the system." Representatives in the Parliament are elected country-wide and do not directly represent a district. The party leaders gain seats in proportion to their party's share of the general vote. Leadership control of the party is not democratic, and leaders or their families stay in office sometimes for generations to enrich themselves. In 1989 the members paid themselves $3,000 monthly, which is forty times the minimum wage, and have blocked all recent reform attempts by President Fujimori.

The legal institutions are inadequate to deal with the suppression and discrimination that the government imposes on the majority of the people. Illegal black market activities are so commonplace that the government has officially accommodated many of its organized functions, such as providing bus transportation and housing, and running small businesses.

Because the government bureaucracy, which in effect runs the country, is almost completely corrupt, their official, but illegal, dealings with the populace have led to a complete disregard for the law.

A complete subversion of means and ends has turned the life of Peruvian society upside down, to the point that there are acts which, although officially criminal, are no longer condemned by the collective consciousness. . . . This infiltration of violence and criminality into everyday life has been accompanied by increasing poverty and deprivation.[20]

The System has caused the creation of a counter system, a "system of extra legal norms," which takes the place of the shortcoming of the official legal system. The official legal system is used as a barrier to prevent competition with the established economic interests. Laws, rules, regulations, and fees have been imposed on anyone who tries to establish a new manufacturing business, build a structure, create a new service, or own or transfer property rights. The counter-system is extremely inefficient because of the subterfuge, bribery, and extra precautions that one has to take to minimize the chance of causing a responsive counteraction by the authorities. For example, the extralegal activities cost ten to fifteen times more in bribes then do legal activities. Because of severe restrictions on obtaining and using capital, the informal marketplace lacks efficient machinery and thus produces less than corresponding legal activities.

The System is run by state bureaucrats and maintained by making cosmetic changes whenever necessary. Laws are changed continually to help a special interest or combine obtain special rights to an economic transaction or activity. These cosmetic changes are made continuously and are the source of power to the bureaucrats. These redistributive laws have politicized all sectors of the population, which organize in self-defense to live at other's expense. Gradually, the special interest groups have become the third leg of the iron triangle.

> The laws enacted as a result of a redistributive agreement between the state and a combine establish a legal system which gradually becomes untouchable because the combine will demand that it be maintained and its demand is supported by the bureaucracy. . . . Combines force the legal system to steadily accumulate laws that prevent access to formal activity, increase the cost of remaining formal, and make it virtually impossible to simplify regulations and reduce bureaucracy.[21]

Canada: The System controls the general quality of life in Canada. The System controls the federal and provincial governments, the constitution, the major political parties, the economy, and the culture of Canada. The Canadian people have abdicated their natural rights (common law) to the central government and thus depend on the government to provide them with the "necessities" of life.

A federal parliamentary state with ten provinces, two territories, and a central government, Canada became a member of the British Commonwealth of Nations when it received its constitution from Great Britain in 1982. The federal government consists of an elected House of Commons, a government appointed Senate, a Premier, various ministries including the armed forces, and the Supreme Court.

Canada's population tripled from 1910 to 1984 and as of 1994 was 29.2 million people. The number of federal government civil servants from 1910 to 1984 increased from about 20,000 to 250,000 people, or 12.5 times.

In 1867, Great Britain passed the British North American (BNA) Act (renamed the Constitution Act of 1867), which established the first self-governing British dominion outside Great Britain. The act established the provinces of Ontario, Quebec, New Brunswick, and Nova Scotia and a Canadian constitution.

All powers not expressly reserved to the Provinces of Canada were assumed by the central Government: the Governor-General, representing the monarch, ruled through Ministers drawn from the majority in her Canadian House of Commons, and Members of the House were elected in numbers proportionate to the population they represented.[22]

The act gave each province exclusive direct taxing powers to raise revenue for provincial purposes and to borrow on the sole credit of the province. Manitoba became a province in 1870, and British Columbia followed in 1871. The opening of the Canadian Pacific Railway in 1885 generated the subsequent significant expansion and growth of Canada.

Canada became a sovereign state on March 29, 1982, when Queen Elizabeth II gave royal assent to the Constitution Act of 1982. The new document:

contains the original statue that established the Canadian federation in 1867, the amendments made to it by the British Parliament over the years, and new material drawing on [Pierre] Trudeau's 1980 proposals and his later discussions with the provincial premiers. . . . A novel part of the document was the Charter of Rights and Freedoms. This set down 34 rights to be observed across Canada, ranging from freedom of religion, to language and educational rights based on the test of numbers. Many of the rights could be overridden by a "notwithstanding clause," which allowed both the Federal Parliament and the provincial legislatures to set aside guarantees in the Charter.

The "notwithstanding clause" has to be renewed every five years to remain in force. The act contains a formula for its amendment:

resolutions of the Canadian Parliament that receive concurrence of two-thirds of the provinces representing at least 50 percent of the country's population are sufficient to approve a constitutional amendment. The act also "committed the central government to provide public services of reasonable quality across Canada by ensuring revenue (equalization) payments to the provinces."[23]

The Charter of Rights and Freedoms was imposed on all Canadians by politicians who had no mandate to create it and who did not consult the people. The people's inalienable rights inherently "protected under the Common Law, are such no more." Although the Charter guarantees Canadians "rights and freedoms, it *specifies* and therefore *limits* them, and subjects them 'to such reasonable limits as can be justified in a free and democratic society.' In short, it grants appointed judges the right to erode or even eliminate those freedoms." Canadian's rights "no longer stand alone, and above judges, in the Common Law tradition, or in an unqualified Constitution" similar to the United States' Bill of Rights. Unlike the U.S. Constitution, which secures the blessings of liberty to the people and their posterity, the Charter defends "peace, order, and good government." The parliament is now subordinate to the Charter of Rights and Freedoms and its reasonableness as determined by a single judge.[24]

The five main political parties in Canada are the New Democratic Party (NDP), Liberal Party, Progressive Conservative Party, separatist Bloc Quebecois Party, and Reform Party, which is conservative. The NDP is Canada's socialist party and is a registered member of the worldwide organization for socialists, The Socialist International. The Liberal Party is similar to the U.S. Democratic Party and advocates more state power to equalize outcomes for different individuals and groups. The Progressive Conservative Party has abandoned its true conservative vision of the world and attempted to win power by outpromising the Liberal Party.[25]

Between September 1990 and October 1991, the socialists (NDP) won control of Ontario, British Columbia, and Saskatchewan, which represent slightly more than half of Canada's 26 million people. Thus while many of the world's socialist countries (such as the Soviet Union, Poland, Czechoslovakia, and Hungary) have renounced socialism as an economic and political way of life, some Canadians will be experiencing the joys of socialism. The NDP's platform includes the following planks:

- Increasing taxes; increasing redistribution of wealth; more government agencies, commissions, and inspectors; and more crown (government owned) corporations
- Modifying and controlling the operations of the great productive organizations
- Providing for an equalitarian society
- Increasing government planning and rejecting of the capitalist theory of supply and demand
- Increasing affirmative action programs whenever possible
- Supporting unilateral disarmament of the West
- Making all conceivable social services universal
- Equalizing incomes, i.e., laws that order increases to equalize wages
- Banishing corporate competition
- Imposing rent controls on all property

The socialist NDP came to power in industrial Ontario with only 37 percent of the vote because the peculiarities of the three-party political System gave it a good majority in the provincial legislature. However, in the federal elections of 1993, the Reform party swept the western part of the country and in 1995 the Ontario provincial elections swept the Conservative party into office. Provincial powers have increased because of the Constitution Act of 1982 and therefore the provincial governments control most of the economic decision making in Canada. The current trend is that Canada will become a province-dominated nation.[26]

However, the provinces agreed during the terms of Prime Ministers Pearson and Trudeau to the "shared cost" of the federal government programs, such as education and Medicare. The provinces thus were allowed to circumvent the BNA Act by borrowing money that the federal government created through the Bank of Canada.

Canadian socialist politicians and bureaucrats have initiated multiculturalism, bilingualism, and immigration policies to follow the ideology of equalitarianism. Their objectives are:

> the eventual achievement of a worldwide equality of social outcomes, a forced equalization of wealth, regardless of merit, and the neutralization of all value-preferences between peoples and cultures. The goal of this policy is to replace all *natural* cultures with the idealistic, artificial, bureaucratic culture of the State itself, to replace moral values with political ones, natural differences with quotas, religious beliefs with secular ones.[27]

The Province of Quebec has for many years tried to protect its French culture and language. Its politicians have as their goal the Francization of Canada or, at a minimum, that Quebec becomes a separate socialist nation. Toward that end, President Trudeau's Languages Act of 1969 forced the rest of Canada to accept official bilingualism. The net result is that a minority French population has succeeded in dominating the linguistic, cultural, and constitutional framework of the nation. Less than fifteen percent of Canadians are bilingual, but the federal government now requires top federal "servants" to be bilingual.

The Department of Immigration has drastically reversed the ethnic composition of immigrants accepted by Canada. From 1946 to 1966, 92.7 percent of immigrants were from traditional countries, such as the United Kingdom, European countries, the United States, New Zealand, Australia, and South Africa. However, from 1968 to 1987, the percentage from traditional sources was deliberately reduced to 31 percent. At the present trend, the percentage of people who say that they are of British extraction will approach zero by the year 2051. Government regulations now permit up to 84 percent of the total immigrants to meet no qualifications.[28]

Trudeau and his socialists slowly revised The System that is now controlled by socialist politicians who maintain and strengthen it at every turn. The System's trend is clear: maximize the government's control over individual lives, equalize everyone especially with regard to income, promote multicultural values, and mortgage the future so that equalitarianism is a permanent fixture in Canada.

Government Institutions in the United States

U.S. Congress: In accordance with the Constitution of the United States of America, 435 Representatives are elected to the House of Representatives every two years, and 100 Senators (two from each state) are elected to the Senate in staggered terms every six years. Each representative now represents approximately 600,000 people from a congressional district in his or her state. Except for age, citizenship, and state residency qualifications, every American is eligible for these offices. Congressmen serve at the forbearance of the House or Senate and may be punished for disorderly behavior or expelled by a two-thirds vote.

Congressmen receive a self-imposed yearly salary of $133,644, yearly cost-of-living increases that are larger percentage-wise than those received by Social Security retirees, health insurance and life insurance benefits, and an extremely generous pension plan. (Ten members who left office in 1994 each will receive estimated lifetime pensions of over $2.3 million.)

Each congressman receives an average of $636,000 a year for staff and office expenses and a franking privilege that has averaged over $220,000 per year. A congressman also receives an office in Washington, D.C., and many perquisites, such as the Congress' gyms, swimming pools, parking garages, subsidized haircuts, interest-free loans, free checking accounts, cafeteria charge accounts, fixed illegal parking tickets, and a yearly income tax deduction of $3,000 for living expenses. The 535 congressmen are aided by 38,696 congressional staff and support people. In 1992, 376 congressional aides made more than $100,000 a year, with more than 1,000 making $80,000 or more a year. The yearly budget for Congress now exceeds $2.8 billion, or over $5 million per congressman, an increase of 150 percent since 1980.

The House and Senate are organized by standing committees and subcommittees that are run by members chosen for their seniority. Committees are organized by the majority party, which establishes the number and ratio of majority to minority members. Committee chairmen are virtual dictators in their committees, controlling committee and subcommittee expenses and budgets and determining what priorities will be assigned to issues that are to be discussed and voted on.

Congressmen are assigned to committees and expected to work with their leadership in promoting the party's policies. A congressman has very little power as an individual and quickly learns that he or she must work with the party's leadership to influence the formation of legislation.

New congressmen are immediately taught that their first priority is to get reelected and to develop a reelection campaign fund supported by the special interests. Their second priority is to maintain an active constituent service whereby potential voters can receive help in dealing with the thousands of government entities that subsidize, regulate, or interfere with their lives.

Congressmen are taught to respond to pressure groups because only they appear to be actively concerned about the government and how laws affect their well-being. Congressional hearings are extremely one-sided with the number of people testifying in favor of government support or regulation greatly outweighing those in opposition. At fourteen typical congressional appropriations committee hearings in 1990, 1,014 witnesses spoke in favor of the spending programs, seven spoke against the programs, and 39 were neutral. The ratio of pro-spending witnesses to anti-spending witnesses was 145 to one. However, this example was apparently atypical, since it is the impression of committee staffers that program advocates outnumber program critics in the committee process by 1,000 to one. In addition congressmen typically receive five or six groups of people in support of a spending program every day during the budget process. The vast majority of pro spending advocates are government officials or former government officials now working for a lobby.[29]

Members of Congress are well aware of this process and the misuse of tax dollars for political purposes. However, Congress also has been very adept at ignoring laws that it has passed. For example, at least two laws have been passed requiring a balanced federal budget, but Congress has used many budgeting, and off-budget tricks to increase deficit spending at unprecedented rates. Until recently:

> Congress has also frequently exempted itself from laws that apply to the private sector: Its members can legally discriminate in hiring and promotion, are exempt from affirmative action and equal employment opportunity laws, can pay their staffs less than the minimum wage, and can legally ignore health and safety regulations.[30]

It is obvious that The System that controls Congress is based on the prolonged exposure of congressmen to progovernment propaganda. This continuous, overwhelming exposure brings "congressmen into the orbit of the bureaucracy, so that instead of checking its growth, they become its patrons."[31]

From 1980 through 1989, Congress enacted an average of 312 laws each year and also passed many bills that died for various reasons. Congressmen, in general, do not know all of the details of most bills on which they vote, and many are surprised when they later find out some of the things they had enacted. On November 27, 1991, the House of Representatives voted 372-47 in favor of the $151 billion, 6-year transportation bill without a single member having read it.[32]

Congress also receives over 3,000 reports a year from over 100 different agencies and cabinets. Although the congressional oversight function is obviously overwhelmed, this does not deter Congress from creating agencies rather than eliminating them.

Congressmen are trapped within The System, which is so strong that Congress cannot even legislate itself to be free of it. Congressmen have learned that all previous reforms were cosmetic and that they cannot make fundamental, structural changes as long as the iron triangle nurtures The System. Senator John Danforth[33] said the following in a Senate speech: "Deep in our hearts, we know we have given our children a legacy of bankruptcy. We have hurt America for the purpose of getting ourselves elected." Senator John McCain[34] earlier said, "We lack discipline. We are spending addicts, and we can't admit it. We can't 'just say no.' We need help."

The attributes of The System within Congress are generally the same as those enumerated in Chapter 2. Top management in this case means the people of the United States, and management means the committee chairman and the party's elected congressional leadership. Although the reproducible attribute does not apply directly, it does apply if the competition to Congress is considered to be the executive and judicial branches and the independent regulatory agencies.

The laws of The System certainly apply to Congress. Even The System's Law of Invisibility holds, since the public is unaware that Congress is controlled by The System. The public is concerned about spending, taxes, and budget deficits and blames Congress and the President for the excesses. Since these unsatisfactory results occur yearly, it is clear that The System is the problem.

The System has been maintaining the status quo for many years. The iron triangle protects and uses The System to further its self interest. Although a few private organizations today are trying to change The System, the last change occurred in 1913 with the passage of the Seventeenth Amendment, which required the popular election of Senators. That change, while fundamental to the Congress, was cosmetic regarding the operation of The System and its effectiveness. On the other hand, an alleged fundamental change in The System is being proposed with the balanced budget amendment, which only lacks ratification by two more state legislatures before it becomes the law of the land.

Government Education: During the first half of the seventeenth century, education was considered a family affair. In 1647, Massachusetts enacted a law ordering that every township containing at least 50 families or householders set up a government run school in which children could be taught to read and write and that every township of over 100 families or householders "should set up a school in which boys might be fitted for entering Harvard College."[35] Every town had an elected school committee whose term of service was three years, with one-third of the committee chosen annually.

Thus The System began with the establishment of a local organization concerned about the management of schools. The school committee initially exercised the management of the town's schools, hired teachers for a term of one year, and established a school budget that had to be approved at the annual town meeting before funds could be expended. The System was very simple and centered about the teachers, parents, and children.

> Because local schools were bound up with family, neighborhood, and community, and because teaching was intrinsically anchored in personal relationships and experiences, people naturally believed that they could and should be able to govern their own educational affairs.[36]

Thus local government school Systems were created throughout America, each reflecting the diversity, culture, and autonomy of that particular locality.

The Constitution of the Commonwealth of Massachusetts, ratified in 1780 by the voters of the towns, established Harvard College as the official state college to be governed by the top state officials and ministers of the six nearby Congregational churches. By this constitution, Massachusetts established its right to be a partner in The System of education.

However, since the beginning of the twentieth century, progressive reformers and educators have been successful in building a nationwide System of education that was supposed to cure all of the so-called ills of the previous local Systems.[37-39] These progressive reformers and educators created a System that:

> was bureaucratic and professional, designed to ensure, so the story goes, that education would be taken out of politics and placed in the hands of impartial experts devoted to the public interest. It was the 'one best system.' During the last few decades, however, scholars have done a thorough job of demolishing their claims. The new educational institutions imposed on the nation were neither inevitable nor uniformly progressive.[40]

Initially, state and local assistance to denominational schools was commonplace until the middle of the nineteenth century, when the advent of compulsory education changed that. Moreover, reading the Bible in public schools was constitutional until the U.S. Supreme Court in 1968 created a new law making such readings unconstitutional.

Beginning in the 1920s, professors of education began using the "look-say" method instead of phonics to teach reading. This method, devised by Thomas H. Gallaudet in 1835 for deaf-mutes, was still used by 85 percent of the nation's schools at the beginning of the 1980s. The progressives remained in full control of The System. The following example, from 1951, is from a paper published in the *Bulletin* of the National Association of Secondary-School Principals:

> We've built a sort of halo around reading, writing and arithmetic. We've said they were for everybody . . . rich and poor, brilliant and not-so-mentally endowed, ones who liked them and those who failed to go for them. . . . The principal has remarked, 'All educated people know how to write, spell and read. . . . The Three R's for children, and all children for the Three R's.' That was it. . . . We've made some progress in getting rid of that slogan. But every now and then some mother with a Phi Beta Kappa award or some employer who has hired a girl who can't spell stirs up a fuss about the schools . . . and ground is lost. . . . If and when we are able to convince a few folks that mastery of reading,

writing and arithmetic is not the one road leading to happy, successful living, the next step is to cut down the amount of time and attention devoted to these areas in general junior and high school courses.[41]

Under the direction of professors of education, book publishers already had been following the above recommendation. One study shows that first readers in the 1920's contained on the average 645 different words; in the 1930's, about 460 words; in the 1940's and 1950's, about 350 words. [In 1962, one edition reached] a low of 153 words. In the 1970's . . . primers contained only 28 percent of the vocabulary presented to their counterparts of fifty years ago.[42]

In November 1991, the Texas State Board of Education realized that there were more than 200 factual errors in the new American history textbooks that were to be used for the 1992-93 school year.

The System of education today is quite uniform throughout the United States. The System's defenders are the usual iron triangle occupants: the politicians (mainly the governors and state representatives but also including the president and congressmen), the bureaucrats (mainly the state and local school regulatory agencies or commissions but also including the U.S. Department of Education), and the special interest groups (mainly the government teachers, school administrators, teacher and other unions, school boards, college departments of education, and book publishers). It should be emphasized that the iron triangle does not include its customers—the children and their parents.

The System has developed a relatively uniform and restricted way of providing educational services to its customers. The System is organized around the state governments, which have enabled it to set up its methods in large school districts. The federal government, although not granted the constitutional right to support education, manages to spend about 6 percent of the $350 billion the United States spends on education annually. Of course, with dollars come regulations on how the states or individuals must comply with the federal government's educational and social policies.

The System's educational policies mainly have been generated, directly or indirectly, by the deans and professors of education, federal and state education officials, superintendents of schools, other school administrators, and teacher unions. "This, more than any other factor, is the nation's education problem." This is because "it is the truth and it should be said: the inferior intellectual quality of the education faculty is *the* fundamental limitation in the field."[43]

The System has restricted the availability of competent teachers by requiring college graduates to obtain a teaching license or certification. This means that a candidate must complete a series of education courses approved by the state department of education (i.e., by The System). Alternate programs have been initiated recently, but The System has managed to limit such programs. "Only about 12,000 teachers in the entire nation have been certified through alternative routes since 1985. That's about 0.5 percent of the 2.4 million teachers now working in elementary and secondary schools."[44]

The System maintains itself by continually increasing its educational budget in spite of copious data suggesting that, if anything, there is a negative correlation between educational expenditures and superior educational performance. Like the schools of education, The System has no interest in the quality of the output of its endeavors with the students, who are its captive customers.

In spite of one of the highest levels of spending (per capita) in the industrial world, the American public school system is generating students who rank 13th out of 13 advanced nations in science and math, and 11th out of 13 in social studies and language.[45] [The System] spent 6.8 percent of the country's gross national product on education in 1986, while the Japanese spent only 5.1 percent, and the West Germans 4.6 percent. Japanese and West German students routinely outperform American students.[46]

Over the past two decades, from 1972-73 to 1992-93, total spending on American education increased from $51.7 billion to

$253.4 billion, a 390 percent increase in current dollars and a 47 percent increase in constant dollars; national enrollment dropped 7 percent; the average yearly teacher's salary increased from $10,164 to $35,334; the number of non teaching staff in government schools increased approximately 40 percent; the average per pupil yearly spending increased from $1,035 to $5,598; and the national average SAT net scores dropped 35 points.[47]

The System uses the civil rights movement to divert attention from poor schooling.

> Educationalists used the movement for their own purposes, which were twofold. One was gain in money, power, and political clout. . . . Two, the civil rights movement provided the rhetoric behind which to hide their lack of a body of pedagogical knowledge. Having failed to develop even effective means to teach reading and arithmetic, educationists adopted the rhetoric of the civil rights movement to move themselves onto a loftier plane. Now they were going to "change society," which to a considerable extent they had already done. By the 1950s, children in public schools were beginning to be noticeably less rigorously educated than their public-school educated parents.[48]

Thus The System uses quotas, affirmative action, and politically correct speech and behavior to maintain its status quo.

The System protects itself by promoting academic freedom, which it defines as anything that enhances its power and longevity. U.S. colleges now maintain a large number of Marxist teachers who still promote Marxism as the preferred way of life for Americans. Education courses are mandated by The System for all teachers so that The System will not be corrupted from within by competent, independent teachers and administrators.

The System continues to expand its scope of activities to maintain its power base. The System initially accomplished its expansion by making school mandatory for children; it did this first in 1852 in Massachusetts and later, by 1918, it was mandatory in all states. Government vocational schools are a good example of this growth in scope of System activities; new courses are continually being introduced—an early example being driver education. In addition to combating racism, the latest "problems" that The System is trying to incorporate into its activities are sexism, discrimination by sexual preference, and the propitiation of academic excellence (elitism).

The System continually generates cosmetic changes in order to deflect any fundamental, structural changes. Examples of cosmetic changes are open classrooms, computerized learning, TV instruction, head start programs, child care programs, parental immersion programs, small class sizes, special education classes, values education, earth day, prevention of nuclear war, flexible modular scheduling, buddy programs, coaching, framework curriculum, animal rights, and whole language.

The System always promotes itself. The System's Law of Hierarchy of Policies (see Chapter 2) has self-protection as its highest priority. Sensing a real threat to its existence by private schools, The System attempts to eliminate or, failing that, to regulate and restrict such schools. The System is against government funding of students who attend nonprofit religious schools. The System uses its major union, the National Educational Association (NEA), to elect and lobby local, state, and federal politicians who are sympathetic to The System.

The System uses its own jargon to establish its professionalism and exclusiveness. John Kenneth Galbraith[49] has written:

Complexity and obscurity have professional value; they are the academic equivalent of apprenticeship rules in the building trades. They exclude outsiders, keep down competition, preserve the image of a privileged or priestly class. The man who makes things clear . . . is a recusant or a scab. He is criticized not only for his clarity but for his treachery.

The System's Law of Bureaucratic Displacement is strongly operable in the government educational system. Over the twenty years ending in 1992-93, the educational bureaucracy and the number of teachers increased, resulting in government spending increases. During this period, however, the enrollment decreased, the number of public schools decreased, and the average Scholastic Aptitude Test (SAT) scores decreased. More important than the drop in SAT scores is the general consensus that the government schools are in worse shape than ever. According to a new Department of Education study, two-thirds of the children in the U.S. cannot read up to their grade level. Thus increased bureaucracy equals decreased output.

When The System is being attacked by a potential fundamental change, The System's sycophants try to obfuscate the idea completely. For example, let's take a look at the voucher System for school choice. The following list presents objections to the voucher system for the purpose of perpetuating The System:

1. Since local control is paramount, limit choice to the government schools in the local school district.
2. The Goals 2000 federal program proposed by President Clinton would impose national input standards on every government school, thus strengthening the educational bureaucracy.
3. The money to establish any voucher System would be diverted from federal educational funds that now go to disadvantaged children—in effect, a shift of funds from poor to middle-class families. (The assumption here is that the present funding programs are giving superior results.)
4. The cheapest way to have school choice is to have one large school building that would house a federation of schools operating and emphasizing individual instruction. (Thus the real problem is inefficient organization and not teachers, programs, and test scores.)
5. The school problem can never be solved until the poverty problem is solved. (Thus being poor prevents one from learning.)
6. The school problem is caused by low teacher salaries. (The implication is that schools would be outstanding if teachers received higher salaries.)
7. School vouchers would promote segregation and elitism.
8. School vouchers would eliminate a comprehensive education experience.
9. School vouchers could negate a state department of education's approved curriculum.

10. School vouchers could prevent health, social, and psychological services on a direct and confidential basis. (This means that parental consent probably would be required.)

11. School vouchers would prevent the implementation of improved programs regarding issues such as birth control, diversity of sexual orientation, stress, suicide prevention, conflict, the environment, multicultural education, and nuclear war.

12. School vouchers would involve support of religious schools and teachings.

13. School vouchers would probably eliminate the elementary counselors now required in many schools.

14. Taking money from teachers' salaries to implement school vouchers would make the situation worse since these funds would decrease. (This implies that teachers in schools chosen by parents and students would not have equal or higher salaries than teachers in the rest of the government schools.)

15. School vouchers would demoralize the students not in such schools and also their educators and parents. (Thus the students who do not exercise school choice would be labeled losers, thereby injuring their growth and well-being.)

16. Because school Systems and schools do not work like free markets: choice will not automatically bring the discipline of the market to bear on education, at least not without a host of other changes that proponents of choice have not grappled with and society thus far has been disinclined to pursue.[50]

17. National testing will lead to national teaching standards and centralized curriculums.

None of the above objections are valid, and all are smoke screens promoted by members of the education iron triangle in order to protect The System.

The System of education in colleges and universities generally lacks quality and is very costly. There are a wide range of colleges and no compulsory attendance laws. In general, The System's Law of Bureaucratic Displacement also holds since government institutions usually have larger student populations, lower tuition and housing prices, and lower output—that is, a much smaller percentage of students graduating compared with private institutions. Since people from middle and upper-income families are two or three times as likely to attend college as people from lower-income groups and go to school for more years at the more expensive institutions, students from high-income families benefit the most from government subsidies of colleges. Thus The System uses government funding of higher education to transfer income from low to high income groups.[51]

Many colleges and universities also are oases "of quasi-socialism" where "America's academic intellectuals are largely insulated from the discipline of free markets."[52] As such, these institutions have transformed themselves:

> from a student centered place of intellectual and emotional development to a place where academic intellectuals . . . rule in their own self interest. . . . Colleges and universities became big business in the 1970s, and in the rush to capitalize on the wellspring of Federal dollars, they forgot their basic mission, educating our children.[53]

Examples of how to change The System of education in a fundamental way are given in Chapter 7, where a change function is proposed that would save the taxpayers billions of dollars each year while improving the quality of education that pupils receive.

Health Care: Health care in the United States has changed both fundamentally and System-wise in the past century. Initiating the changes was the proof in the 1880s that diseases are caused by germs. The development of antiseptics and heat sterilization in the 1880s and 1890s led to the development and expansion of hospitals, which up to that time were considered to be very unhealthy and only good for treating the poor. "The resulting growth in the number of hospitals was staggering. In 1873 there were only 149 hospitals in the U.S. In just 50 years, by 1923, the number had soared to 6,830." By 1973, the number had increased to 7,438 hospitals, but by 1987 there was a leveling off of hospital growth and an actual decline to 6,821. In 1870, there were only

64,414 physicians in the United States, or one for every 617 people. By 1970, there were 348,328, or one for every 602 people. By 1987, there were 612,000 physicians, or one for every 397 people, resulting in a 75 percent increase in the number of physicians in just 17 years. In 1987, total health care expenditures were $500.35 billion, of which 41.4 percent were paid by federal, state, and local governments. The Department of Commerce estimated that national health expenditures increased to $838 billion in 1992, an 11.5 percent increase over the previous years.[54]

The health care System for Americans before the 1930s mainly depended on either the individual's ability to pay for services that were needed (about 80-90 percent) or aid from other private individuals, churches, or mutual aid societies. The federal and state governments' health care aid was very limited. In 1929, total health care expenditures were $6.85 billion, of which 11.4 percent were paid by federal, state and local governments.

By the early 1900's, many fraternal societies began to institute formal health and accident insurance as well. In 1917, an estimated 45 of 59 fraternal orders in California offered a sickness or accident benefit, as did 140 of 159 in Illinois. Before the Depression, fraternal societies thoroughly dominated the health insurance market (at least among the working class). The secret of their success as compared to their commercial competitors lay in their enviable ability to check the threat of "moral hazard," the bane of the insurance businesses, and an especial problem for health insurance because of the difficulty of verifying claims of sickness. [The fraternal society had several weapons in its arsenal to guard against moral hazard.] The Social Insurance Commission of California noted in 1917 that the mutual benefit nature of the societies undoubtedly tends to counteract the tendency to malinger. Persons who might be unscrupulous in dealing with a commercial company are apt to be more careful when dealing with an organization whose financial condition is a matter of direct concern to themselves.[55]

In addition, fraternal members usually were friendly with each other, which ensured constant contact (and thus conformation) in times of ill health. Probably most import was that the fraternal societies had a strong religious tone to their activities and most members were God-fearing, righteous individuals who were not willing to violate the Ten Commandments.

Since the 1930s, mutual aid societies have been eliminated allegedly because of actuarial problems, although other factors were probably more responsible for their demise. State governments, in response to doctors' lobbying, passed laws forbidding fraternal societies from forming health maintenance organizations by contracting with doctors. The first hospital insurance plan was introduced in 1929 and, due to its success, many other plans were generated throughout the country in the 1930s. At about that time, the government started its metamorphosis into a welfare state, which eventually eliminated or minimized the self-help and mutual help actions of society and replaced them with the paternalistic programs of the government and its growing legions of social bureaucrats.[56]

From the 1930s, the federal and state governments have passed many laws concerning the governments' support of health care. There are now over 700 state laws, some of which are hundreds of pages long, that govern all health care providers. These laws, which are considered by many to be entitlements, now cost the taxpayers $675 billion per year and are increasing each year at rates greater than 10 percent per year.

The System of health care in the United States is run by the usual iron triangle of politicians, special interests, and medical care providers. Figure 4-1 shows the health care iron triangle, with the customer (the patient) merely the vehicle that permits The System to function in its and the triangle's behalf.

The System of health care in the United States is very complicated. Figure 4-2 is a flow chart of The System that exists today; it shows the following: (1) the movements of four types of patients who are medically treated; (2) the flow of the costs derived for the types of patients; (3) the material from suppliers and the input regulations and restrictions from the governments, insurance companies, and businesses; and (4) the four potential

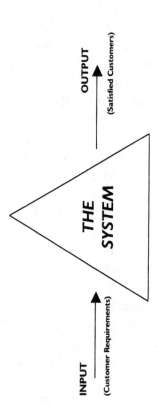

THE IRON TRIANGLE OF
THE SYSTEM OF HEALTH CARE IN THE UNITED STATES

- Physicians
- Nurses, Medical Technicians
- Hospitals, Clinics, Nursing Homes, etc.
- Medical Equipment Manufacturers & Suppliers
- Drug Companies & Suppliers

OUTPUT
(Satisfied Customers)

THE SYSTEM

INPUT
(Customer Requirements)

- Federal Politicians
- State Politicians
- Their Staffs

- Government Bureaucrats
- Regulatory Agencies
- American Medical Association
- American Hospital Association
- Health Insurance Association of America
- Other Organizations
- Lobbies

Figure 4-1

FLOW CHART OF THE SYSTEM OF HEALTH CARE IN THE UNITED STATES

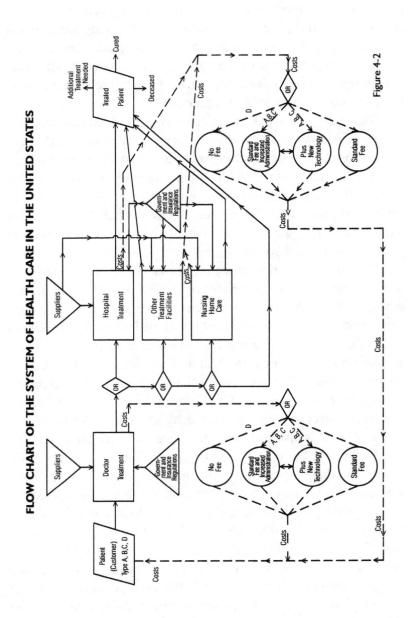

Figure 4-2

paths for the patients that result from the medical treatments received from this process. The patients' movements are depicted by lines. The patients are shown by parallelograms, and the iron triangle members are shown as triangles or rectangles. The costs are shown as circles, and the path of costs are dashed lines. Decision points are noted as diamonds.

There are four types of patients: type A individuals purchase private insurance; type B individuals earn group insurance through the institution for which they work, and may or may not have private insurance; type C individuals receive group insurance through the U.S. or state governments, such as Medicare, Medicaid, military or civil service, or the Department of Veterans Affairs, and may or may not have private insurance; type D individuals do not have insurance.

The treatment that three of these types of patients may receive could depend on the cost or treatment that the insurance supplier allows. Although there may be a standard fee for each type of treatment or service, the standard fee is not applied for one of three reasons. The first reason is that some people (type D) are too poor to pay for treatment and are not insured. The costs for the treatment they receive are therefore transferred to paying customers, types A, B, and C. The second reason is that doctors now must increase their fees for each service in order to pay for the large liability insurance they are forced to carry because of the permissive laws being exercised by an army of lawyers. The third reason is that hospitals, other medical care facilities, and physicians also need to recover the costs for their new technology.

According to the AMA, the average doctor in 1990 had an income before taxes of $314,300, worked 59.1 hours per week, and took five weeks vacation. Average expenses were $150,000 for supplies, rent, personnel, and insurance, leaving a net income before taxes of $164,300. In 1991, the average doctor saw 118 patients a week; general and family practitioners saw the most (144), and surgeons the fewest (107).

The doctors, hospitals, and other treatment facilities or personnel are influenced in their diagnoses and treatments by inputs from the state and federal governments and insurance providers. These iron triangle members interact with one another to optimize the growth of The System of health care in the United States, which also results in their own growth. Expansion of services to the elderly and the poor is the main thrust that drives The System, along with the creation of new or improved equipment or processes.

In addition to hospitals, treatments are available in clinics, outpatient centers, nursing homes, and other facilities. These treatments also have suppliers and inputs from the insurance providers, and their costs follow the same process as the doctors' costs.

There are no natural brakes on costs in this System. Table 4-2 gives reasons why medical care in the U. S. is so expensive.

The patients have been programmed by The System to demand more and better services, which they know will not directly cost them anything significantly proportional to the services they receive. Doctors know this also and have been increasing the price of their services. For the first time in the history of the United States, in November 1991, doctors in a New York City municipal hospital went on strike for higher salaries.

Doctors and hospitals have very little incentive to prevent or limit costs in treating customers. The for-profit insurance providers have an incentive to minimize costs, but the government and the nonprofit medical care providers have very little incentive to do so since most of their fees are on a cost-plus basis. In addition, there are fewer for-profit facilities compared with the nonprofit facilities, and thus there is no real perception of competition.

Health care costs have been rising not solely because patients are excessively increasing their transactions but because of the large increase in new technology, improved facilities, and improved

Table 4-2 Reasons Why Medical Care Is So Expensive

1. Past government restrictions on the supply of physicians, and present government restrictions on the number of medical schools and licensing of physicians
2. Increased demand due to government funding of Medicare, etc.
3. Increased demand due to third-party insurance
4. Soaring medical malpractice insurance costs
5. Resultant increases in so-called defensive medicine
6. The large percentage (90%) of not-for-profit hospitals
7. The availability of new, very expensive technologies
8. Government restrictions on permitting health care services by others rather than M.D.s, e.g., midwives
9. Government restrictions on the introduction of new medicines and techniques
10. Government funding of research and development of "preferred" medical problems, e.g., AIDS vs. cancer
11. The excessive use of illegal drugs and the resultant exorbitant treatment costs involved, increased criminal activities resulting in medical costs, and the birth of drug-dependent babies
12. Government policies and funding of welfare, leading to a life style dependence on welfare support (especially welfare mothers)
13. Government tax policies which in effect limit the research and development of new medicines and technologies, and cause businesses to provide health-care insurance to their employees in lieu of higher wages that would be taxable to them
14. The monopolistic control of the entire medical profession by a union of physicians, i.e., the AMA
15. The AMA's restrictions on doctors' advertising their services
16. Government mandates on insurance underwriters

medical care personnel. The government's Health Care Financing Administration estimates that new technologies and facilities consumed at least 40 percent of the growth in real hospital spending.[57]

Moreover, the Florida Health Care Cost Containment Board issued a report in August 1991 stating that at least 40 percent of the doctors practicing in Florida have invested in joint medical ventures to which they can refer their patients. For example, only three diagnostic imaging centers of the 160 surveyed were not partially or wholly owned by doctors. In addition, full-service clinical labs owned by referring physicians perform an average of 3.3 diagnostic tests per patient compared with 1.7 tests per patient in non doctor-owned labs. This figures out to an average charge of $43 per patient versus $20 per patient, respectfully. The report also indicated that the joint venture labs provided a lower quality of services compared with non doctor-owned labs.

The System tries to maintain its status quo by promoting cosmetic changes that help it grow incrementally. The federal government (in this case Congress, the Department of Health and Human Services, and the President) is trying to be all things to all people at all times. These members of the iron triangle are trying to expand government-supported health care to the poor, the elderly, children, and welfare recipients. While they are causing an increase in demand for free health care services, they are trying to decrease the costs of these services by either limiting the costs of treatments or restricting treatments that require very expensive technologies.

The System understands this dichotomy and is prepared to relax its principles and growth rate to maintain its control of health care. Most of the proposed changes that have been discussed during the past few years are cosmetic, and they would not change the basic nature of The System. Problems today, such as increasing costs, restrictions on the quality of health care, and rationing of high technology health care, will continue to be problems tomorrow as long as The System remains in control.

Postal Service: The System that controls the U.S. Postal Service has roots that are over 200 years old. Although many changes have occurred to The System throughout those years, it is stronger than ever.

The U.S. Postal Service is an example of a government supported monopoly in which cosmetic changes are made continually. From 1739 to 1774, Benjamin Franklin was the Postmaster General for the American colonies as the representative of the postmaster general of England but was dismissed because of the political situation in the colonies. On July 26, 1775, the Second Continental Congress passed a resolution establishing an American postal System known as the Continental Post. "Not until the Articles of Confederation went into effect, March 1, 1781, was Congress recognized as having a monopoly over the postal service." It was assumed that postal rates would be established by Congress which would cover all expenses of the Postal Service. On September 17, 1787, the U.S. Constitution authorized Congress to establish post offices and post roads.

"The first Congress under the Constitution was too busy to make formal provision for the postal system and continued the establishment as it had been defined in the ordinance of 1782." On September 22, 1789, Congress and the President approved an act that established a temporary post office that would have the same power as under the previous Second Continental Congress. On February 20, 1792, a law established the postal system as a government monopoly and set postal rates that were based on distances.

In 1799, the Post Office administration consisted of nine people who supervised 677 post offices and the transportation of mail over more than 1,600 miles of post roads.

President Monroe in his annual message to Congress, Dec. 2, 1823 . . . discussed the Post Office. . . . He pointed out that there were now 5,240 post offices and 88,600 miles of post roads, that the receipts amounted to $1,114,345.12 and the expenditures, $1,169,855.51[58]

Various improvements in the mail service increased its efficiency, such as free city delivery (1868), postal money orders (1864), the sorting of mail on mail cars *en route* (1864); postal cards were first issued in 1873, special delivery letters were authorized in 1885, free rural delivery in 1896, motor vehicle service in the larger cities in 1914,[59] [a postal savings system in 1910 (now defunct), the parcel post system in 1912, and air mail in 1918.]

On April 18, 1950, Postmaster Jesse Donaldson reduced residential service to one delivery a day and business service to two a day. In spite of this reduction, in fiscal year 1951, the Postal Service's expenditures were $2.27 billion and the deficit was $565 million. The next year, expenditures were $2.61 billion and the deficit increased to $720 million.

Appointed in 1953, Postmaster General Arthur Summerfield modernized the Postal Service's antiquated accounting system, saving $25 million a year in man-hour expenses. He decentralized the Postal Service's operations, created a Bureau of Personnel and a Research and Development Department, and attacked the problems of plant obsolescence, inadequate transportation, and inefficient and wasteful procedures. Looking at the Postal Service as a public utility, his objective was a yearly balanced budget. In 1960, the Postal Service's annual report announced that it would improve its service and meet "the ultimate objective of next-day delivery of first class mail anywhere in the United States."

On April 3, 1967, Postmaster General Lawrence O'Brien suggested "that the Post Office should become a nonprofit government corporation managed by a professional executive and that the postmaster general should cease to be a member of the president's cabinet and should be a businessman, not a politician." On August 12, 1970, the United States Postal Service (USPS) became an independent establishment of the executive branch of government. The USPS is directed by a Board of Governors appointed by the President with the advice of the Senate. These nine governors serve for nine-year terms and appoint the postmaster general and deputy postmaster general, who also become board members. The USPS can sue, be sued, enter into contracts, and buy, sell and hold property. The USPS employees are no longer in the U.S. Civil Service but are members of the new postal career service. By 1984, the USPS was supposed to be self-supporting, with any surplus invested for the benefit of the USPS. Congress retained the right to determine what is non mailable.

Postal rates are set by a special rate commission of five professionals appointed by the President for six-year terms. The proposed postage rates can be rejected only by unanimous vote of the nine governors appointed by the President. The postage rates are also subject to judicial review. "Rates of pay are to be comparable to rates and types of compensation paid in the private sector of the economy of the United States."[60]

"Far from solving the postal problems, the reorganization appeared to make them worse."[61] R.J. Myers notes that the USPS managers have become a self-serving elite and the postal unions have managed to ratchet up the average employee's wages and benefits to over $40,000 a year.

Bovard suggests that the February 1991:

> four-cent hike in stamp prices will help finance the greatest intentional mail slowdown in U.S. history. The average first-class letter now takes 22 percent longer to reach its destination than in 1969. . . . In July 1990 the Postal Service began sharply reducing its delivery standards for first-class mail. . . . The revised standards could add 10 percent to the average delivery time for first class mail. . . . When asked at a September (1990) hearing of the House Post Office Committee about the costs of the slowdown to the American public, Postmaster General Anthony Frank declared, "I don't think it costs the American public anything.[63]" [The Postal Service is the only delivery business that believes speed is irrelevant.]

According to Dr. Richard Lesher,[64] President of the U.S. Chamber of Commerce:

> [the USPS's] restrictive work rules make it virtually impossible for the Postal Service to reap the benefits of its massive investment in new technology. For example, it is common practice for postal employees to use old inefficient machines because union rules specify that 90 percent of the employees must work full time.

The Postal Service has demanded and received an exorbitant increase in rates to sustain a reduction in service. It is only through the magic of a government imposed monopoly that such miracles are made possible.

It is clear that the reorganization was merely cosmetic and strengthened The System. The cosmetic changes have resulted in much poorer mail service at an increasing cost ($8 billion per year) to the user and taxpayer. Moreover, the agency posted a deficit of $1.5 billion in 1991 and over $1 billion in 1992. Part of this deficit was caused by the USPS sponsoring the 1992 Olympics, which cost the taxpayers $122 million. Due to rate increases, the USPS had a profit of $1.77 billion in 1995 and $1.57 billion in 1996.

The present postmaster general, Marvin Runyon, initially vowed to eliminate 30,000 positions in the Postal Service with no loss of service. However, he recently requested his staff to review the possibility of reducing home delivery to just four days a week, omitting Tuesday, Thursday, and Sunday. It is obvious that The System will not change its basic monopolistic ways and that a change function must be applied by the voting public through its agent, Congress.

Supreme Court: The System of government in the United States was ordained and established by the ratification of the Constitution by eleven states in 1788 and the inauguration of George Washington as the first President of the United States on April 30, 1789. The Constitution is unique in the history of constitutions of various countries of the world, with most of the actual provisions being purely American in their origin.[65]

Our whole system of government is based on the assumption that there are certain absolutes, referred to in the Declaration of Independence as "the Laws of Nature and of Nature's God." This maintains that there *is* a God, not less so because we may not fully appreciate His laws, nor fully understand His logos.[66]

The Constitution embodies many provisions that already were part of several state constitutions and the Articles of Confederation. The Constitution's chief principles are as follows:[67]

• The division of government into three separate and distinct branches: the Executive, the Legislative, and the Judicial.

• The plan of representative government

• The superiority of local self-government, in that the new federal government would not control matters that could be adequately dealt with by the states

• The division of the elective Legislative into two branches that are equal

• The election of the Executive directly or indirectly by the people

• The powers given to the President were largely the powers vested by the State Constitutions in the Governors of the existing States

• The appointment of the judiciary by the Executive, by and with the advice of the Senate

• The jurisdiction given to the Judiciary over national matters

• The provisions regulating the methods of action by Houses of Congress, and the modes of election, were largely mere mechanism of government; they were not matters of fundamental principle; and most of this mechanism was also taken directly from the State Constitutions.

• The written limitations on the power of the Congress and the President included in the Bill of Rights

The Constitution was created with checks and balances on its constituent parts.

Small States secured equal representation in the Senate, and the large States proportional representation and the origination of revenue bills in the House; that through which the Northern States secured Federal regulation of commerce, and the Southern, prohibition of Federal interference with importation of slaves for twenty years, and representation of three-fifths of the slaves in election to the House.

The executive branch had limited authority but could veto a bill passed by Congress, and the president's term of office was set at four years. Congress could override the president's veto by a two-thirds vote in each House. The Supreme Court judges could declare an act unconstitutional and served under the condition of good behavior. Each representative served a two-year term and each senator served a six-year term.

Article III of the Constitution established that:

judicial Power of the United States, shall be vested in one supreme Court, and in such inferior Courts as the Congress may from time to time ordain and establish. [The Article states that the judges] shall hold their offices during good Behavior [and shall] receive for their services, a compensation which shall not be diminished during their continuance in office.

The Article limited the supreme Court's power as follows:

- To all Cases, in Law and Equity, arising under the Constitution, the Laws of the United States, and Treaties made, or which shall be made, under their Authority.
- To all Cases affecting Ambassadors, other public Ministers and Consuls.
- To all Cases of admiralty and maritime Jurisdiction.
- To Controversies to which the United States shall be a Party.
- To Controversies between two or more States; between a State and Citizens of another State; between Citizens of different States; between Citizens of the same State claiming lands under Grants of different States; and between a State, or the Citizen thereof, and foreign States, Citizens or Subjects.
- To all Cases affecting Ambassadors, other public Ministers and Consuls, and those in which a State shall be a Party, the Court shall have original Jurisdiction.
- In all the other Cases before mentioned, the supreme Court shall have appellate Jurisdiction.
- Power to declare the Punishment of Treason

Article III also listed the law regarding trials and treason as follows:

- The Trial of all Crimes, except in Cases of Impeachment, shall be by jury.
- Such Trial shall be held in the State where the said crimes shall have been committed.
- But when not committed within any State, the Trial shall be at such Place or Places as the Congress may by Law have directed.
- Treason against the United States shall consist only in levying War against them, or in adhering to their Enemies, giving Aid and

Comfort. Testimony of two witnesses to the same overt Act, or on Confession in open Court are required for conviction.

The federal judicial System was established by the Judiciary Act of 1789 wherein three levels of courts were created: district courts, circuit courts, and the Supreme Court. The Supreme Court initially was composed of a chief justice and five associate justices. The country was divided into 13 districts with a district court in each. These districts were grouped into three circuits. A circuit court was to be held twice a year in each district, which was to be ruled by two justices of the Supreme Court and by the district judge. The justices had to ride the circuit by stagecoach, gig, sailing vessel, or steamboat.

As the country expanded, so did the courts. In 1855, Congress created a court of claims that rules on claims brought against the United States. By 1869, Congress fixed the number of Supreme Court justices at nine.

The Supreme Court entertains appeals and writs of error or grants writs of certiorari (directions to the courts to send the federal question to it) from the circuit courts of appeal, the district courts, the court of claims, and the state courts. During its first 150 years, the Supreme Court acted as the appellate court that was established by the Constitution. By 1936, the Court had declared much of the New Deal legislation unconstitutional. In reaction to the Supreme Court's decisions, President Franklin Roosevelt proposed:

> that for each member of the Supreme Court who was over seventy years of age, and did not elect to retire, the President would be empowered to appoint an additional justice to the Court and thereby enlarge the Court's membership up to a total of fifteen.[68]

This plan was defeated resoundingly, in spite of the very large majority the Democrats enjoyed in Congress. Because of retirements and deaths, however, Roosevelt was able to name six new justices to the nine-man Court.

Over the next forty years, the Supreme Court created many new laws that ignored the intent of the signers of the Constitution and the Court's 150 year legislative history. The "rule of law" became the "rule of men" while the Supreme Court usurped the legislative function of Congress. The basic constitutional tension between the local or state governments and the federal government was destroyed, with the federal government assuming the basic rights and privileges reserved for the states.

This trend has decreased slightly from 1982 to 1992 because of the appointment of new Supreme Court justices. However, the federal government still controls or regulates many activities covered by law. Moreover, many of today's laws would have been declared unconstitutional during the first 150 years of the United States' existence.

The Supreme Court System basically has remained unchanged since Franklin Roosevelt's presidency. Cosmetic changes include salary increases (now $159,000 per year for associate justices and slightly more for the chief justice) and four or five legal staff members instead of one or two. About 150 decisions a year are handed down, and about 5,000 are passed upon. Justices may retire with a government pension at age seventy after serving ten years as a federal judge or at age sixty-five after serving fifteen years of federal services. The System maintains itself against all proposed changes, and only a change function properly applied could result in a New Supreme Court System that would reinstitute the rule of law that the country enjoyed for its first 150 years.

PRIVATE INSTITUTIONS IN THE U.S.

Large Manufacturing Business: The System in a large manufacturing business resides in each department and covers each function, such as manufacturing and services, sales and marketing, accounting and finance, research and development, engineering, quality, human resources, and top management. The System manages each entity differently.

Top management uses The System to maintain its informal policies and procedures and special perks and rewards. The System is used, even unwittingly, by these top managers to maintain the status quo of the organization. Management uses the traditional financial measurements to determine the status of the business. Monthly, quarterly, and yearly performance data are scrutinized, and decisions are based primarily on such data.

The System's cost accounting system is used to prepare monthly, quarterly, and annual financial and tax statements for top management, outside shareholders and investors, creditors, and government and regulatory agencies. However, effective process control and product cost accounting systems, and effective measurements of non inancial indicators are rarely part of The System's repertory of financial controls.[69]

The System's tools are used to direct and control the organization and "solve" its problems. Chief among these tools are cost savings programs, cash flow programs, capital equipment restrictions, research and development limitations, and lower level layoffs. These tools are used repeatedly whenever the company's performance wanes, since The System repeats those things that have been accepted in the past and require no real change in the basic operations. The System encourages and maintains group-think, wherein the group serves itself and not the organization. "Group-think is unfortunately most rife at the top and centre of organizations where the need for 'keeping things close' seems more important."[70]

The System maintains the high salaries, bonuses, and perks for top management. These hygiene or maintenance factors, as Herzberg et al.[71] call them, come with position and are relatively independent of the company's actual performance, especially in companies ten years or older.

The middle managers are caught in a dilemma caused by top management's ignorance of The System's existence. Figure 4-3 depicts the concept of The System being composed of similar components in each of the organization's departments or functions but also having a major component for top management. The System fills the entire organizational structure with a component in each major and minor department or function. The top management portion of The System is generically the same as the other portions but has different details.

The organization's work-flow usually is sequential, with each department tasked with a particular function of the business. The marketing, sales, engineering, manufacturing, quality, finance, and administration departments usually are independent of one another and have their own departmental objectives. The departments by tradition meet periodically to coordinate activities, although each one usually optimizes its own output based on an approved annual plan.

Marketing, engineering, and manufacturing usually are sequential in their planning operations. After engineering receives marketing's objectives, it completes research on the product and then develops working models that meet marketing's requirements. These models and their drawings are then transferred to production, which is then supposed to manufacture the product according to orders obtained by the sales department. Manufacturing must have the capacity and material to meet its production schedules. Because of The System, manufacturing tries to have extra capacity and sufficient inventory to meet the variable production schedules it receives for the many products it produces. The quality department ensures that an acceptable quality level of product is shipped to customers.

Middle managers must live with The System in their departments, which means that everyone in the departments also has incorporated The System into his daily work routines. However, the middle manager has to deal with one or more top managers who are operating within their special portion of The System. The middle manager can be buffeted by directions from

SCOPE OF THE SYSTEM

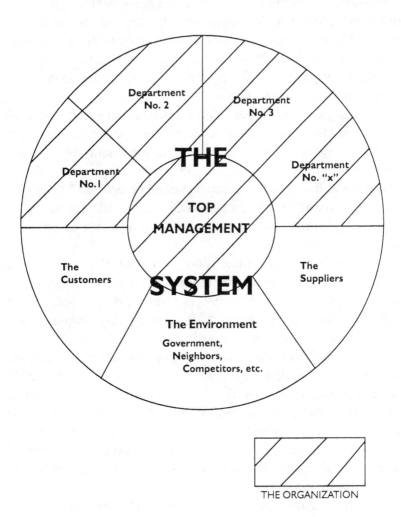

Figure 4-3

top management according to its System of operation, and these instructions can contradict The System in all of the other areas. Both the manager and the people in the department recognize the ambiguity of the situation and try to finesse the proposed changes whenever possible. This dichotomy is maintained until top management understands the situation, decides to change The System, and implements real changes.

The System in a large organization usually is a composite of the Subsystems that control each major division or part of the organization. The System becomes modified in each division, plant, or function, especially as the company matures. Each Subsystem is consistent with The System and reacts with The System and top management to maintain its status quo.

The scope of The System includes all groups within the organization and those outside that interact with the organization. Top management may not be aware of the many internal and external interactions that occur. However, The System is aware of these interactions and optimizes them in its own best interest, that is, stability first and growth and longevity second.

All of The System's attributes and laws apply to a large business. Different laws may apply in different major divisions or units at various times. The company's objectives may affect The System depending on the approach taken by top management to implement the objectives. The System will determine if the proposed changes are cosmetic or real and react accordingly.

Illicit Drugs: The U.S. Government has declared that certain drugs are illegal except under a physician's care. Because of this restricted supply of drugs, the price that consumers pay for such drugs is high, and consequently the profits for the manufacturer, distributor, and seller are increased significantly.

High profits in any industry attract competition. Therefore, there is an underground economy of many illegal suppliers, distributors, sellers, and buyers of illicit drugs. The more the central and state governments try to eliminate the drug trade, the higher the prices of drugs become, resulting in an increased supply of drugs and number of drug suppliers.

At least fifty-five U.S. Government agencies or departments are directly concerned with the illicit drug problem. Table 4-3 lists the eighteen federal agencies and their proposed fiscal year 1993 budgets for anti-drug activities.[72]

Table 4-3   1993 Federal Drug Control Budget Summary

1993 Budget Request   (Millions $)

1.	Dept. of Justice	4,704.5
2.	Dept. of Health & Human Services	2,222.3
3.	Dept. of Defense	1,223.4
4.	Dept. of The Treasury	1,105.2
5.	Dept. of Education	7522.0
6.	Dept. of Transportation	724.1
7.	Dept. of Veteran Affairs	590.6
8.	The Federal Judiciary	429.9
9.	Dept. of State	314.6
10.	Agency for International Development	260.9
11.	Dept. of Housing & Urban Development	168.2
12.	Office of National Drug Control Policy	79.1
13.	Dept. of Labor	72.6
14.	Dept. of The Interior	42.7
15.	Dept. of Agriculture	16.1
16.	ACTION	13.4
17.	U.S. Information Agency	8.4
18.	Small Business Administration	0.7

Total Federal Drug Program (millions $)   12,728.7

1.   **The Department of Justice** is responsible for the U.S. Bureau of Prisons, Drug Enforcement Administration, Office of Justice

Programs, Assets Forfeiture Fund, Organized Crime Drug Enforcement Task Forces, FBI, U.S. Marshals Service, U.S. Attorneys, support of U.S. Prisoners, Immigration and Naturalization Service, Criminal Division, INTERPOL, and Tax Division.

2.   **The Department of Health and Human Services** is responsible for the Alcohol, Drug Abuse, and Mental Health Administration, Health Care Financing Administration, Administration for Children and Families, Indian Health Service, Centers for Disease Control, and the Food and Drug Administration.

3.   **The Department of Defense** is responsible for the detection and monitoring of aerial and maritime transits of illegal drugs into the United States; the integration of the command, control, communications, and technical intelligence assets of the federal government into an effective communications network dedicated to drug interdiction; the improvement and funding of the state governors' plans for expanded use of the National Guard in support of state drug interdiction and enforcement operations; the drug prevention and treatment of department personnel; and the research and development of specialized automated data processing equipment, advanced detection systems, and improved sensor systems. The funding given in Table 4-3 does not include the costs of active duty military personnel, except National Guard and reserve components.

4.   **The Department of the Treasury** is responsible for the U.S. Customs Service, Bureau of Alcohol, Tobacco, and Firearms, Internal Revenue Service, U.S. Secret Service, Federal Law Enforcement Training Center, and Financial Crimes Enforcement Network (FinCEN).

5.   **The Department of Education** is responsible for drug-related prevention activities in elementary and secondary schools. Funding is granted to states for vocational rehabilitation of drug dependency. The department administers state programs for children with disabilities due to prenatal exposure to drugs, including preschoolers.

6.   **The Department of Transportation** is responsible for the drug interdiction and related activities of the U.S. Coast Guard, Federal Aviation Administration, and National Highway Traffic Safety Administration.

7.   **The Department of Veterans Affairs** is responsible for the drug treatment and medical care of veterans in VA hospitals and outpatient clinics.

8.   **The Federal Judiciary** is responsible for drug-related civil and criminal cases in the U.S. courts and a drug abuse treatment program for defendants awaiting trial and convicted criminals, including parolees, probationers, and supervised releases.

9.   **The Department of State** is responsible for developing, implementing, and monitoring U.S. international counter-narcotics strategies and programs, including funding various drug-related programs in other countries.

10.   **The Agency for International Development** is the principal provider of U.S. funds for counter-narcotics activities in various South and Central American countries.

11.   **The Department of Housing and Urban Development** provides funds for drug prevention, control, and elimination at public and Indian housing developments.

12. **The Office of National Drug Control Policy** is responsible for providing the President with comments and recommendations on drug issues and the government's various drug programs. It provides oversight and policy development for federal agencies, as well as hundreds of state and local government and private organizations. It provides funds for government agencies in the high intensity drug trafficking areas of New York, Los Angeles, Miami, Houston, and the Southwest border. It administers the Assets Forfeiture Funds as directed by Congress.

13. **The Department of Labor** administers the Job Training Partnership Act programs for drug abuse prevention, which includes the Job Corps and drug-free workplace programs for state and local government employees, nonprofit employers, and veterans.

14. **The Department of the Interior** is responsible for the anti-drug programs of the Bureau of Indian Affairs, Bureau of Land Management, U.S. Fish and Wildlife Service, and National Park Service.

15. **The Department of Agriculture** is responsible for the research and development of controlled substances to reduce growth, inhibit production, or completely eradicate the worldwide illicit drug crop. It also is responsible for the U.S. Forest Service's drug control program.

16. **ACTION** administers and funds anti-drug activities for the federal volunteer service programs, including Drug Alliance, VISTA, Foster Grandparents Program, and Retired Senior Volunteer Program.

17. **The U.S. Information Agency** is responsible for informing other countries about the government's anti-drug activities.

18. **The Small Business Administration** is responsible for assisting and counseling small business to eradicate drugs from the workplace.

The illicit drug problem has lead to serious side effects, such as AIDS from shared drug needles, babies born with drug additions, increased crime to support drug habits, and lost opportunity costs in health and law enforcement areas.

The federal government has been fighting the war on drugs for many years. In 1981, the government's funding for the drug war was $1.46 billion. By 1986, it had doubled to $2.83 billion. By 1990 it had increased 6.6 times to $9.69 billion, and by 1993 it had increased to $12.73 billion, which included funding for 70,135 full-time people.

The illicit drug System in the United States is obviously very large, very expensive, very complicated, and self-propelled. Over 100 federal and state agencies are involved in the war on drugs. Each agency has a System that it protects and succors. These 100 plus Systems interact with one another in ways that optimize their own interests and responsibilities. Also interacting with The System are The Systems of many foreign countries. Coordinating the objectives, policies, procedures, and practices of the country's war on drugs is the Office of National Drug Control Policy. The top managers of The System are Congress, which determines the laws that The System follows, and the President, who provides the executive management (leadership) for The System. The owners of The System are the people of the country.

In spite of, or maybe because of, the increased costs of the drug war being waged by the federal government, The System has maintained itself by assimilating all the cosmetic changes that the iron triangle has generated. It is clear that unless a change function is introduced to destroy The System, the illicit drug System will continue unabated.

SUMMARY

This chapter discusses various examples of The System. Russia, Japan, Peru, and Canada were chosen as being representative of most of the larger, important countries. Congress, public education, health care, the postal service, the Supreme Court, a typical manufacturing business, and the illicit drug culture were selected as representative of the most important institutions that affect the quality of life in the United States.

Each example typifies The System in complex institutions. Large institutions and organizations usually are subdivided into many small organizations, which are further subdivided into many smaller groups, such as countries, providences, states, counties, cities, towns and villages, or divisions, centers, departments, sections and teams.

The System that controls a large complex organization usually is made up of many smaller systems, or subsystems, that can control much of the organization's activities. However, these subsystems are basically the same as The System, except that the details of operation and control of the scope and type of activity (work) differs.

The Systems of the Russian, Japanese, and Peruvian governments are similar in some overall respects. Each country has a top management that is somewhat undefined and unofficial in practice. The politicians and bureaucrats control their respective interests or activities within their iron triangle which determines how The System operates in their country. The constitutions and systems of laws are managed and controlled by these two iron triangle components. Canada, on the other hand, has a more unusual iron triangle wherein all three participating groups interact within The System under an authentic legal System based on the rule of law.

The relative strengths of the iron triangle groups vary for each country. Table 4-4 gives their relative order of the iron triangle groups' strength: Strongest, Average, and Weakest. Although one group typically has more power, all member groups as a whole still control The System that rules and runs their country.

Table 4-4   Relative Strengths of Iron Triangle Groups

	Politicians	Bureaucrat	Special Interests
Russia	Strongest	Average	Weakest
Japan	Weakest	Strongest	Average
Peru	Strongest	Weakest	Average
Canada	Strongest	Average	Weakest

The five U.S. government controlled institutions are similar in that their iron triangle members overlap in many instances. The federal, state, and local politicians are the same groups of people. The government bureaucracies and the special interest groups concerned with each institution are different for each institution. Thus, if one were to describe The System that controls how the people of the United States are governed, one would have to understand the interaction of The Systems that control the federal, state, county, and local governments and agencies and the various special interest organizations of the many iron triangles.

The typical service or manufacturing company has its own System that usually is in control of the company. Some references in this book also contain descriptions of such Systems and the change functions applied by their top management: e.g., Chapter 2, ref. 5; Chapter 3, ref. 73; and Chapter 6, ref. 2. In addition, the Michael Hammer and James Champy book, *Reengineering the Corporation*,[73] gives four companies' experiences on introducing the concept of "discontinuous thinking" [i.e., change functions] in order to replace their respective Systems.

PART 2

§§§

HOW IT SHOULD BE

CHAPTER 5

How To Change The System

If you want to make enemies, try to change something.
—*Woodrow Wilson*[1]

This chapter studies the concept of two kinds of change: cosmetic and fundamental. Cosmetic changes are usually superficial and therefore not significant in the long term. Fundamental changes are usually permanent and structural. It is noted that change does not necessarily imply control, and vice versa. The concept of control of a process is discussed in the context of variations of the output parameters of the process. Statistical Process Control (SPC) is defined and explained in some detail. SPC must be utilized to determine whether the process is operating reproducibly or The System needs to be changed. Change from external sources also can affect The System. Although The System usually is successful in maintaining the status quo, eventually the organization, and thus top management, becomes aware that the external environment can cause unsatisfactory results for the organization. An action plan is outlined for this situation. To change The System, one must plan an approach that can be successful in both its application and results. A dozen general approaches are given, one of which is acceptable for a manufacturing process or service organization. A seven-phase action plan is suggested for successfully changing The System.

151

INTRODUCTION

To understand how to change The System, one first needs to understand the concept of The System and how The System actually controls the organization and the workplace. Although everyone is familiar with the concept of change, one should also be cognizant of the kinds of change and their potential impacts.

One needs a plan or an approach to implement changes to an organization. After a comprehensive, thoughtful approach is selected, including a vehicle for implementing the process, several other steps have to be taken to activate the program.

This chapter discusses steps that one might take to understand The System better. The two types of real, significant changes are discussed and compared with cosmetic, superficial or insignificant changes. The concept of control is explored in more detail, especially with regard to a process. The critical importance of understanding and undertaking statistical process control for most processes is discussed in detail. The strategy of using external changes to the benefit of the organization is outlined. A dozen competing approaches and an action plan for changing The System are proposed.

The concept of a change function, which is the vehicle used to implement the process of changing The System, will be discussed in detail in Chapters 6 and 7. While people in an organization can suggest changes to The System, they cannot individually implement such suggestions. However, within large organizations there are usually smaller groups or departments in which many of the ideas about changing The System can be applied locally without top management's knowledge or approval. Middle management and other supervisors also may have the authority and ability to change a process within The System that is within their jurisdiction.

UNDERSTANDING THE SYSTEM

One should understand that each System is unique and usually has many facets or modes of operation in the various parts of an organization. The System usually manifests itself as an unofficial way of operating the organization, but in some cases, such as a country or government, part of The System is recognized as the official management process, allegedly controlled by the top managers of the organization.

One must first understand that The System exists and has understandable and predictable characteristics. Seven steps that one can take to understand the characteristics of The System are given in Table 5-1.

Table 5-1 Seven Steps to Understanding The System

1. Define The System: how it grew, how it operates, and maintains itself.
2. Identify its scope, strengths, and weaknesses.
3. Confirm the applicability of The System's attributes and Laws.
4. Determine what The System is now changing, or ignoring.
5. Discover the basic objectives of The System, and who its proponents and opponents are.
6. Identify The System's customers, suppliers, and protectors.
7. Compare The System's actual results with the organization's stated long-term objectives.

1. **Define The System:** First describe how The System operates. Analyze how The System grew in each of the major areas of the organization. Discover how The System maintains itself in spite of management directives to the contrary. Analyze the root causes of persistent problems.

2. **Identify The System's Scope, Strengths, and Weaknesses:** Study The System's methods in each area and determine if the

output (results) of its operations is efficient, profitable, and desirable from the organization's viewpoint. Analyze The System's strengths and weaknesses in each major area. Rate The System's influence in each area compared with top management's leadership, direction, and control.

3.   Confirm the Applicability of The System's Attributes and Laws: Analyze the intensity of each of The System's attributes. Determine the validity of each of The System's laws. Compare actual cases of previous actions taken following the laws.

4.   Determine What The System Is Presently Changing or Ignoring: Analyze how The System has reacted to the latest management announcements or initiatives. Study the changes initiated by The System and determine why the changes were adopted.

5.   Discover the Basic Objectives of The System and Who Its Proponents and Opponents Are: Compare the objectives of the organization with the objectives of The System. Analyze who in the organization supports The System and how that support is manifested. Determine who opposes The System and their objections to it. Identify specific examples of objection to The System and determine whether they are valid.

6.   Identify The System's Customers, Suppliers, and Protectors: Determine whether The System's customers and suppliers are consistent with the organization's goals. Identify any discrepancies between how customers are treated and the organization's objectives regarding its customers and customer services. Determine whether internal customers are treated differently than external customers. Determine which managers are content with The System and which would like to change it.

7. **Compare The System's Actual Results with the Organization's Stated Long-Term Objectives:** Most organizations have an annual plan and probably have multiple year plans and objectives. However, very little effort is made to analyze the actual results of the plan and what they mean to the organization.

To facilitate real, permanent change, the results should be analyzed with respect to The System and its statistical control of the organization's activities. Analyzing the output through The System's filter should reveal whether the results are consistent with the original long-term objectives. The analysis should also lead to a new understanding of cause and effect.

As a consequence of becoming aware of The System and the results of its control on the organization, one may become aware of the acute need to change The System. Therefore, because some changes are ineffective when implemented, one must understand what type of change can be effective.

UNDERSTANDING CHANGE

The dictionary says that change means to alter, vary, modify, or make or become different. From the moment of birth, humans become aware of change. Change is ubiquitous, continuous and unending. Organizations, like life, are always in a state of change.

Change in organizations may be purposeful, directed, managed, and controlled. Conversely, change in organizations may be haphazard, random, undirected, impetuous, and irrepressible. When The System is in control of the organization, change is purposeful, directed, managed, and controlled. Moreover, change is usually either minimized or optimized to protect The System's status. While an organization is continually changing, "any particular change has its own pattern, with a discernible direction, magnitude, pace, and duration."[2]

There are two basic types of significant or real change: permanent or structural and temporary or cyclical. Structural change is an important reordering, increase, or decrease in the aggregate of elements that comprise the structure. It is usually nonreversible and requires permanent adjustment to the previous status. Cyclical change is a temporary or periodic change in a qualitative parameter from a level or state to which it is likely to return. Cyclical changes usually are not inherently structural and usually are repeatable, self-limiting, and reproducible under similar conditions.

While cosmetic change, on the other hand, may be either permanent or temporary, in its long-term potential it is not basically significant. In poorly led organizations, most changes are both cosmetic and cyclical with an irregular period. Cosmetic changes usually do not have long-term effects on the organization but may adversely affect some people in the organization. The System promotes and accepts cosmetic changes by management because they do not threaten The System in any way. In reality, cosmetic changes only serve to reinforce The System's longevity since they indicate that management does not wish to make structural changes that would challenge, alter, and probably overturn The System's power base.

There is a basic conflict between the concepts of change and control. Change does not necessarily imply control, and control does not necessarily imply change. When discussing cyclical changes, Martel observes that:

> less regular and uniform, but still exhibiting cyclical patterns, are many changes resulting from human behavior. The characteristic that makes most of these changes cyclical is their recurrence over fairly narrow ranges within self-limiting boundaries. What happens is that when the level of an activity approaches a boundary (established by previous experience), information to that effect causes an alteration in the amount of pace or direction of the activity, returning it to a previous state.[3]

The above scenario is an example of a process. Any process is only effective and efficient if it is under control with respect to its inherent natural tendencies. A process is said to be under statistical control:

> when, through the use of past experience, we can predict, at least within limits, how the phenomenon may be expected to vary in the future. Here it is understood that prediction within limits means that we can state, at least approximately, the probability that the observed phenomenon will fall within the given limits.[4]

The concept of the statistical control of a process (or statistical process control* or statistical quality control) is extremely important because when the concept is understood and used, one is alerted to the need for action or non action depending upon the values of the output parameters measured. Moreover, if statistical process control is ignored, changes may be made when they shouldn't be.

There are two causes of change. The type due to The System is called chance, common, normal, natural, or random. The type due to a specific, determinable cause outside The System is called assignable, special, abnormal, or non random. If the process is under control, then the variations of the output parameters are usually within the inherent capability of the process, and thus the variations are natural or random in their values. For a process under control, these variations might get the attention of top management. If management does not understand that all the data, including the undesirable results, are what the present process will always generate when it is under statistical process control, then management is likely to change something in order to eliminate the undesirable results.

For example, if the monthly sales of a division of a large company were those given in Table 5-2, a question might arise about the 26th month's sales of $0.2 million, which were much lower than any of the previous months' sales. A question also

---

* Statistical process control charts are also called Shewhart control charts after their creator and promoter, Walter A. Shewhart.

Table 5-2 Monthly Sales by Quarter (in million $)

Quarters	1st	2nd	3rd	4th	5th	6th	7th	8th	9th
1st mo.	6.0	5.0	3.5	2.3	3.2	3.1	3.3	2.0	3.1
2nd mo.	3.0	3.0	2.5	4.7	7.0	6.1	5.5	4.0	0.2
3rd mo.	2.0	2.0	6.5	2.2	3.0	2.1	2.2	7.5	?
Total	11.0	10.0	12.5	9.2	13.2	11.3	11.0	13.5	?

might arise if the next month's (27th) sales were $8.1 million.

If the manager understands SPC, nothing special would be done since an analysis would show that the sales process was under SPC, and thus both the $0.2 million and the $8.1 million sales figures should be expected statistically. This means that the sales process is reproducible within its inherent process boundaries, with monthly sales expected between $0.2 million and $8.1 million.

However, if the 27th month's sales were $8.8 million instead of $8.1 million, then the sales process would be out of control and the manager would have to look for a special cause that was responsible for the sales figure being larger than The System (the process under SPC) expected.

If management's response ignores the statistical aspects of the past data (measurements), the action taken is likely to be a baseless change, which could easily lead to increased variation of the output data and increased *undesired* results. If the process is under statistical control, then The System is controlling the process. The only way to effect real change, therefore, would be to change The System that controls the process.

If the process and The System are out of control, then an assignable or special cause of change exists. Finding the assignable or special cause will enable management to address the change, especially if it is an undesirable one. Unless the special cause (root cause) is identified and appropriate action taken, the process may continue its out-of-control output at a later time. Thus management must change The System and act accordingly.

In order to eliminate the acute problem, The System usually is changed locally. However, The System in the organization's other activities generally is not changed. Although the changes are apparently permanent, they are usually small compared with the total output of The System that runs the organization.

Martel[5] proposes the following strategy for mastering change:

We need a new strategy for planning for the future, a strategy that assumes that change is more likely than continuity and that enables us to understand the changes that are coming and to make use of them. [He proposes a process of five steps:]

- Recognize that change is occurring.
- Identify the changes likely to affect one's particular business, profession, or personal plans.
- Determine the type and probable pattern of each identified change.
- Rank the changes by the importance of their effect and the likelihood of their occurrence.
- Make use of the changes.

The first step is to recognize that change is occurring both inside and outside the organization. The natural bias in favor of continuity means that The System maintains the status quo in spite of external changes. "The expectation of continuity has a further, even more stultifying, consequence. It breeds inactivity." Martel points out the fallacy of assuming that the present trends will continue indefinitely. Therefore, management should avoid projections based on business as usual. In fact, "business as usual is unusual. It almost never happens."

The second step is to identify changes that are likely to affect the organization, including those that affect both supply (upstream) and demand (downstream). Changes that affect supply include new information, new technology, new work force requirements, increases in resource costs, increased competition, and political and environmental concerns. Some changes that affect demand are improved communications, educational levels, population status, changes in societal values, and the economic environment.

The third step is to determine the structural and cyclical changes and understand how they will affect the organization short term and long term. "The pace of a change is at once its most important dimension and the most difficult one to discern."

The fourth step is to rank the changes according to their potential importance, discounted by their improbabilities. This step serves as a guide for allocating time and resources.

The fifth step is to acknowledge and react to the changes affecting the organization. This usually means that The System has to be changed, which is a formidable task. Structural changes require rethinking the strategies for the organization, and cyclical changes require tactical responses that are timely and integrated into the organization's daily workflow.

APPROACHES FOR CHANGING THE SYSTEM

Once the leader of an organization understands that The System has to be changed because of top management's unacceptable, inadequate performance in the past and that a strategy for mastering change has been developed, the next step is to determine what approach should be taken to change The System. The approach should incorporate the general concept that is to be followed regarding the change desired. A dozen potential approaches are listed in Table 5-3 and summarized on the pages that follow. One or more of the first eleven approaches have been attempted by some companies and have resulted in limited successes. The last approach is being used by a relatively small number of companies that are in the process of successfully replacing The System.

Table 5-3   Approaches for Changing The System

- Management-by-Objectives Approach
- Technological Approach
- Sub-standard Approach
- Explorer's Approach
- Piecemeal Approach
- Automation Approach
- Surgical Approach
- Economic Approach
- Selective Approach
- Legal Approach
- Socialistic Approach
- Productivity Improvement Approach

Management-by-Objectives Approach: The organization's leader sets the new revenue and profit objectives and assimilation occurs. Some managers even promote planning and the generation of five-year plans by the major elements of the organization. However, the main emphasis of this approach is establishing new financial objectives for the organization. These new objectives are thought to be sufficiently clear to generate improved motivation for change throughout the organization. The members of the organization are then supposed to make changes in their policies and procedures that will meet the new objectives. Nevertheless, in most cases the members are not in control of their work and cannot make changes to The System.

This approach is illusory. The System will accept the new objectives as valid directions or goals but will not change the basic way it works, because it knows that objectives always change, and therefore maintaining and strengthening itself is its main duty.

The organization's leader, allegedly understanding that change must occur, is not willing to disturb The System to change it in a fundamental way. The leader's strategy for mastering change is faulty and unworkable. The approach is superficial and eventually might lead to downsizing. Since it is a cosmetic approach to change, the organization's long-term performance will not be enhanced significantly.

Technological Approach: Top management assumes that the organization's problem is caused by poor or inadequate performance of the technology used by the organization. The department or group responsible for the technology is therefore the source of the problem. The approach for changing The System is to replace the technology with better technology. Thus the problem will be resolved by the technological improvement of the offending unit.

The technological approach usually will be insufficient to effect a major change in the entire System, which will absorb the new technology and generate the appropriate outputs. Although The System can be changed significantly within the technological group affected, it is basically unchanged and continues to maintain the status quo throughout the rest of the organization.

On rare occasions, the new technological paradigm is so dynamic and omnipotent that it revolutionizes the organization and The System. This can be seen with the auto replacing the horse drawn carriage, airplane travel dominating rail travel, and the electric light replacing the candle. These are exceptions, however, and the leader who counts on a technological improvement in the organization's services or products to make a structural difference in The System most likely will be disappointed. At best, the technological change could improve the organization's output by 10 to 20 percent; at worst, it could decrease the output by the same percentages. Most likely the change will be unsubstantial, and any improvement will be in the 5 to 10 percent range.

Substandard Approach: Every organization has a group of people that is directly responsible for building a product or producing a service for customers. This group is usually a minority of the organization but is very visible with respect to the organization's output. Because of its visibility and intimacy to the customers, top management assigns the cause of the organization's problems to this group's alleged marginal performance. The solution is obvious—reform the substandard group by improving the management and the people in the group. However, even after the group is apparently improved, it is still thought to be substandard.

The most obvious and common example of this type of thinking is found in manufacturing companies. In some companies, it is asserted that manufacturing is considered to be the undesirable area where marginal people work. It is thought that most problems that the company has are due to manufacturing. Thus poor quality, excessive costs, shipment delays, and field failures and returns are caused by the manufacturing department's poor management and the poor performance of its members.

If top management tries to reorganize the manufacturing group by replacing its manager, the resultant will be mixed. The new manager may try to change The System by introducing cosmetic changes or real changes. In the former case, the output probably will be similar to the previous trend. In the latter case, if the vehicle for changing The System is valid, the results could be positive as long as the other arms of the System do not prevent the changes from occurring. However, since the problems (poor quality, excessive costs, shipment delays, and field failures and returns) caused by the manufacturing group are probably less than 30 percent, any real change in The System also must affect all of the other groups in the process. This means that marketing, sales, engineering, purchasing and material control, finance, and human resources departments also must change the way they work. If The System is not changed across all functions, the resultant performance will not be optimum and may even be marginal.

Explorer's Approach: In the explorer's approach, management discovers a major problem within the organization and attacks it and then discovers another major problem and attacks it. This continues until the situation is considered to be satisfactory. With this approach, periodic revivals of problems are possible and even predictable.

This approach is an attempt to improve an organization's performance by solving the most critical problem at hand. If the symptoms are cured, it is assumed that the disease (the problem) was overcome. The immediate changes that are introduced to solve the problem are not necessarily associated with changing The System, and thus probably can be considered to be cosmetic. This approach is repeated with each problem, and the changes instituted are not necessarily applied across the organization since it is thought that the problems are independent of each other.

The System reacts to each of these changes locally. A change in one area in a particular process will not be acknowledged or used in another area that has a similar process. Since The System is not threatened with this approach, it follows its Rule of Alternate Efficiency. The status quo is followed and maintained because The System and the people know that these new changes are cosmetic.

Although problems are solved at the time, the root causes of the problems most likely are not identified. Therefore, the problems recur at a later time, thus confirming their cyclical nature.

Piecemeal Approach: Having determined to change The System, management implements change by increments, starting with the alleged most successful group and allowing it to lead the way to change. The thinking is that this superior group will be able to teach the other groups or departments how to improve their performance using the principles and techniques that the superior group had demonstrated leads to success. This approach is a series type of program in which departments or divisions are brought on sequentially. In this approach, The System is to be changed incrementally over a period of time. It assumes that the departments are independent of one another and thus changes in one department will not adversely affect another department.

This approach is similar to the explorer's approach, except that a successful group rather than a problem within the organization is chosen as the target for change. The System treats this approach in a manner similar to the substandard approach. However, management supports the group and its management in its budget justifications for capital equipment, education, and training.

This sequential approach to change also assumes that The System in the groups not undergoing changes will not adversely affect the group undergoing changes. Since the bulk of the organization is under control of The System, the targeted group will have a problem influencing the other groups to change their direct input and output interactions with it. This piecemeal approach probably will take at least twice as long to implement throughout the organization compared with an organization-wide approach, which alone is a sufficient reason for rejecting it.

Automation Approach: Apparently having unwittingly decided that McGregor's Theory X is the correct management philosophy, management eliminates many of the people who cause the organization's problems. Thus management automates wherever possible, because it believes that machines can be programmed to work correctly, efficiently, and continuously. It believes that automation can eliminate or significantly reduce problems and mistakes. This approach assumes that people cause most problems and ignores the fact that The System is the cause of most problems and that automating The System will not cause the problems to disappear but will merely obscure the old problems and generate a new batch of problems.

An example of this approach is the $40 billion automation program instituted by General Motors a few years back. Because the GM management never understood The System, the approach failed to make a significant improvement in the company's performance and prevented the proper approach from being considered and implemented.

The automation approach is really a variation on the technological approach. This specific, company-wide application of technology usually does little to change the fundamentals of The System.

Although many processes can be improved by automation, the integration of most processes requires people to interact. Processes that require people to interact also can be automated. The Japanese have introduced the *kanban*[6] (display card) method mainly to control the amount and pace of production. This very successful method of control is usually a manual operation.

Unless The System is changed such that all of those covered by The System are supportive in a very positive, long-term manner, machine automation will do very little except move bottlenecks and inventory to different points of the process.[7]

Surgical Approach: This approach is popular with many CEOs, especially newly appointed ones. It consists of looking at the performance records of all major divisions or groups in the organization and eliminating the units within them that have unsatisfactory records. Thus major units are sold or discontinued. This downsizing of the organization supposedly will have a positive impact on profits and cash flow. The approach ignores the fact that The System is the cause of most of the problems and that most of the units could have a positive potential if The System were changed.

The approach also ignores the fact that The System is still in charge in the other units. Members of the remaining units, knowing that The System still exists and is in (de facto) charge, will fear losing their jobs and thus will not make any waves. Rather they will perfect The System in order to isolate and protect themselves. The remaining units thus will become more passive with respect to customers and competitors.

It is clear that top management using the surgical approach does not understand The System and the need to change it. These managers are captured by The System and therefore continue to carry out the types of changes that they used in the past. Although the drain on cash is abated, the long-term potential of the organization is not significantly enhanced and may be reduced because of the potential reduction of future new customers.

Economic Approach: The economic approach involves expanding the organization's business into profit-making activities that compete with competitors. Although the organization's top manager agrees that major changes must be made regarding The System, the basic approach is to increase the organization's external thrusts while maintaining The System's internal status quo. The economic approach expands the organization's activities such that the incremental increased costs are less than the revenue that the new activities generate. Although the organization's operations are altered, The System is not changed in any basic manner. As far as The System is concerned, the changes are all cosmetic.

The economic approach ignores changing The System because top management's priority is expansion by either acquisition, internal growth, or entrepreneurial activities. Thus the chairman of the board, president, CEO, and COO become engrossed in the problems associated with the rapid expansion of the business. This becomes critical in many cases when the new businesses are not completely familiar to the top managers, and thus problems and the risks taken consume much of top management's time. In the remaining operations, The System maintains itself and protects itself from the adverse effects (such as a reduction in available capital from the organization) that may occur with this approach.

This approach may occupy top management's time and efforts for three to five years or longer. The System, meanwhile, follows its own Law of Oligarchy. The organization's long-term performance and potential therefore are not actively addressed by The System. As far as top management is concerned, the organization's long-term performance and potential are found mainly in the new areas of economic activity. The System exists in these new areas in a different form but is also ignored by top management.

Selective Approach: The selective approach entails changing The System only in those parts of the total environment that adversely affect the organization. The total environment includes the customers, competition, business conditions, and political, social, and local circumstances. The basic thrust of this approach is to concentrate the organization's efforts on changing The System's performance in these areas. The concept of a holistic System is not considered. The changes introduced in one area are contradicted by The System in other areas. Thus this approach to change is very ineffective and inefficient and would take a very long time to implement throughout the organization.

The selective approach is cosmetic and cyclical in nature and a variation of the management-by-objectives approach.

Legal Approach: The legal approach to changing The System entails changing the organization's existing policies and procedures. Once top management understands that The System must be changed, it starts by reviewing and revising the old corporate policies and procedures. The thought is that because changes have occurred since the initial policies and procedures were established, it would be a good idea to update them.

This approach assumes that The System can be legislated out of existence or at least legislated out of its control of the organization. This is the classic cart-before-the-horse mistake.

Management is attempting to exert its authority by means of its position in the organizational chart.

This approach is doomed to fail because The System will immediately recognize that it is cosmetic, and thus everyone will treat it as such. The new policies and procedures will document some of the changes that have occurred since they were last written or revised. Although these changes are more efficient and useful than the previous procedures, they most likely are procedural in nature and do not make any structural changes to The System. Thus this approach will not result in any long-term major improvement to the organization. Actually, this approach will delay the possibility of major change occurring in the organization.

Socialistic Approach: The socialistic approach is favored by government agencies and many nonprofit organizations because their existence as special interest groups depends on the government's protection. The bureaucracy and The System are mutually protective in these organizations. Any real change in The System of one of these organizations will be directed toward improving The System's connections with its benefactor, the government. Changes will be made to strengthen the organization's competitive position against private industry or other nonprofit organizations. The System will be used to support the other members of the iron triangle. Most changes directed toward the organization's customers will be illusory because there is a negative incentive to become too dependent on these customers for the long-term existence of the organization.

The primary thrust of all change for these organizations is to maintain and improve their survival and longevity. Since the need for profits is nonexistent in these organizations, the incentives for change are directed toward social, political, or technological changes. In these organizations, top management and The System are intertwined, and each serves as a protector to the other.

For example, President Bush in January 1992 asked the heads of government agencies to weed out unnecessary and burdensome federal regulations. This confirms the comments in the preceding paragraph, since such regulations never would have been issued if the agencies thought that they were counterproductive to the agencies' missions. Weeding out implies a small number of changes, that is, cosmetic changes. If significant change had been desired, the President could have directed the agencies to reduce the number of regulations by fifty percent during the next six months.

The socialistic approach to change is also the favorite approach of those outside a particular nonprofit organization or government agency if they are part of a similar iron triangle. In other words, those in local iron triangles also support, at least politically and vocally, all the other similar iron triangles. The socialistic approach to change is promoted by their mutual support and the active support of much of the media and the entertainment industry.

The management of nonprofit organizations and government agencies will never consider changing The System because it would not be in their personal interests. Thus a higher authority must change The System in these institutions. The public must institute the desired changes in government organizations, which usually can be done only by the ballot box.

However, there are occasions when only other methods can work. For example, the iron triangle in the American colonies (England's King and Parliament, the government bureaucracies in England and America, and the Tories and the favored economic interests) was changed forcibly in 1776 by the colonists.

Productivity Improvement Approach: The productivity improvement approach also could be called the prevention approach, customer approach, total quality management (TQM) approach, or total cycle time approach. Its basic thrust is a conceptual and actual revolution in the way that all the members of the organization perform their jobs. Prevention of problems, mistakes, omissions, and errors and the complete support of customers' short-term and long-term requirements are also goals of this approach.

Since most organizations are in business to satisfy customers, The System must be changed so that it becomes extremely responsive to the needs and requirements of customers. Everyone's job will be changed under this approach. Strict organizational or functional lines will be obliterated, and everyone will have a responsibility to ensure that customers receive products or services that they want and purchase.

This approach requires that the organization practice TQM and time-based management. Total quality management is "the overall, company-wide program for attaining the goal" of establishing "an effective system for integrating the quality-development, quality-maintenance, and quality-improvement efforts of the various groups in an organization so as to enable production and service at the most economical levels which allow for full customer satisfaction."[8]

Time-based management or time-based competitiveness[9] is an organization-wide program for minimizing the time it takes to supply a product or service from the expression of a customer's need until that need is satisfied. This entails drastically reducing the marketing, engineering, manufacturing, and sales loop by significantly cutting the lead time to produce a product or service. Shorter lead times are accomplished by introducing improved engineering designs, flexible manufacturing, short production runs, minimization of the number of components, improved quality, reduced handling of parts, and employee decision making on the factory floor.[10]

This approach requires looking at the entire organization as embodying The System. The System must be replaced with a new responsive System that is controlled and maintained by all members of the organization.

This approach has been tried to some extent by some companies. An International Quality Study[11] reviewed 945 management practices in over 500 organizations, including those in Canada, Germany, Japan, and the United States. The study revealed that "organizations that use process improvement practices—process value analysis, process simplification, and cycle time analysis—generally tend to perform better than others." The study also analyzed (1) the benefits of benchmarking, broad-based employee empowerment, general and specific quality training, and compensation related to overall quality and team performance that can and have accrued in some organizations and, (2) why similar benefits have not happened in other organizations.

ACTION PLAN FOR CHANGING THE SYSTEM

A plan of action can be developed to change The System in any organization using the seven phases outlined in Table 5-4. The first four phases were originated by William E. Conway,[12,13] president of Conway Quality, Inc., who before retiring and forming his own consulting company, successfully implemented these steps as president and CEO of Nashua Corporation.

Table 5-4   Seven Phases for Changing The System
1. Understand that it can be done.
2. Be willing to do it.
3. Make resources available.
4. Determine and then make the structural changes.
5. Control and maintain the changes.
6. Analyze the changes and their results.
7. Repeat the process.

1. **Understand That It Can Be Done:** The first phase is to understand that one or more major problems exist. One then must realize what the root causes of the fundamental problems are and that structural changes are required. One must understand the concept of The system and the concept of changes, and why and how they should be implemented. Top management must propose, articulate, and continuously nurture a vision of the future of the organization that should exist after The System has been changed.

2. **Be Willing to Do It:** The second phase is that management must be willing to implement a major change in The System, or create a new one. All managers must be dedicated to the continuous effort of changing The System. Management must believe in the concept of sustained improvement throughout the entire organization.

Intent is not sufficient. To understand these concepts requires knowledge of actual practices, analytical statistical theory, and enlightened human resources and tools. McGregor's Theory X must be discarded in favor of his Theory Y.* True belief and

---

* According to McGregor's Theory Y

1. The expenditure of physical and mental effort in work is as natural as play or rest.

2. External control and the threat of punishment are not the only means of bringing about effort toward organizational objectives. Man will exercise self-direction and self-control in the service of objectives to which he is committed.

3. Commitment to objectives is a function of the rewards associated with achievement. The most significant of such rewards, e.g., the satisfaction of ego and self-actualization needs, can be direct products of effort directed toward organizational objectives.

4. The average human being learns, under proper conditions, not only to accept but to seek responsibility.

5. The capacity to exercise a relatively high degree of imagination, ingenuity, and creativity in the solution to organizations problems is widely, not narrowly, distributed in the population.

6. Under the conditions of modern industrial life, the intellectual potentialities of the average human being are only partially utilized. . . .The limits on human collaboration in the organizational setting are not limits of human nature but of management's ingenuity in discovering how to realize the potential represented by its human resources.

understanding are based on experience doing these things. Belief begets doing; doing begets belief. It is imperative that most individuals believe that they can contribute to a real change in the organization. Management and the rest of the organization must be relentless in an ongoing drive for increased quality and productivity in every process of the organization. The entire process of improvement (change in The System) must be constantly advocated by all management levels and almost all the other members of the organization.

3. **Make Resources Available:** The third phase involves actuating the human resources of the organization. Everyone must be educated in the concepts of The System and change and learn that structural changes in the organization can lead to significant improvements in their well-being. People will need to work in a more demanding, active, and participatory environment. Therefore, teamwork will be a key to making it all happen.

People will have to be educated and trained in new techniques and procedures for making continuous improvements. It is necessary that most people understand how to use available tools and equipment, and the theory for improving the quality and productivity of the processes used within the organization. Once the problems are identified and quantified, the following techniques can be used to initiate changes: surveys, imagineering, principles of work (industrial engineering), simple analysis (charting), and sophisticated statistical tools.[15,16]

4. **Determine and Then Make the Structural Changes:** The fourth phase is for top management to change The System formally. Management must create, develop, or use a change function (see Chapter 6) to introduce the changes desired. In some cases, two different fundamental problems have to be changed before The System can be replaced with a New System. There is usually one fundamental problem that must be eliminated before

the second one can be addressed. For example, an organization may have two product lines or businesses, one of which is becoming obsolete or already has a marginal future. Top management should address that issue and resolve it, such as by selling the product line or business, before attempting to solve the other fundamental problem.

In most businesses, the change function should include the productivity improvement approach. Management must issue new objectives, policies, and procedures, communicate its intentions, and demonstrate its dedication to the proposed structural changes. Management must demonstrate its ongoing commitment to the process of improvement for the organization and its members.

Management must recognize the need to reorganize the workflow and the material throughput of the organization to reduce inventory, reduce cycle time, and eliminate the bottlenecks and constraints, which are the ultimate limitations of the overall output of the organization.[17]

It is imperative that management be intimately involved in initiating these changes. If management is not convinced that such changes are necessary for the survival of the organization, the entire process of change will either fail or be postponed until management becomes enlightened and committed. Implementing this phase of the action plan requires specific process steps, which are discussed in detail in the next chapter.

5. **Control and Maintain the Changes:** The fifth phase is for top management to make sure that everyone in the organization clearly understands the objectives of the proposed changes. However, as originally stated by Drucker:[18]

control is an ambiguous word. It means the ability to direct oneself and one's work. It can also mean domination of one person by another. Objectives are the basis of control in the first sense; but they must never become the basis of control in the second, for this would defeat their purpose. Indeed, one of the major contributions of management by objectives is that it enables us to substitute management by self-control for management by domination.

It should be clear that changing The System requires not only top management's relentless support but also management by self-control by everyone in the organization. New, unique, original, and enduring changes are possible to The System only if most of the people involved in The System feel that they have some degree of self-control of their work. It is top management's responsibility to make the necessary changes that will allow the activation of self-controlled members of the organization.

Management must ensure the introduction of improved measurements that relate to the outputs of the various processes in operation throughout the organization. Management must ensure that statistical techniques are used to improve the processes in an efficient, ongoing manner.

Control can be maintained only if people are trained, useful and meaningful measurements are made and recorded, and statistical techniques are used to analyze the state of the processes being monitored (hopefully under statistical process control).

6.   **Analyze the Changes and Their Results:** The sixth phase is the feedback process wherein the effects of changes are measured and analyzed. The data should be analyzed from both a short-term and long-term perspective. All data must be analyzed for statistical significance to see if they are of sufficient magnitude and gathered over a significant amount of time to determine, with a high confidence level, whether the results are meaningful. The usual financial data, while very accurate, may not be too significant with regard to the organization's long-term growth or survival.[19,20]

After the changes have been analyzed and found to be significant, management must study the results of the changes. The results of changing The System may be noticeable almost immediately but may not be financially significant in the short term. However, real changes to The System should yield noticeable, significant improvements within a year. By the end of the second year, financial projections should look promising, and there should be clear indications that the longer term future looks rewarding.

7.   **Repeat the Process:** The seventh phase requires top management to make sure that the improvement process continues indefinitely. There must be a change in The System such that the old status quo is not acceptable and ongoing and relentless changes (improvements) in every process are expected, required, and implemented. This step must be discussed with everyone at the initiation of the overall program so that the concept of continuous change is understood and eventually accepted.

SUMMARY AND CONCLUSIONS

This chapter discusses the nuts and bolts of how to change. It lists seven steps that one should take to understand the characteristics of The System. This is followed by an analysis of the two types of changes that can be applied to alter The System. The desired changes should be permanent or structural in kind; instead, most changes introduced by top management are cyclical or temporary.

The major concept of a process being under control is highlighted. A process is under control only if it is under statistical control. This means that past measurements taken on the process are shown to be within the material, inherent limits of the process, and that one can predict statistically that the process if under control will remain within such limits. This basic concept is ignored most of the time in most organizations. Ignorance of this basic concept causes untold costs and labor to be wasted in these organizations.

A basic strategy for identifying that change in an organization is needed is presented. Only the Productivity Improvement

Approach for changing The System is recommended by the author as being potentially most effective and efficient. This approach entails the empowerment of all members of the organization and the practice of total quality and time-based management.

An action plan of seven phases is given for changing The System. Unless The System is changed thoroughly, any fragmentary changes will only serve to maintain The System and the status quo. Albert Einstein knew the approach that must be taken to change The System: "The significant problems we face cannot be solved at the same level of thinking we were at when we created them."[21]

As The System is structurally changed by top management, it becomes a New System. The key to success of the New System is everyone's acceptance of the concept of ongoing change. The System no longer is the major independent force in the management of the organization because after it is destroyed another New System is generated which is in partnership with top management and the rest of the members in the organization.

To change The System a unique change function should be applied to it. The change function should incorporate as part of its basic foundation the elements of the productivity improvement approach. It must be initiated, nourished, and maintained by top management if it is to be successful in replacing The System with a new one that is significantly different. As Peters has said, the changes required are in effect a necessary revolution: "Excellent firms don't believe in excellence—only in constant improvement and constant change."[22]

CHAPTER 6

Changing The System

It isn't the incompetent who destroy an organization. The incompetent never get into a position to destroy it. It is those who have achieved something and want to rest on their achievements who are forever clogging things up. To keep an industry pure, you've got to keep it in perpetual ferment.

—*Henry Ford*[1]

This chapter analyzes the process of changing The System and expands upon the changes that can occur to The System that runs an organization or controls a process. It is particularly important to recognize that the output of any organization is a result of many concurrent and sequential processes. Moreover, each process is supposed to be controlled by The System. That is, the process generates an output that depends on the various procedures, parameters, and factors predetermined by The System. If the process is under statistical process control (SPC), then the output of the process results in well-defined goods or services. An example is given of the consequences of a process not being under SPC. The principles of how to solve problems within The System are explained. The relatively obscure principle of how to change The System is discussed in technical terms. The concepts of first-order changes and second-order changes are reviewed in detail to indicate how one goes about trying to change The System. A four-step procedure for solving problems is outlined. The concept of a change function is presented for the first time as the critical management tool for implementing significant change. Examples of various change functions that have been or could be utilized to change The System are discussed. The importance of management leadership, vision, and nonmanagement participation and commitment is stressed. The critical steps for changing The System are identified.

179

INTRODUCTION

The concept of changing The System is completely different from the concept of changing elements within the organization. It entails a process that requires an eclectic understanding of how The System exists and is maintained. Without an understanding of the basic influences and transactions that occur, one cannot hope to solve the problem. Deciding to buy a car from manufacturer A rather than manufacturer B will not change how manufacturer A or manufacturer B operates. Their Systems are impervious to changes of this type.

After presenting a conceptual understanding of the principles relating to change, this chapter discusses the usual emphasis given to cosmetic changes, and the need to make fundamental changes when conditions make it necessary. The case for higher process yields is given for a multistep process in a manufacturing process or service process. An example is given of an analysis that was made from the numbers and types of mistakes that truck drivers made for a trucking firm. These two examples illustrated the fact that The System in each case had to be changed if improved performance was to be obtained in the future.

How the concept of change affects people is explained. The basic principles of problem solution are analyzed in detail. Revealed are the answers to the questions: (1) How does this undesirable situation persist? and (2) What is required to change it? The difference between first-order changes and second-order changes is explained, and a simple example given. It is shown that second-order changes can serve as the vehicle for changing The System. Various ways of conceiving such second-order changes are established. The principles of problem formation are stated that enable new solutions to be discovered to persistent problems.

It is shown that second-order changes can lead to permanent or structural solutions of problems related to The System. I have coined the term "change function" to mean the application of a second-order change to a System problem. Eight examples of unusual problems to which change functions were applied are presented. In each case, the implementation of the change function solved a major System problem.

Management leadership is shown to be required in order to implement System changes in an organization. The various aspects of how individuals change are given.

The implementation of a change function to an organization is outlined in detail. A critical path for this is submitted. Problem elimination techniques are proposed.

CONCEPTUAL UNDERSTANDING

Appreciation of Cosmetic vs. Fundamental or Structural Changes

Cosmetic changes occur at the margin of an activity because they are the only changes that the local activists can make successfully. The System prevents any fundamental changes from being made because such changes are potentially threatening to The System's existence. Therefore, The System facilitates cosmetic changes because they satisfy the people that initiate and implement them and are an outlet for the people who are unsatisfied with the status quo. If such cosmetic changes are perceived to have positive benefits, then all the people with such perceptions likely will try to generate additional cosmetic changes. Thus cosmetic changes beget cosmetic changes and suppress the realization that more funda-mental changes are required.

Fundamental or structural change may occur "only when there is a confluence of changing values and economic necessity."[2] We have seen that the former Soviet Union is in a period of changing values and severe economic decline. It is an example of a System that knows it is in trouble and that is resisting the initiation of fundamental, structural changes. The System is generating a series of cosmetic changes to buy time in the hope that The System's proponents can reestablish political control of the country and thus maintain The System's hegemony. Fortunately, but belatedly, the propagation of additional cosmetic changes only increases the people's awareness of the need for permanent change.

As mentioned in the previous chapter, it is important to understand why and when to change something. In any organization, whether it supplies a manufactured product or a service, repetitive transactions occur. These transactions are called a process, and a manufacturing line or a service activity may contain a series of minor processes or steps, each of which adds value until the overall process is completed.

A process may consist of a hundred or more separate steps or minor processes. Suppose that *each* step was performed correctly 99 times out of 100. If you think that the total good output of the process would be 99 times out of 100, you would be wrong for the following reason. Let us perform the first step of the process on a lot of 1,000 items. Since our acceptance rate is 99 of 100, or 0.99, then the number of acceptable units available after the first process step would be 990 (1,000 times 0.99). If in the second step we wait until we have 1,000 ready for processing and then performed the second step process on the lot of 1,000 items, we would obtain the same acceptable results (990). However, if we do not wait but perform the second step process on the output of the first step process, then we would obtain a total two-step yield of 990 times 0.99, or 980.1. Thus the yield of the entire process can be obtained by multiplying the yields of each separate step. In this example, we would have an output yield of acceptable items of $(0.99)^{100}$, or 0.99 times 0.99 one hundred times. This total yield would be 0.366 or 36.6 percent.

If a hospital or manufacturing plant had an efficiency of 99 percent in each step of a process, then the total output efficiency would be 36.6 percent for a 100-step process. Therefore, 63.4

percent of the resources applied to the total process were wasted or, if possible, reworked and made acceptable. In either instance, the cost of such poor yields might be very high and might not be acceptable in the overall scheme of things.

Assuming that the poor yield was unacceptable, one would want to change the process. Suppose that the yield for each step improved so that 999 of 1,000, or 99.9 percent, were acceptable units. Then, the total output yield would be $(0.999)^{100}$, or 90.5 percent for a 100-step process. In this case, only 9.5 percent of the resources of the total process were wasted or reworked.

The above discussion about the efficiency or output of a process in a service or manufacturing organization is an example of information that is required to make an intelligent decision about why and when to make a change in a process. However, all is not sanguine with the above scenario, which assumed that the measurements of acceptability were correct and that the individual steps and the total process were under statistical process control (SPC).

There are relatively simple procedures and analyses that one may perform to ascertain if the process is under SPC. To reiterate what was said in Chapter 5, one must first know if the process is in control or out of control. A process being in control or out of control refers to the process itself and not to the people or machines that perform or monitor the process.

Therefore, to make an intelligent decision about when and how to change a process, one must know if the process is under SPC. If the process is under SPC, then one must change The System of the process in order to alter future results. If the process is not under SPC, then one or more special causes that are adversely affecting the process must be eliminated or changed so that the operator can regain or establish statistical control of the process.

The W. Edwards Deming's book, *Out of the Crisis*,[3] discusses a service industry (trucking freight) as an example of the use of

SPC. In a typical trucking firm, truck drivers pick up shipments and transport them to a terminal for reloading and delivery by other drivers. Their trucking operation is one step in a long chain of operations (a process). Every step offers a chance for a truck driver to make a mistake. An analysis showed that the 150 drivers in one terminal made 7 different types of mistakes for a total of 617 mistakes in one year. For a twenty terminal trucking firm, almost $1 million a year of additional cost was generated due to driver mistakes. The distribution of the number of drivers that made "X" number of mistakes is shown in Figure 6-1.

Figure 6-1   Distribution of Mistakes Made by Drivers

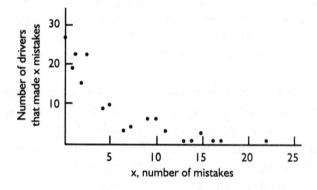

(Reprinted from *Out of the Crisis* by W. Edwards Deming by permission of MIT and the W. Edwards Deming Institute.)

Deming's analysis shows that the upper limit for this process if it is under control would be 11 mistakes. Thus it became clear that the process was not under SPC and that many mistakes by some of the drivers were caused by special events that were outside of The System controlling the process. Seven drivers each with more than 11 mistakes accounted for 18 percent of the mistakes, and the 143 drivers each with less than 11 mistakes made 82 percent of the mistakes. The System was to blame for the 505 mistakes, and the seven drivers accounted for 112 mistakes. Therefore management was responsible for the 505 mistakes since they were generated by The System that was under management's complete control.

This example illustrates the acute need for management to understand SPC and the concept of The System being under control, while it still was generating unwanted results that the employees were unable to change. Because The System is responsible for most of the mistakes, top management must understand that it is responsible for most of the problems that occur within The System that it established. Thus only top management can change The System by instituting structural, basic, and company-wide changes that are not cosmetic.

How the Concept of Change Affects People

An individual working or living under a System can do very little to change that System. Any changes that people manage to institute are usually accepted by The System as being nonthreatening. Having interfaced with The System over a long period, people become resigned to the fact that The System exists and they cannot change it. Apathy results from the concept that "you can't beat The System."

Because people understand that The System is in control, they usually do not blame anyone who works either within or, even illegally, against The System. When The System is in control, some may think that it is fair to get around it any way possible since they are not directly hurting, injuring, or wronging another person by such actions. Cosmetic changes also usually are acceptable to almost everyone, since they probably do not upset the status quo and may be even marginally helpful.

However, fundamental or structural changes usually cause great concern, mainly because the consequences of such changes are not understood or are thought to be threatening to one's welfare. Argyris[4] notes that people's defense mechanisms are primarily related to experiences of anxiety, conflict, frustration, or failure. The defense mechanisms that could be activated include aggression, guilt, discriminating decisions, delay, denial, repression, suppression, inhibition, conversion into personal problems, overcompensation, rationalization, identification, projection of blame to others, vacillation, ambivalence, and continuation mentally of another choice. In all but the smallest or newest of institutions, there is a natural tendency to resist change, which Thompson[5] calls cultural lag. He notes that all members of an organization eventually become socially specialized. That is, they become specialized in working with the various individuals with whom they are in daily contact. "Consequently, any suggestion for change must be measured against its effect on the cooperative system as a whole."

The people who work or act within The System know how to use it to deflect or defeat a fundamental or structural change imposed by top management. Unless management understands and plans to prevent such behavior, the change will be resisted by most people.

The key to instituting fundamental or structural change without also creating massive resistance is to develop a change function that automatically prevents such resistance. How The System problem is formulated determines the approaches that can be created and used.

Principles of Problem Solution

Watzlawick, Weakland, and Fisch[6] have elucidated a theoretical perspective on the questions of persistence and change in human affairs. Their book, *Change Principles of Problem Formation and Problem Resolution,* is a very important contribution to understanding how to resolve social problems and is very germane to understanding how to change The System.

They note that:

for example, whenever we observe a person, a family, or a wider social system enmeshed in a problem in a persistent and repetitive way, despite desire and effort to alter the situation, two questions arise equally: "How does this undesirable situation persist?" and "What is required to change it?". . .[7]

They have answered these questions by using analogically two abstract and general theories from the field of mathematical logic: the Theory of Groups and the Theory of Logical Types.

Group Theory is concerned with the relationships between the elements of a group and the whole group, providing the group has the following properties:

a. [The group] is composed of *members* which are all alike in one common characteristic, while their actual nature is otherwise irrelevant for the purposes of the theory. [The members of such a group must have the common denominator that] any combination of two or more members is itself a member of the group. . . . The term *combination* refers to a change from one possible internal state of the group to another. . . . Thus this first group property may allow for myriads of change *within* the group (in fact, there are so-called infinite groups) but also makes it impossible for any member or combination of members to place themselves *outside* the system.

b. Another property of a group is that one may combine its members in varying sequence, yet the outcome of the combination remains the same. . . . One might, therefore, say that there is changeability in process, but invariance in outcome.

c. [The third property of a group is that it] contains an *identity* member such that its combination with any other member gives that other member, which means that it maintains that other member's identity. [This property means] that a member may act without making a difference.

d. [The fourth property is that for] any system satisfying the group concept, we find that every member has its reciprocal or opposite, such that the combination of any member with its opposite gives the identity member; e.g., $5 + (-5) = 0$ where the combination rule is addition. Again we see that on the one hand this combination produces a marked change, but that on the other hand this result is itself a member of the group (in the present example the positive and negative integers, including zero) and is thus contained within it.

The authors have used the Theory of Groups to provide: a valid framework for thinking about the peculiar interdependence between persistence and change which we can observe in many practical instances where . . . the more that something changes, the more it remains the same thing.[8] [Unlike the Theory of Groups, the Theory of Logical Types gives one] a model for those types of change which transcend a given system or frame of reference.

The Theory of Logical Types also concerns collections of things, in this case called *members*, and the totality of that collection is called *class*. The essential axiom of this theory is that: whatever involves *all* of a collection must not be one of the collection; or conversely: if, provided a certain collection had a total, it would have members only definable in terms of that total, then the said collection has no total. We shall call this the "vicious circle principle," because it enables us to avoid the vicious circles involved in the assumption of illegitimate totalities.[10]

Some examples of classes for which the Theory of Logical Types applies follow: "Mankind is the class of all individuals, but . . . it is not itself an individual. . . . Conversely, in totalitarian ideologies the individual is seen only as a member of class, and thus becomes totally unimportant and expendable . . ."[11] The economy is the class of all financial transactions, but it is not itself a financial transaction. Health is the class of all human physiological processes, but it is not itself a process. Socialism is the class of all government owned functions for the production and distribution of goods and services, but it is not itself a function.

Watzlawick et al. explain that extreme problems can occur whenever one ignores the difference between a class and its members and thus treats one like the other. For example, Zeno's paradox of the motion of an arrow: "At any one instant in time, the arrow is in a fixed position at rest. Therefore, it is not moving." This paradox, like most paradoxes, is generated because of the confusion between class and member, and the fact that motion is not one of the members of the class of positions but is of a "higher" level or class. Thus, in order to accomplish fundamental change, the situation must be elevated to a completely different level or framework or class. A stationary arrow may occupy an infinite number of positions, since the infinite number of positions is the class of all stationary objects. In order to change this situation, the class must change, and in this case to a higher or more sophisticated level or state. The new class is that of motion, which is class of all changes of position with time. The solution to understanding the "moving" arrow paradox is to conceptually shift to the next level of class that should then lead to the elimination of the original problem.

In discussing the cybernetic properties of a machine with input, Ashby notes that:

it will be seen that the word "change" if applied to such a machine can refer to two very different things. There is a change from state to state. . . . which is the machine's behavior, and there is a change from transformation to transformation, . . . which is a *change of its way of behaving*, and which occurs at the whim of the experimenter or some outside factor. The distinction is fundamental and must on no account be slighted. [12]

According to Watzlawick et al.:

There are, then, two important conclusions to be drawn from the postulates of the Theory of Logical Types: 1) logical levels must be kept strictly apart to prevent paradox and confusion; and 2) going from one level to the next higher (i.e., from member to class) entails a shift, a jump, a discontinuity or transformation—in a word, a change—of the greatest theoretical and . . . practical importance, for it provides a way out of a system.

In summary, group theory provides a theoretical framework for understanding "the kind of change that can occur within a system that itself stays invariant." For example, bicycle riders must engage in small steering movements to maintain their equilibrium. These small changes are required for The System to remain in control.

The Theory of Logical Types is not concerned with what goes on inside a class, i.e., between its members, but gives us a frame for considering the relationship between member and class and the particular metamorphosis which is in the nature of shifts from one logical level to the next higher. . . . It follows that there are two different types of change: one that occurs within a given system which itself remains unchanged, and one whose occurrence changes the system itself.[13]

The authors call the change within The System *first-order change* and the change from The System to outside The System *second-order change*. "Second-order change is thus change of change."

Thus to change The System, a second-order change must occur. The second-order change is always a discontinuity or a logical jump; it often appears to be illogical, paradoxical, unthinkable, highly unlikely, strange, or improbable.[14]

The authors give an example of second-order thinking in the solution to the following abstract geometrical problem. In Figure 6-2, item A consists of a square of nine dots on a flat surface of paper. The object is to connect all nine dots by drawing only four straight lines without lifting the pencil from the paper. Most people will attempt to solve this problem by applying first-order principles to The System. Configurations B, C, and D are examples of first-order attempts to connect all the dots with four straight lines connected together. All other similar configurations will fail also because the solution is not among the first-order set of elements given.

Figure 6-2 Example of First-order Thinking

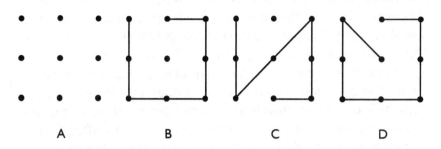

A   B   C   D

The solution is found in the use of second-order elements, which by definition are not part of the first-order elements. The reader is invited to create a second-order element and thus solve the problem. (The answer is given on page 197.)

Herbert Butterfield notes that the discovery and initiation of significant change in the field of science may be likened to:

picking up the other end of the stick, [which is a process that involves] handling the same bunch of data as before, but placing them in a new system of relations with one another by giving them a different framework.[15]

Arthur Koestler[16] has analyzed the art of creation by the comic, the scientist, the artist, or the writer. He suggests that for a successful creation (unique change) to occur, the situation or idea must be perceived "in two self-consistent but habitually incompatible frames of reference." He uses the concept of two planes that intersect, with each plane containing the idea or situation in its own class. Where they intersect, the idea or situation exists in both dissimilar planes or classes. Thus the situation or idea:

is not merely linked to one associative context, but *bisociated* with two. [Koestler] coined the term *bisociation* in order to make a distinction between routine skills of thinking on a single "plane," as it were, and the creative act, which . . . always operates on more than one plane.

Koestler revised his usage of the term "frames of reference" and other similar terms for the expression "matrix," which is a shorthand version for either "matrices of thought" or "matrices of behavior." He uses the word "matrix" to denote any ability, habit or skill [and] any pattern of ordered behavior governed by a "code" of fixed rules.[16]

After considerable justification from many examples, he notes that "the *bisociative* patterns found in any domain of creative activity are tri-valent: that is to say, the same pair of matrices can produce comic, tragic, or intellectually challenging effects." He means that two matrices may collide (interact) in various ways and thus give various types of results.

The use of a second-order change has the following consequences:

> The confrontation with an alien matrix reveals in a sharp, pitiless light what we failed to see in following our dim routines; the tacit assumptions hidden in the rules of the game are dragged into the open. The *bisociative* shock shatters the frame of complacent habits of thinking; the seemingly obvious is made to yield its secret.
>
> [Koestler explains that] problem solving is bridging a gap between the initial situation and the target. [One then usually searches] for a matrix, a skill which will bridge the gap. The matrix is found by way of analogy (or association by similarity) that is to say, by recognizing that the situation is . . . the same as some past situations. [One then tries] to apply the same skill which helped in those past situations, to the present lie of the land.[18]

Koestler calls first-order change associative thought or habit and second-order change *bisociative* thought or originality. The main distinguishing features of these two approaches are summarized in Table 6-1.[19]

Principles of Problem Formation

First-order changes are applied in most cases of attempted significant change; usually this results in unsatisfactory solutions because they are really members of the same group and thus are not different in any major aspect from the original situation. Only when the proposed first-order change solution is reframed within another class or level can the ultimate solution—the change function—be realized.

Table 6-1   Features of Associative and *Bisociative* Thought

Habit (First-Order Change)	Originality (Second-Order Change)
• Association with the confines of a given matrix	• *Bisociation* of independent matrices
• Guidance by preconscious or extra conscious processes	• Guidance by subconscious processes normally under restraint
• Dynamic equilibrium	• Activation of regenerative potentials
• Rigid to flexible variations on a theme	• Super-flexibility
• Repetitiveness	• Novelty
• Conservative	• Destructive−Constructive

Watzlawick, Weakland, and Fisch summarize second-order change as follows:

a. Second-order change is applied to what in the first-order change perspective appears to be the solution, because in the second-order change perspective this "solution" reveals itself as the keystone of the problem whose solution is attempted.

b. While first-order change always appears to be based on common sense (for instance, the "more of the same" recipe), second-order change usually appears weird, unexpected, and uncommonsensical; there is a puzzling, paradoxical element in the process of change.

c. Applying second-order change techniques to the "solution" means that the situation is dealt with in the here and now. These techniques deal with effects and not with their presumed causes; the crucial question is *what*? and not *why*?

d.   The use of second-order change techniques lifts the situation out of the paradox-engendering trap created by the self-reflexiveness of the attempted solution and places it in a different frame. . . .

Many who are professionally engaged in affecting change attempt to answer the first-order question "why" because they believe that its answer is the key to the solution or change that they seek. However, it is clear that this approach is not necessary or even desirable in many cases. For example, "mathematical statements are best understood as interrelated elements within a system. An understanding of their origin or causes is not required to grasp their significance and may even be misleading."[21]

According to Watzlawick et al., many problem-solving scenarios:

have an identical structure: an event, (*a*) is about to take place, but (*a*) is undesirable. Common sense suggests its prevention or avoidance by means of the reciprocal or opposite, i.e., (not-*a*) (in accordance with the group property) but this would merely result in a first-order change "solution." As long as the solution is sought within this dichotomy of (*a*) and (not-*a*), the seeker is caught in an *illusion of alternatives*, and he remains caught whether he chooses the one or the other alternative. It is precisely this unquestioned illusion that one *has* to make a choice between (*a*) and (not-*a*), that there is no other way out of the dilemma, which perpetuates the dilemma and blinds us to the solution which is available at all times, but which contradicts common sense. The formula of second-order change, on the other hand, is not (*a*) but also not (not-*a*).[22]

Second-order changes require that a change in the present matrix or a reframing of the situation be accomplished:

To reframe . . . means to change the conceptual and/or emotional setting or viewpoint in relation to which a situation is experienced and to place it in another frame which fits the "facts" of the same concrete situation equally well or better, and thereby changes its entire meaning. . . . What turns out to be changed as a result of reframing is the meaning attributed to the situation, and therefore its consequences, but not its concrete facts.[23]

The authors suggest the following four-step procedure for solving problems:

1) a clear definition of the problem in concrete terms;
2) an investigation of the solutions attempted so far;
3) a clear definition of the concrete change to be achieved;
4) the formulation and implementation of a plan to produce this change.[24]

Max Black[25] describes the use of metaphors in developing second-order solutions to problems:

A metaphor has the power to bring two separate domains into cognitive and emotional relation by using language directly appropriate to the one as a lens for seeing the other; the implications, suggestions, and supporting values entwined with the literal use of the metaphorical expression enabled us to see a new subject matter a new way. The extended meanings that result, the relations between initially disparate realms created, can neither be antecedently predicted nor subsequently paraphrased in prose. . . . Metaphorical thought is a distinctive mode of achieving insight, not to be construed as an ornamental substrate for plain thought. . . . Use of a particular model . . . may also help us to notice what otherwise would be overlooked, to shift the relative emphasis attached to details—in short, *to see new connections*.

A good example of this type of thinking is shown by Ikujiro Nonaka,[26] who recently reviewed how highly successful Japanese companies have become knowledge-creating companies and how they have quickly incorporated new technologies and products by disseminating such new knowledge. He notes that creating new knowledge depends on:

tapping the tacit and often highly subjective insight, intuitions, and hunches of individual employees and making those insights available for testing and use by the company as a whole. . . . The knowledge-creating company is as much about ideals as it is about ideas. . . . The essence of innovation is to re-create the world according to a particular vision or ideal.

Nonaka points out that such a situation can occur if all employees are committed to change, innovation, and the enterprise's identity and mission. He shows that powerful things are possible when tacit and explicit knowledge interact. The role of figurative language is important in elucidating the tacit and explicit concepts at the same time. He states that:

one kind of figurative language that is especially important is metaphor. . . . Metaphor is a distinctive method of perception. It is a way for individuals grounded in different contexts and with different experiences to understand something intuitively through the use of imagination and symbols without the need for analysis or generalization. Through metaphors, people put together what they know in new ways and begin to express what they know but cannot yet say.

Metaphor accomplishes this by merging two different and distant areas of experience into a single, inclusive image or symbol—what linguistic philosopher Max Black has aptly described as "two ideas in one phrase." By establishing a connection between two things that seem only distantly related, metaphors set up a discrepancy or conflict.

The metaphor is used to trigger the knowledge-creating process, which is followed by a process that reconciles contradictions and makes distinctions by analogy. The analogical process clarifies "how the two ideas in one phrase actually are alike and not alike. . . ." This step leads to logical thinking and action.

This process is one of changing The System by introducing a second-order change function. It is extremely important because it shows how a change function can be generated for a process or a situation that needs to be changed for one or more reasons. Nonaka gives three examples where this knowledge-creating process was successful in creating three new, highly acceptable products.

Figure 6-3 gives the solution to the nine dot problem by invoking a second-order change that uses two imaginary dots outside the framework provided to draw the lines. This solution to a simple problem is typical of the thinking that must be applied to problems in The System.

Figure 6-3   Solution to the Nine-dot Problem

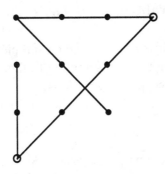

In sum, we have seen that one must initiate a second-order change to change The System. One does this by using a second-order matrix or reference frame (reframing) in which a proposed change can occur naturally. The implementation of a proposed fundamental change to The System is called a change function.

The following section gives some examples of problems that have unusual change functions applied to them, resulting in the generation of acceptable solutions.

CHANGE FUNCTIONS: VEHICLES FOR CHANGE

A change function may be very simple and short or very complicated and long. But in every case, it is a method or procedure whereby if followed eliminates the original problem. The change function, or second-order change, may be related only slightly to a first-order change solution. The change function may seem nonsensical or irrelevant to someone who is part of The System problem. For any System problem, an infinite number of change functions may exist. Many of them may be inappropriate, impractical, or may simply not yield desired results. The challenge is to find the optimum change function—one that works, that is simple, and that is acceptable to management and the people in the organization.

Examples of Problems and Their Change Functions

The pages that follow present eight examples of problems that have unusual change functions applied to them, which resulted in the generation of acceptable solutions.

The Bible contains many examples of the use of second-order change:

• A bedridden man with palsy was taken to Jesus through the roof of a house. Jesus, recognizing his faith, said, "Man, thy sins are forgiven thee." The Pharisees who witnessed this objected because only God can forgive sins. Jesus answered them by saying that it is easier to say "Thy sins be forgiven thee" than to say "rise up and walk." Jesus then commanded the palsied man to arise, take his couch, and go home, which he did. Thus Jesus heals a man by commanding him to rise and walk away. This reframing of the matrix of healing by another matrix of God's power was God's way of illustrating His glory to all people of the area.[27]

• In talking to the people and his disciples, Jesus said, "For whosoever will save his life shall lose it; but whosoever shall lose his life for my sake and the gospel's, the same shall save it."[28]

• "And Moses stretched out his hand over the sea, and the Lord caused the sea to go back by a strong east wind all that night, and made the sea dry land, and the waters were divided. And the children of Israel went into the midst of the sea upon the dry ground: and the waters were a wall unto them on their right hand, and in their left."[29] Thus the Lord created another miracle (change function) to save the Israelites who were fleeing Egypt and Pharaoh's army.

Koestler[30] gives three examples of very famous and important incidents that have significantly altered the welfare of the world. In each incident, a change function was needed to give the individual a new insight to the solution he was seeking.

Johann Gutenberg invented a printing press with movable type in 1450. Until his invention, print was transferred from carved wooden blocks by rubbing the reverse side of a page that was placed on top of the inked blocks. The matrix required for that operation necessitated carving blocks of wood into letters or pictures. Gutenberg searched for years for alternate methods to replace the laborious carving and explored the possibility of using a steel coin punch, but this method just replaced the wooden blocks and did not alter the rest of the printing process. One day at a wine harvest, he noticed the power of the grape press. At that moment it occurred "to him that the same, steady pressure might be applied by a seal or coin—preferably of lead, which is easy to cast—on paper, and that owing to the pressure, the lead would leave a trace on the paper—Eureka!" The second-order change, or *bisociation,* was the combination of the coin or seal with the wine press. Gutenberg generalized the concept of the wine press and instantly recognized the change function that would solve his problem.

Johannes Kepler discovered the laws of planetary motion in 1609. Before Kepler:

> [astronomy] had been a purely descriptive geometry of the skies. The motion of stars and planets had been represented by the device of epicycles and eccentrics—an imaginary clockwork of circles turning on circles turning on circles. . . . Kepler, who served his apprenticeship under Tycho (de Brahe), was given the task of working out the orbit of Mars. He spent six years on the task. . . . He found to his dismay that certain observed positions of Mars differed from those which the theory demanded by magnitudes up to eight minutes arc.

This was considered a catastrophe and required a new theory of astronomy.

Kepler realized that the circles of the existing theory did not describe the actual motion of the planets and concluded that the paths were oval. He was already a believer in the Copernican theory that the sun, and not the earth, was the center of the universe. He also was encouraged:

by that beautiful analogy between the stationary objects, namely, the sun, the fixed stars, and the space between them, with God the Father, The Son, and The Holy Ghost. [Twenty-five years later he modified his analogy significantly:] the sun in the middle of the *moving* stars, himself at rest and yet the source of motion, carries the image of God the Father and Creator. He distributes his motive force through a median which contains the moving bodies, even as The Father creates through The Holy Ghost.

In his revised analogy, the planets were part of the scheme, and the Holy Spirit became an active force like the active force from the sun that drives the planets. Using this newly discovered idea of the force of the sun, he developed a theory that included a second force and described the motions of the planets uniquely and accurately.

The change functions that Kepler discovered was the idea that the force of the sun influenced and controlled the planets like the Father influenced mankind through the Holy Spirit. Since everyone until that time believed in the geometric matrix of astronomy, it required Kepler to see the *bisociative* matrix (the second-order plane) that allowed the physics of motion to be the new matrix for astronomy, aptly named celestial physics. Kepler changed the entire concept of the motion of heavenly bodies and thus laid the foundation for the Space Age.

Koestler describe a third example, Charles Darwin, as:

perhaps the most outstanding illustration of the thesis that "creative originality" does not mean creating or originating a system of ideas out of nothing but rather out of the combination of well-established patterns of thought—by a process of cross-fertilization, as it were.

Even at the time of Aristotle, there were two opposite schools of thought about the evolution and immutability of species. By the end of the eighteenth century, similar views on evolution were promulgated in at least three European countries:

that is, fifteen years before Charles Darwin was born. The controversy continued unabatedly and Darwin was well aware of the controversy when he decided to become an evolutionist after his voyage on the Beagle, which ended in 1836 when he was twenty-seven years old.

Darwin studied the standard works on evolution and noted that the theories lacked cohesion, rigor, and proof of correctness. Darwin decided to collect facts about domestic breeding and construct a theory that explained the facts collected by many people. He tried various ideas within the familiar matrix of the known properties and theories at that time. According to Koestler, for amusement Darwin read Malthus' *An Essay on the Principle of Population,* which had been published more than forty years earlier in 1797. In this book "he saw in a flash the 'natural selector,' the causative agent of evoluting for which he had been searching." It is interesting to note that Darwin had completely misunderstood Malthus. "What Darwin Found in Malthus' essay he had read into it himself. . . ."

An idea written by another author over forty years earlier was used to construct the second-order matrix that provided the change function that Darwin had long sought. It should be noted that at the time Darwin was discovering his theory, Alfred Russel Wallace also remembered Malthus' essay, which produced a "flash of insight which led immediately to the simple but universal law of the 'survival of the fittest'. . . ." Wallace and Darwin were friends and wrote a joint paper that was read at the Linnean Society meeting on July 1, 1848, under the title *On the Tendency of Species to form Varieties; and on the Perpetuation of Varieties and Species by Natural Means of Selection.* "When the paper was read there was no discussion and no sign of interest. . . . In November of the next year *The Origin of Species* was published, and only then did the storm break." Thus Darwin unjustly received the sole credit for the change function—the theory of natural selection.

In the 1880s, Bohm-Bawerk[31] discovered the answer to the "value paradox" of goods and services. Until then, classical economists such as David Ricardo and John Stuart Mill had analyzed:

> the economy in terms of 'classes' rather than the actions of individuals. As a result the classical economists could not find the correct explanation of the underlying forces determining the values and relative prices of goods and services; nor could they analyze the actions of consumers, the crucial determinate of the activities of producers in the economy.[32]

Bohm-Bawerk showed that the value paradox was explained by analyzing the decisions made by individual consumers. He showed that:

> no productive activity, whether of labor or of any productive factors, could confer value upon goods or services. Value consisted in the subjective valuation of the individual consumers.[33]

Thus Bohm-Bawerk generated a change function that allowed him to distinguish between the actions of individuals and the concept of aggregates of economic transactions.

A virtual example of a change function involves a teacher who had insomnia for years and tried all the known remedies unsuccessfully. A friend, understanding the need for a change function that will enable the teacher to lose her insomnia, asks the teacher to follow a simple procedure each night with her alarm clock that will cure her insomnia within 2½ months. Starting that night when she goes to bed, the teacher sets the alarm clock for five minutes later, turns off the lights, and then tries to fall asleep. The second night, she is to set the alarm clock for ten minutes later. Each night she sets the alarm for five minutes later than the previous night. This is done whether or not she falls asleep.

By initiating a second-order change—the setting of an alarm clock that will wake up a sleeping person—the problem is taken to a new level of reference. This is a second-order change because the teacher now has a vehicle that is related to but obviously not the cause of her insomnia—the alarm of the clock.

Assume that the teacher is awake when the alarm rings the first night. She repeats the process for two weeks and is also awake when the alarm goes off after 70 minutes. The next night the alarm goes off after 1 hour and 15 minutes, but she was asleep and was awakened by the alarm. The next night she is awakened after 1 hour and 20 minutes, and the third night after 1 hour and 25 minutes. This continues until she decides that it is silly to be awakened from a sound sleep each night. Since this decision is reached way before she sets the alarm for six hours later (that would be 72 days), she is cured before the 2½-month period.

The above eight examples demonstrate unique change functions in operation. In practical cases, such as changing the long-term performance of a business or a government agency, a unique change function will also have to be created.

MANAGEMENT LEADERSHIP

Initiating Change

Top management must be convinced that fundamental or structural changes are required for it to change The System. Although top management may not initiate the need for such change, top management must initiate changing The System if it is to happen in a timely fashion throughout the organization.

The key to changing The System is for top management to find, create, or modify a change function that forces The System to change and meet the desired goals set by top management. Although many organizations are in the process of attempting improvement, most are run inefficiently and ineffectively and are struggling to accomplish significant long-term performance objectives.

Chapter 4 described The System for a typical large business, which could have a dozen or more departments or business centers that are each controlled by The System in a unique way. The problem top management has is to determine a change function that will be effective in all areas of the organization.

Beer, Eisenstat, and Spector[34] note that the usual attempts at change by top management are not fundamental and include "acquisition and divestiture, trimming excessive costs, rationalizing assets, introduction of new manufacturing systems, and new organizational revitalization." These and others, such as layoffs, early retirement programs, reduced sales promotions, and revised overhead and inventory accounting procedures, are cosmetic changes.

They state that fundamental changes are required, such as:

flatter, less hierarchical, more flexible organizations; empower employees to take initiative in reducing costs, improving quality, and responding to customer needs, . . . different patterns of management, and employee commitment; plus redefinition of the corporation's culture.

Their studies suggest that programmatic changes, that is, programs mandated by the CEO down to the lowest elements of the organization, were unsuccessful. What went wrong, they suggest, is that the corporation's "emphasis on values or culture did not take into account the organization as a total system."[35]

Top management must initiate fundamental change through the smaller organizational units—plants, divisions, departments, or business centers. The emphasis should be:

focused on the business' central competitive challenges as the means for motivating change and developing new behaviors and skills. We call this successful approach "task alignment". . . . Task alignment works by aligning the organization's ad hoc structure with its critical business problems.[36]

The basic concept of this approach is first to change the behavior of everyone by applying multiorganizational or functional teams to tasks related to critical business problems. "After behavior is changed then attitudes and knowledge will change."

Drucker[37] states that U.S. manufacturers need to:

change drastically the way new products and new models are conceived, designed, made and marketed, with the process eventually being telescoped into months from years. What these needs require are changes in behavior. But "changing culture" is not going to produce them. Culture—no matter how defined—is singularly persistent. . . . In fact, changing behavior works only if it can be based on the existing "culture."

The desired approach for introducing a change function in large businesses is by mandating new corporate goals and objectives that the managers of major groups must meet within a specified timeframe. This must be done with the understanding that the managers of the groups will initiate new ways of energizing people and breaking down The System. These new ways would have to be directed toward solving business problems that the groups have and most likely would include improving competitiveness by reducing the total cycle time of their work.[38]

Management, Vision, and Reality

To accomplish a change in The System that controls the organization, almost everyone in the organization will have to be affected. If a specific process is out of control, the process must be changed for that System. If the process is only a local one, a special change function for that local System must be found and implemented. Changes at the local levels can be accomplished best if the formal organizational structure and management are modified so that individuals have the opportunity to contribute in their unique ways to the business of the organization. Restructuring tasks into ad hoc teams that are multifunctional, self-directing, and self-governing appears to be the most effective way to initiate behavioral changes. Individuals and teams should have the authority to get the job done effectively and efficiently. This means that the ad hoc teams must be able to circumvent, ignore, overcome, or dismantle old policies and procedures and, more importantly, The System.

Since the root of most problems is The System and a management that slights or overlooks The System, teams and individuals must be able to bypass these barriers whenever they hinder their ability to solve problems in a timely fashion.

Once the business strategies are laid out for the entire organization, Peters recommends that everyone in the organization be completely immersed and involved in everything that they encounter. A climate must be created that encourages everyone to demonstrate spontaneous initiative. Everyone should understand that "there are no limits to the ability to contribute on the part of a properly selected, well-trained, appropriately supported, and above all, committed person."[39]

Peters makes it abundantly clear that an inherent part of any fundamental change for businesses must be the new concept of "total customer responsiveness" in which every individual in every element of the business is mainly concerned with totally satisfying each customer's total requirements. Therefore, each individual in each part of the business must be concerned with innovation and constant improvement in the workplace.[40]

An applied change function will automatically affect everyone in the organization, directly or indirectly, in addition to those who have input to the organization and those who are affected by its output. Those individuals who are not directly affected by the new changes will find themselves in a very small minority with limited chances for rewards and satisfaction.

Since most businesses are run by managers who are concerned with short-term results, such as monthly and quarterly sales and profit, top management's timeframe is almost always a year or less. Changing The System in a business usually takes longer than three years. As noted in Chapter 2, it takes varying amounts of time to learn to work with The System, depending on one's organizational level and experience within the organization and The System in place. To change The System, the behavior of individuals must be changed such that the old System no longer can control their behavior and their output.

Crosby[41] suggests that it usually takes four or five years for an organization's improvement process to be successful. The manager who initiates a process to change The System must be patient, persistent, and consistent.

> The most difficult lesson for the crusader to learn is that real improvement just plain takes awhile to accomplish. The urgency of the need, the obviousness of the cause, and the clarity of the solution have little to do with getting things straightened out. . . . [The way that significant change can occur is] to lead people gently toward what they already know is right. Otherwise, they just will not cooperate.[42]

Crosby explains that the way to get people to change their behavior in an acceptable manner toward improving their work is to involve them in a technique related to their work rather than involve them in the concept of change for improvement's sake. Therefore, the key is to involve everyone in developing techniques to solve their local problems and improve their local processes, which if done correctly, eventually leads to a change in behavior. Crosby points out that there is a risk to this process if done incorrectly. "The key negative aspect is that the people can get the idea that the system will work regardless of how much personal effort they put in or don't put in."[43]

Because there is continual change in the external environment, Beer et al. believe that the renewal process for a company could take ten or more years.[44] Considering the complexity of change required by the former Soviet Union, for example, it is obvious that the process of changing The System in the new republics could easily take ten or more years. However, for a company owned by stockholders, the timeframe should take less than five years because it does not have to interface with and satisfy an iron triangle of partners. A company under outstanding management that follows Parkinson's Law* ought to operate so efficiently and effectively that it will generate positive results and

---

*Parkinson's Law: Work expands so as to fill the time available for its completion. Its corollary is: Work contracts if there is limited time available for its completion.

increased profits within three years, and in five years at least double its profits.

Peters has shown that some companies have accomplished such results. For significant change to occur, top management must look at the entire organization from a zero-base viewpoint. The present organizational structure, policies, and procedures cannot be permitted to limit or prevent significant and rapid change. In practice, if management concerned itself with reducing the time it takes for each process or transaction, the benefit would be reflected in higher productivity and energized people, as well as synergistic improvements in customer satisfaction, quality, and reduced inventories.

However, using the concept of time reduction to improve the organization's performance is not sufficient to inspire vision and motivation in most people. What is first required is the vision of a changed future for the organization and everyone in it. Top management must articulate and demonstrate its commitment to that vision. The acceptance of such a vision by the other people in the organization depends on whether or not they believe that (1) the vision would be good for them, (2) management is really serious about making the vision come true, and (3) management will back that determination with *consistent* actions.

Peters concludes that companies must change their visions drastically to be successful and to survive in the increasingly competitive future. Table 6-2 lists Peter's *Eight Bold Goals*[46] that should be accomplished within a two to five year timeframe.

These are goals that The System cannot handle because they are not cosmetic. The System can stretch only ten to fifteen percent before its built-in procedures limit its output. Therefore, goals proposed by Peters and others cannot be achieved by piecemeal changes to the policies, procedures, and processes that are presently in place. To implement these goals, The System has to be completely destroyed and reconstructed by means of a change function. The introduction of a change function requires everyone in the organization to change his or her behavior.

Table 6-2   Eight Bold Goals For Businesses

Productivity	Increased by 100% to 200%
Quality	Defects reduced by 95%
Development Cycle	Shortened 75% to 90%
Order Lead Time	Reduced 90%
Inventory	Reduced 90%
Layers of Management	Reduced 75%
Span of Control	Increased by 500%
Training Budget	Increased by 200% to 300%

How Individuals Change

According to Schein,[47] "most theories of influence or change accept the premise that change does not occur unless the individual is *motivated* and *ready* to change." Schein points out three ways that individuals change their attitudes. An individual changes "because he is *forced* to change by the agent's directed manipulation of rewards and punishments." An individual has a strong motivation to rise in the organization hierarchy and thus is "eager to accept the attitudes and acquire the skills which he perceives to be necessary for advancement." The third way is what he calls "influence as a process which occurs over time."

The last way is the same approach that Crosby suggested. Schein notes that there are three phases to the influence approach. Paraphrasing Schein the phases are:

- *Unfreezing*: an alteration of the forces acting on the individual, such that his stable equilibrium is disturbed sufficiently to motivate him and to make him ready to change.
- *Changing*: the presentation of a direction of change and the actual process of learning new attitudes. This process occurs by either

internalization or *identification*. *Internalization* is the way one learns new attitudes by being placed in a situation where new attitudes are demanded of him as a way of solving problems which confront him and which he cannot avoid; he discovers the new attitudes essentially for himself. *Identification* is the way one learns new attitudes by . . . emulating someone who holds those attitudes.

• *Refreezing*: the integration of the changed attitudes into the rest of the personality and/or into ongoing significant emotional relationships.

Recognizing that there are creative ways of approaching System problems, Naisbitt and Aburdene[48] list four steps suggested by Roger Von Oech that an individual should apply to break out of his or her traditional modes of thinking:

• Challenge the rules.

• Inspect your own rules.

• Fall out of love with your own rules and ideas.

• Think frivolously. Make jokes about the problem on which you are working.

These four steps are similar to those suggested by Koestler where he shows that second-order change may be introduced by the development of jokes or puns.

Charles Handy[49] suggests that we are now in an age of discontinuity, of change everywhere. Discontinuous change he identifies as:

change not part of a pattern. . . . Discontinuous change requires discontinuous upside-down thinking to deal with it, even if both thinkers and thoughts appear absurd at first sight. [He notes that thirty years ago Donald Schon[50] argued that creativity comes from the] "displacement of concepts"—from taking concepts from one field of life and applying them to another in order to bring fresh insights.

The creation of a change function for an organization is required to change The System but is only the beginning. The critical task is to create a climate of change within the entire organization that will automatically energize everyone toward new goals and objectives that are challenging, futuristic, and self-rewarding. This climate must create a framework for cooperation among all functions of the organization. It must permit individual growth and satisfaction to occur without being imposed upon by a supervisor or manager. The climate must enhance and promote self-actualization while enhancing and promoting the objectives of the organization. We have seen that introducing teams, which in effect informally changes the organizational structure, is conducive to introducing real change.

IMPLEMENTATION OF CHANGE

The Choice of a Change Function

After top management decides to change The System, it must establish the goals that have to be met. The goals must be very challenging yet possible to accomplish. All members of the organization must be required to stretch their commitment, their work performance and, most important, their thinking and creativity about how best to advance their personal skills and knowledge. The ultimate output of the revitalized organization will depend on the goals chosen and the intermediate objectives that are generated in response to the goals.

Top management must create or chose a change function that will eliminate The System and also automatically allow the goals of the organization to be met. For example, top management for the U.S. Congress (the American people) must create a change function that automatically allows congressmen to break out of their present mold of self-promotion. Top management for the Soviet republics (the people of the various republics and their elected representatives) must create a change function that prevents the Communist party, the KGB, the military, and organized crime from exercising overriding controls on all aspects of the country. Top managers for Japan (the people) must create a change function that institutes a government that truly represents the people and not the iron triangle that controls The System. For a business, top management must introduce a change function that prevents The System from continuing its control over the work habits of the employees.

The key to changing The System is the change function—the second-order change that prevents The System from controlling the performance of the organization. Choosing the correct change function is paramount. An inappropriate change function, one that does not automatically eliminate the root cause or causes of the problems, will only exacerbate the situation and delay the possibility of changing The System.

A good example of a faulty change function is the one initially proposed by Gorbachev in the Soviet Union. His proposal appeared to give freedom to the republics but actually maintained the control of The System by the Communist Party. Although Gorbachev suggested that he was changing The System, he was doing everything in his power to maintain it by making various cosmetic changes; these changes preserved the basic ground of The System—of one party (the Communist Party) control.

A second example of a faulty change function was President George Bush's American 2000 program for improving the public elementary and secondary schools in the United States. That program did not propose to change The System in any significant way. It merely proposed cosmetic changes that appeared to be fundamental but in reality maintained the iron triangle's tight grip on The System.

A Critical Path to Change

A business can be revitalized in many ways, but experience and studies have shown that there is an optimum way for large organizations to introduce real change. Beer et al.[51] call this optimum way "the critical path to corporate renewal." The idea is to initiate the process in the smaller, self-contained divisions or plants of a large organization where the manager of that division or plant can be involved in making the process work.

One plant manager put it this way:

> We put this concept (employee participation) into the plant. The only reason it worked to start with was because I personally was overriding the system. I was in the plant every damned day . . . so I personally made it work. The minute I took myself out (of my plant) . . . bingo, it was right back to where it was. . . . After that happened it took me about a year and a half to realize that no matter how much training you do, how much teaching you do, no matter what the hell you do, if you don't permanently change the organization's structure, the infrastructure to force behavior change, it isn't going to happen. The organization, that structure, is stronger than anything else you can do and it's going to pull it right down to the old environment unless you permanently change it.

Beer et al. describe a process of six overlapping but distinctive steps that leads to the implementation of the change function previously chosen. They call these steps the *critical path*:

> This path develops a self-reinforcing cycle of commitment, coordination, and competence. The sequence of steps is important because activities appropriate at one time are often counterproductive if started too early. Timing is everything in the management of change.[52]

The six steps to the process of putting into effect the change function are discussed below.

1.   **"Mobilize commitment to change through diagnosing the problems that prevent competitiveness."** Once the top managers are convinced that fundamental and structural change must occur for the organization to become more viable and successful in the future, they must make that information available to all the members of the organization. People must develop a diagnosis of what the problems in the organization are and how they can be solved or what has to be done before they can be solved.

2.   **"Develop a shared, task-aligned vision of how to organize and manage for superior performance."** Once a core group of people

are in general agreement about what the basic problems are, the general manager can lead people "toward a task-aligned vision of the organization that defines new roles and responsibilities." Cross-functional teams are formed to identify the root causes of problems and to propose solutions. The teams are also charged with interacting with other teams whenever a boundary retards the flow of information or the performance of the team. Inherent in a team-structured organization is elimination of supervisors or unit managers. Teams that are self-contained become self-managed. Supervisors and unit managers have to become consultants, trainers, or specialists whom the teams use when needed.

The development of task-oriented teams leads to a flattening of the management structure of the organization. This flattening does not have to happen immediately but should occur after the teams have been operating successfully for six to twelve months and a de facto reorganization has already taken place in the minds of most team members.

3.   **Develop and support a "consensus for the new vision," help enhance the competence and faith of the people who have bought into the process, and supply the cohesion needed to move the process toward dismantling The System.** The general manager of the division or plant must make it clear that top management endorses and encourages member involvement and the team approach. For middle managers and other managers who support this approach, the general manager should create or authorize alternative job opportunities that are required in order to implement the organizational changes or to ensure future growth. They should agree to transfer elsewhere in the corporation those cannot support this new approach, or offer them generous outplacement arrangements.

The general manager should provide or authorize training wherever needed. Programs regarding team development, team leadership, quality and statistical quality control, sales, customer service, job training and basic and advanced education should be authorized. All employees should be treated as potential career employees.

4. **"Spread revitalization to all departments" and functions that supply members to the task-oriented teams.** With ad hoc teams developing improved processes and defining root causes of problems, the departments to which they belong must support their roles as team members and also their team decisions that affect the departments. This is critical to the individuals who form the teams. While the team members believe that their respective department managers have a major effect on their future promotions, wage increases, and careers in the company, they also believe that some of the team activities and decisions may hurt projects in their own departments.

The initiation of revitalization in some departments might not be as rapid as in others. This problem should not be solved by direction of the general manager. Rather the general manager should identify with any such department the very critical needs and support requirements that it must fulfil in a timely manner. In short, the management and the people of such a department must be given new, clear objectives to be met within new time-frames. The new vision of the organization's future and how this affects them must be articulated.

For example, the engineering department in a manufacturing business might be such a department, since it traditionally is relatively isolated from the rest of the organization. The engineering department has to learn from the general manager that by some specific time its development cycle for new products must be reduced, while at the same time the products are manufactured more easily at a reduced cost but with improved reliability. It also has to learn that the product must be able to be made with various sets of specifications to reflect different customer requirements. This might necessitate not only a drastic reorganization of the department's work arrangements but also a retraining of some of the engineers.

5.   **Consolidate the changes by establishing new policies that reflect and support the goals of the organization.** This should only be attempted when it becomes evident to *almost* everyone that a New System—controlled by the management and members of the organization—is now in place. The new procedures and processes should permit the maximum flexibility of individuals in their task-related jobs. (This step differs from the one suggested by Beer et al. in that operating procedures and the organizational structure are not formalized. See Peters[53] for the need to stamp out the bureaucratic rules and procedures.)

This step should reinforce the goals of revitalizing the organization and consolidate the critical needs for flexibility, innovation, and superior quality. The general manager eventually may have to reorganize the management structure to reflect the new changes that have occurred in the organization. The organization should be optimized to maximize its response to its customers.

The concept of narrow job descriptions should be eliminated.[54] Performance appraisals should be ongoing, and remuneration should be based on both the individual's and the team's performance. Once the change process is working and growing, bold financial incentives should be available to everyone in the organization through the teams or work groups.

6.   **Monitor and adjust the process of change.** The process should be adjusted to respond to problems that develop, the changing competitive environment, and opportunities that arise as a result of the fundamental and structural changes that occur in The System. Measurements should be developed that reflect what is important to the growth of the business, especially those associated with the generation of revenue and growth of customers. Emphasis should also be on measuring, evaluating, and promoting the

improvement of all processes, using SPC as the fundamental tool for evaluating quality. Processes should be changed only as a result of completing the formal "design of experiments" process.

Following these six steps in sequence is very important because it allows time for people to adjust to the changes in their work and the implications of how these changes will affect them in the future. The people must believe that changing The System is possible and that the changes they are partaking in could lead to fundamental changes to The System.

Top management must be very consistent and persistent in promoting the changes, goals, and future of the organization. Any inconsistent behavior or actions by top management could seriously delay the process of change by at least a year and probably two or three years.

Measurements and Evaluation

Everyone must be able to monitor the results of the process to change The System. Peters[55] notes that the usual measurements are short-term oriented and not related to the long-term performance of the organization. He suggests that six elements are usually missing in the ongoing progress reviews of the average organization:

(1) simplicity of presentation
(2) visibility of measurements
(3) everyone's involvement
(4) undistorted collection of primary information throughout the operations area
(5) the straightforward measurement of what is important, and
(6) achievement of an overall feel of urgency and perpetual improvement.

The first five elements are necessary to ensure that the evaluations of work processes are completely understood by those who perform the work and are affected by the input to or the output of the work.

Measurements and analyses relating to the quality of the output of each process, which are understood by each individual involved in the process, are key to determining what to do and when to do it, such as whether to continue the process with no change in anything or to determine what changes should be made in the process to improve its output.

These kinds of measurements and their evaluations are the tools that will foster innovation, flexibility, extraordinary responsiveness, and total integrity from each individual who is involved in the process of changing The System.

Problem Elimination Techniques

Box[56] points out three simple strategies that can be used to eliminate problems in any process. The first strategy, which he calls corrective feedback, "occurs when the study of system faults leads to their eradication." The simplest way to study the process is to measure its performance and capture that data. The data should be captured in the form of a run sheet—a tabulation or graph of data versus time or run number. A study of the data using check sheets, Pareto charts, cause-and-effect diagrams, histograms, stratification, scatter plots, and yield data can lead to eliminating problems in the process.[57] The data can be evaluated using Shewhart SPC charts to determine when the process is out of control and thus when the process has to be changed. Using these various measurement tools, the output of any process can be maintained or improved, depending on the output that one desires.

The second strategy he calls preemptive feed forward (PFF), which "is a process whereby careful forethought prevents faults from occurring." This process refers to eliminating problems before they occur—like picking up objects on a floor so that people cannot trip over them, or putting two first-class stamps on an envelope that contains a four-page letter. "PFF might be used temporarily while a fundamentally better system is devised. However care must be taken to see that PFF is not used as a substitute for fixing the system."[58] The process should be changed so that things automatically are done correctly. Thus people should be taught to not drop things on the floor and to weigh a four-page letter to determine its correct postage.

The third strategy for eliminating problems is simplification. Simplification of a process may be possible, especially if it contains many steps or has been in place for years without change occurring. Many processes over time become more complicated without necessarily becoming more effective. Box notes, "Because complication might provide work and power for particular bureaucrats, the process of simplification must not be in their hands nor subject to their obstruction." Simplifying a process might be accomplished by a cross-functional team. A flow chart may be very useful in determining how the workflow could be simplified or made more efficient. New machines or tools could be used or created to replace present multiple steps in a process. The process might be replaced with a different one that performs the same function quicker, better, and/or cheaper.

One of the most important types of processes that could be simplified is the manufacturing process of setup and breakdown for complicated tools or processes. Simplifying such types of processes can save a considerable amount of time when changing a process from one type of a product to another.

Most routine or administrative processes have been established based on The System, whereby little or no planning or analysis was done originally. Many such processes could be simplified if someone (or a team) studied the process and then introduced changes that prevented problems from occurring or saved a considerable amount of time and effort of people who were in the process flow.

SUMMARY

Implementing changes to The System is very difficult, mainly because The System supports the people who work within it and makes them feel very comfortable. People will partake in attempting to change The System if they believe that it needs to be changed and that it can be changed by them with top management's direction, blessings, or acquiescence. If the proper change function is applied, The System can be fundamentally and structurally changed. However, The New System must be continually evaluated by taking effective measurements that are analyzed and acted upon if needed.

We have seen that changing The System requires not only top management's approval and staying power but also the generation of a change function that will cause the desired change in The System. For most businesses a change function based in large part on the Productivity Improvement Approach is probably the best approach. For other organizations, more detailed, specialized, and dynamic change functions are required. In many cases, very significant problems exist, but no System changes are being attempted because of the iron triangle's ownership of The System. Thus to change The System sometimes requires destroying, eliminating, or making ineffectual at least two of the elements of the triangle. However, top management (which is sometimes the people) can introduce change functions that overcome the hegemony of the iron triangle and thus change The System.

The adoption and use of a change function may be extremely difficult and time consuming. Schon[59] notes:

> It is always a painful and wrenching experience to confront a confusing situation and to break with a way of structuring it that had been deeply held, however joyous and exhilarating the resultant insight may be. It is no surprise, then, that a law of least change operates in all the interactions among our structures, the world, and us. Conservatism is our characteristic pattern. The little skirmishes with the new on which we focus attention are rare exceptions in our lives.

CHAPTER 7

Examples of Change Functions

There are more things in heaven and earth, Horatio,
than are dreamt of in your philosophy.
—Shakespeare[1]

This chapter considers proposed change functions for six important U.S. institutions: Congress, Education, Health Care, Illicit Drugs, the Post Office, and the Supreme Court. It also contains proposed change functions for the governing Systems of Japan, Peru, Canada, and the republics resulting from the dissolution of the Soviet Union central government. The change functions described in this chapter, like all change functions that propose to destroy The System, are quite controversial and hard to implement. In most cases, it will take five or more years for people to even seriously consider them.

INTRODUCTION

As discussed in the previous chapter, a change function has the effect of changing The System in such a fundamental or structural way that it is replaced with a new one. Ideally a change function is triggered by a single, simple concept, such as that of the wine press for Gutenberg. Countless examples have shown that many inventions, discoveries, and creations are generated by a single, simple idea. However, to change The System in many complex organizations a more complex change function is usually required.

Each of the following proposed change functions is offered as a potential solution to The System problem that exists in the

221

organization or institution. Some of these proposed change functions are futuristic—it will take a considerable amount of time before the pressure on top management forces the introduction of a change function on The System. Some are not politically correct and therefore could not be attempted in the near future.

Although the following proposed change functions are not the only ones that could destroy and renew The Systems in the organizations being discussed, they represent the best approaches. Some of these change functions are quite complex, with many concurring and interlocking elements. This is because simpler ones could not destroy The System and thus eliminate the problem that it generates. Many of the proposed change functions could be very controversial because the proponents of the status quo—the members of the iron triangles—would be very active in denouncing such changes. The members of the iron triangle always support and try to take over The System. The System tries to balance out these supporters in order to protect itself long-term wise.

UNITED STATES INSTITUTIONS

Change Function for Congress

Congress is a classic example of a government body in which The System completely controls the operation of the organization. Congressmen are trapped in The System that causes them to expand government activities and the budget every year. The spend-and-elect philosophy is the motivating force in their jobs. Most congressmen believe that if they do not implement that philosophy, then they will be replaced by someone who will. Since congressmen believe that they can best help govern the country, they therefore reluctantly accept the spend-and-elect philosophy. An example of this philosophy was Senator Nancy Kassenbaum's promise to serve only two terms when elected as senator from Kansas in 1978. In May 1989, however, she changed her mind, concluding that her seniority could be put to "good and worthwhile purposes."[2]

A change function is required that will cause congressmen to replace their self-perpetuating philosophy for one that optimizes the general welfare of the country. Their present philosophy maximizes the specific welfare of the iron triangle.

Such a change function could be one that limits the time a congressman may serve in Congress. This concept is not a new one. On November 15, 1777, the Continental Congress in the Articles of Confederation agreed that "no person shall be capable of being a delegate for more than three years in any term of six years."[3] This concept was also introduced during the drafting of the Constitution and in the First Congress but was dropped because of more pressing business. The Constitution for the Commonwealth of Massachusetts declares:

> In order to prevent those, who are vested with authority, from becoming oppressors, the people have a right, at such periods and in such manner as they shall establish by their frame of government, to cause their public officers to return to private life; and to fill up vacant places by certain and regular elections and appointments.

Thus the concept of term limitation was expressed in 1780 when that Constitution was adopted.[4]

The change function needed in this case is two new amendments to the U.S. Constitution. These amendments will have to be initiated and approved by the states since the Congress, embraced with The System, will not vote to initiate a constitutional convention to change The System. The following are my two proposed amendments that will stop the course of runaway government and enhance the general welfare and blessings of liberty in all of the United States.

The First Proposed New Amendment:
[Amendment No. 28 to the Constitution]

Title: **Terms and Conditions of Service for Congressmen, Supreme Court Justices, the President, and the Vice President.**

Preamble: In as much as the President, Vice President, Representatives, Senators, and Supreme Court Justices are considered to be stewards of the commonweal of the people of these United States, therefore these offices should be considered to be those of public service and not of lifetime employment. In this spirit of public service, the terms and conditions of such service are hereby established.

Section 1. The terms of the members of Congress shall henceforth be limited to a single, unrenewable term in each house of Congress. Each member of the House of Representatives shall be elected to a single, unrenewable three-year term of office. A three-year term election will coincide with the presidential election once every twelve years. Each member of the Senate shall be elected to a single, unrenewable term of office. For each state, the terms shall continue to be staggered.

Section 2. Congressmen, at the time of this amendment's ratification, are permitted to run for reelection for only a single, unrenewable term or are permitted to run for election to the other House for a single unrenewable term when the next election takes place.

Section 3. The Supreme Court justices shall be limited to a single, unrenewable term of twelve years. The present Supreme Court Justices' terms will be staggered based on length of service on the Court at the time of this Amendment's initiation. Those justices who have already served their twelve or more years shall be eligible to serve a maximum of an additional six years, upon which time their service shall expire. Those justices who have served less than twelve years shall be eligible to serve a maximum of eighteen years, upon which time their service appointments shall expire. Upon the resignation, death, or removal of a Justice from the Court, a new Justice shall be appointed for a twelve-year term by the President with the consent of the Senate in accordance with established procedures. Upon completion of their service on the Supreme Court, justices will be eligible for nomination by the President to serve on another federal court.

Section 4. Newly elected Congressmen and newly established Supreme Court justices shall henceforth not receive nor accrue any new or additional pension and any other additional government benefits, such as health care, insurance, or Social Security or retirement benefits. The sole total remuneration of these officials shall be their salary, which shall be established by the preceding Congress.

Section 5. Congressmen and Supreme Court Justices, except for remuneration or investments already determined by contracts established before the acceptance date of this Amendment, shall not receive nor accrue any other remuneration from any individual, organization, corporation or government during the time of their government service as Congressmen or Supreme Court Justices, respectively, except as provided in Section 7. Congressmen shall not be eligible for any salary increase during their term of office. Those Congressmen who are in office at the time of the adoption of this Amendment shall be affected by the terms of this Section and the entire Amendment when and if they are reelected to Congress.

Section 6. The newly elected President and Vice President shall henceforth receive only a salary as total remuneration for his or her term or terms of service as President or Vice President. The President or Vice President shall not receive nor accrue any government-funded pension and any other government-funded benefits, such as health care, insurance, or government Social Security or, retirement benefits, during his or her term of office. Congress shall establish the total remuneration for the President or Vice President before any presidential election takes place.

[This section could also begin with this sentence: "The terms of office for the President and Vice-President of the United States shall be a six-year, unrenewable term." This six-year term limit was suggested by President Rutherford B. Hayes in his Inaugural Address of March 5, 1877, because he believed that the sitting President should be above party politics and that it would be easier to reform the government bureaucracy if just one, six-year term were in effect rather than the potential of two four-year terms. Ex-President Jimmy Carter, writing in the May/June 1987 issue of the American Heritage, also proposed a single six or seven-year term for the president. In this alternative, the elections for Representatives would run concurrently with the election of the President only every six years, and only one third of the Senators would run concurrently with the President's six-year term.]

Section 7. The President, Vice President, Congressmen, and Supreme Court Justices may, during their respective terms of office, receive remunerations from blind trusts and other entities established by law passed by a two-thirds vote of both houses.

Section 8. For all federal primaries and elections, a NOTA (None of the Above) line shall be available for the voter. If a plurality or majority of voters choose NOTA, then the election shall be rerun. Those candidates on the ballot who received less than 10 percent of the total vote cast shall be barred from candidacy for that rerun election. If the rerun election results in a plurality or majority of voters choosing NOTA, then all previous candidates on the ballot shall be ineligible for the subsequent rerun election. This election process shall continue until a candidate is chosen by the voters. (If the original election date cannot be met, then a special election on a subsequent date shall be held.) If no candidate is found acceptable, the state shall determine the procedures for establishing a new list of candidates.

The Second Proposed New Amendment:
[Amendment No. 29 to the Constitution]

Title: **Economic and Financial Limitations of the Government.**

Preamble: In accordance with the preamble of this Constitution, the general welfare of the citizens of these United States shall be enhanced by limiting or restricting the government in the following areas:

Section 1. Except in time of declared war, the government spending each year shall be limited to the official anticipated revenues for that year. Deficit spending is prohibited. Any inadvertent shortfall in revenues shall be made up the next year by a reduction in the proposed spending for that year. If the deficit for the year is one percent or more of the year's revenues, then each Congressman, the President's, and the Vice President's total salary for the year shall be reduced by a percentage equal to five times the percentage deficit for that year.

Section 2. Only a single comprehensive budget account shall exist for the government. No off-budget funds are permitted.

Section 3. The government's deficit shall be repaid in full during the next two decades.

Section 4. Gold coin and bullion shall be legal tender and may be used to satisfy contracts between two parties who have freely agreed to such a contract. The government shall not limit or regulate the legal commerce of such coin and bullion and shall not tax these items. Private gold coinage and private 100 percent gold-based certificates shall be permitted as legal tender, and all contracts that require payment in such tender shall be enforceable in a court of law.

Section 5. The government's tax on the income that individuals receive shall be limited to the use of a single tax rate with no deductions or credits except a single standard deduction for each individual covered by the form. The form shall be limited to the size of one side of a single standard postal card. For this tax, compensation is defined as actual payments of wages, salaries, and pensions and includes fringe benefits paid by employers.

Section 6. The government's tax on taxable business income shall be limited to the same single tax rate set for individuals.

Taxable business income is defined as "business receipts less the cost of business inputs, less compensation paid to employees, and less the cost of capital equipment, structures, and land. . . . Organizations exempt from the business tax are: (a) state and local governments, and their subsidiary units; (b) educational, religious, charitable, philanthropic, cultural, and community service organizations that do not return income to individual or corporate owners."[5] The business tax form shall be simplified to fit on one side of a form twice the size of a single standard postal card.

Section 7. Except in time of declared war, the government's tax revenue each year shall be limited to a maximum of 15 percent of the sum of the annual taxable individual income and the annual taxable business income. This limitation may be temporarily increased for a single year by approval of at least 95 percent of the members of each House of Congress and by the President.

Section 8. Congress shall fund all mandates; and all laws passed by Congress or its agencies shall apply to Congress.

Section 9. The President shall have veto power over any item, complete sentence, or complete paragraph of any bill or resolution submitted by Congress. Congress may override such a veto in accordance with previously established procedures.

The first proposed amendment, the 28th, is the most critical of any potential amendment to the Constitution. It will function to change The System of the federal government in the United States and create a new type of public servant or statesman in the Congress. In addition to the usual candidates who partake in congressional elections, there would be an outpouring of many other candidates from various professions and life situations. For example, many businessmen, teachers, scientists, doctors, retailers, salesmen, manufacturers, retirees, housewives, or state legislators would be willing to invest three or six years of their productive lives to serve their country. Many of those Congressmen who are presently able to be reelected will completely change their spend-

and-elect philosophy into a philosophy of what is best for the country.

Anyone elected under this Amendment would have no incentive to satisfy the lobbyists and special interests in lieu of the country's overall interests. Since there would be no seniority rights or long-term committee chairmen to wield power over proposed legislation, Congress would become a true deliberative body that could strive to balance the long-term interests of the country with the short-term interests of its citizens. Legislation would be developed that would be eclectic. The government's interference in the economy would be minimized, because the special interest groups that require subsidies and special tax consideration would be a minority and would receive fair treatment under the law rather than special treatment at the expense of other people in the country.

The second, or 29th, Amendment would shape and limit the Congress' ability to expand the federal government's control over the individual. It would force Congress to define priorities within specific spending limits. It would also force Congress to analyze which government agencies continue to generate rules and regulations that are unconstitutional or have economic and financial consequences, such as limits on growth, jobs, revenues, and profits for most individuals and businesses. Thus, the new congressmen would challenge the basic inefficiencies inherent in government controls or operations; they would then go on to develop programs to enhance the individual's capabilities and opportunities.

The 29th Amendment would change The System rapidly; with both amendments in place, significant results would become evident after 3-5 years. With only the 28th Amendment enacted, it would probably take 5-10 years to get equivalent results.

A congressman's remuneration should be limited to a total salary predetermined by the government because eliminating the other benefits, such as health, Social Security, and pensions, would isolate congressmen from voting on programs that directly concerned their present remuneration. What is more important, since congressmen would serve only one term, they would be considered temporary government employees or self-employed consultants and thus would not be eligible for any additional government benefits.

The gerrymandering process that occurs every ten years would not be needed if congressmen were limited to a single term. Congressional districts eventually could reflect natural economic or social areas rather than being drawn up solely to maximize the reelection of a candidate from the political party presently in control.

Single-term congressmen no longer would be inbred partners with the government bureaucracy since the bureaucracy could not help them get reelected. Eventually, congressmen would realize that the government bureaucracy and special interest groups usually promote legislation that is beneficial to their own interests and detrimental to the public's interests. Thus, for example, there would be no vote trading wherein congressmen agree to support various special interests to ensure their reelection.

To get elected, a candidate for Congress would have to appeal to the majority of voters rather than the special interest groups and PACs. Since no candidate would be an incumbent, at least two and probably three or four candidates would be running in each congressional district. The public would perceive that a real choice was available, and thus the percentage of voters in each election would increase. (The NOTA provision would help also.)

In addition to improving the federal government's operation, the concepts embodied in the two amendments would be applicable to the various state and local governments. Although many state legislatures probably would not attempt to limit the terms of state legislators, popular initiatives are feasible in some states and could be used to change The System of state government.

An alternative change function that would eliminate the need for the 29th Amendment would be to modify the 16th Amendment, which now reads as follows: "The Congress shall have the power to lay and collect taxes on incomes, from whatever source derived, without apportionment among the several States, and without regard to any census or enumeration. . . ." This Amendment would be modified by adding the following sentence: "No person, family, or business shall be taxed by Congress at a higher rate than 10 percent of their respective total incomes from whatever source derived."

This alternative would be effective only if the total rates were limited to 10 percent or lower, which would force the government to cut back on its spending, borrowing, and subsidies to the iron triangle members. Congress would be somewhat limited in its ability to buy votes, and forced to eliminate many nonessential government-supported programs that are not mandated by the Constitution. However, without a private gold-based legal tender, Congress could borrow its way to excessive spending and large deficits and thus cause the Federal Reserve to inflate the economy.

Other possible change functions could change The System but are all limited in their scope of effectiveness or require drastic limitations and controls on the individuals involved. For example, one alternative change function would be to limit the terms of congressmen to two, three, or four terms. Such a limitation would tend to reduce the spend-and-elect syndrome by half, a third, or a fourth but also keep intact the lobbying and funding of the special interests and PACs. In essence nothing would change since most congressmen would be trying to get reelected most of the time. Most congressmen appear to want a minimum term limit that extends at least twelve years. Real term limits will become possible only if the states initiate constitutional conventions for a term limits amendment to the Constitution.

A third alternative change function would be to have the government finance the election campaigns of all candidates for

Congress who receive at least 5 percent of the vote cast in the primary. The problem with this alternative is that funds would be required for the primary campaigns and thus PACs and other special interests would be used by incumbents to get reelected, keeping The System essentially unchanged. This approach would not eliminate the spend-and-elect syndrome that presently affects every congressman.

A fourth alternative change function would be to ban donations over $100 given to a candidate for Congress by any individual or group. This approach could favor the candidate who has ample funds to run for office. Wealthy candidates could have an overwhelming advantage over candidates who have to count on supporters' funds for their campaign. Alleviating this problem would require banning or limiting the amount of one's own funds that could be spent for one's campaign. Such a law would be clearly unconstitutional and against the natural right to own and use property. It also does nothing to eliminate the primary interest of most of today's congressmen.

A fifth alternative change function would be to repeal the 17th Amendment,[6] that instituted the elections of U.S. Senators by the popular vote of eligible voters in a state. Prior to its ratification, U.S. Senators were chosen by the state legislatures. If it were repealed, state legislators again would have the right to reappoint incumbent senators. Ironically, Senators' continuance in the Senate would depend upon a single special interest. Although senators would not have to raise campaign funds from the PACs and other special interests, their focus would be related primarily to the politicians that run their state. Since state politics are always part of an iron triangle of special interests, senators indirectly would be reliant on those special interests. This alternative change function unfortunately would be merely a cosmetic change that would not alter the senators' behavior.

A sixth alternative change function could be a modification of the proposed 28th Amendment. Everything would be the same except that the President's and Vice President's term of office would be limited to a single, nonrenewable four-year term. The Vice President would be eligible to be a candidate for the Presidency and serve a four-year term. This proposed change would elevate the job of the Vice President, since the Vice President would be eligible for a promotion. Therefore, the choice of a vice presidential candidate before a national election would become almost as important as the choice of a presidential candidate.

A seventh alternative change function would be an amendment that increases the number of representatives.[7] This would not solve the basic problem of self-interest on the part of Congress, and would not address the primary incentive of congressmen to get elected at any cost.

Based on the incorrect assumption that The System problem is that of divided government, (the majority of both houses of Congress not belonging to the same political party as the President), Sundquist[8] proposes a multi-part change function that allegedly would eliminate the problem of an ineffective (noninterventionist) federal government. His main suggestions follows:

1. Make ticket splitting (voting) impossible. One would have to vote for the President and Vice President and the representative and senator on a party ticket and not as individuals.

2. Change the ballot format. Allow the choice of voting for a straight ticket or for each individual.

3. Change the election schedule. Have the election for congressmen two weeks after the election for President.

4. Pass a constitutional amendment that lengthens the terms of representatives to four years and of senators to eight years.

5. Pass a constitutional amendment that assigns the winning presidential candidate enough Senate and House seats to outnumber the opposition.

6.   Pass a constitutional amendment that authorizes Congress to call a new presidential election by law, which would require a two-thirds majority in each House to become a law.

7.   Pass a constitutional amendment that would permit Congress to remove the President by a no confidence vote of 60 percent of each House, which would then require a new election of all congressmen as well as the President and Vice President.

None of these seven proposed changes would change The System that controls Congress. Instead, they would render congressmen even more venal because of their increased sense of security and longevity. These seven proposed alternate change functions therefore would protect and strengthen The System.

In summary, the key to changing The System in Congress is the proposed change function, i.e., the 28th Amendment. There appears to be no other viable alternative to this particular change function. The key to expediting the change that would occur from the ratification of the 28th Amendment is to ratify the 29th Amendment. Implementing these two amendments would lead to an unprecedented, large, non-inflationary growth of wealth that would be shared by every social and economic group in the country. With this increased wealth throughout the country, the need for government restrictions, laws, and controls would be limited. For example, the federal government would not need to support and control health care because sufficient funds would be generated by individuals, charities, and the states to satisfy the basic health needs of the country.

Change Functions for the Education System

In the 1988 presidential election campaign, President Bush wanted to be known as the education President, the President who was responsible for making significant improvements in the education of school children. Eventually in 1991, his Secretary of the Department of Education, Lamar Alexander, proposed a six-part facade to reshape the country's educational System by the year 2000. It was an attempt to preempt and direct the states' educational Systems. The first five parts of the programs were cosmetic changes.

1. Establish 535 experimental New American Schools that "would serve children from age 3 months to age 18."[9] This would mean one school for each congressional district plus two others for each state, presumably for the patronage of the two U.S. Senators.

2. Establish a government-sponsored national achievement test that could lead to an alleged voluntary form of educational standards.

3. Increase government-funded family planning, health care, day care, and head start programs.

4. Change teacher certification rules.

5. Lengthen both the school day and the school year.

The sixth part of the program was to promote school choice. It proposed to award $ 1,000 scholarships to 500,000 first-to-twelfth-year school children, which could be used in any schools whether public, private, or religious. This was a pseudo school-choice proposal because of the limits regarding per pupil costs and the widespread but sparse distribution of the scholarships. Therefore, it would have become another educational program veneer in the never ending circle of educational fads. The changes to The System, had they taken place, would have been merely cosmetic.

All parts of the program easily could have been adopted by The System, since the first five would have strengthened The System's control over public education. In fact, depending on the standards that might have been imposed on private schools chosen by students, the *America 2000* program could have set back real change in The System of primary and secondary education.

The Clinton administration's *Goals 2000: Educate America Act* is a sophisticated, reversal of the Bush program. Instead of a program in which national performance standards would be set at world-class levels and statewide testing would evaluate children's mastering of the curriculum, *Goals 2000* stresses the "opportunity to learn" and measures the *inputs* to each school System. Thus a new Federal National Education Standards and Improvement Council would direct the establishment of "opportunity standards," which is a code term for spending targets on federally designated items for each school System. The law requires "race norming," prohibits using testing as a criterion for graduation or promotion, and requires teaching methods to meet "content standards." The only choice states would have in this program would be whether or not to accept the federal funds for the program, which would lead to more direct influence and control of the schools' operations by the federal government.

If, however, congressmen were limited to a single term, fundamental changes could be made to The System by eliminating the federal government's involvement in education. Therefore, the most likely way to change The System is by passing new state laws that eliminate the bureaucracy's and special interests' control of The System. The key to changing The System lies in the introduction of a change function that uses the dual concept of privatization and parental choice.

In 1955, Milton Friedman first suggested a voucher plan to reduce the government's control over education and return it to parents, who originally had such control. Friedman argues that a free enterprise economic System is essential to a democratic political System. Therefore, it is essential for the protection of our individual freedoms that services be provided through our economic System instead of our political System. He reasons that government funding of education was acceptable because of its "neighborhood effects."[10] He also states that just because the government pays for a service does not mean that it should provide the service. Friedman notes that The System of education is poor because it is a government-sponsored monopoly controlled by a large, unresponsive bureaucracy.

He explains that the lack of competition is responsible for the bureaucracy's performance. Therefore the solution is obvious: introduce competition. Free enterprise market forces could be introduced to provide alternate educational services that are better than the governments' services and therefore would attract parents and students.

Friedman proposes that the government should provide parents with educational vouchers that could be redeemed for cash by any school that enrolled the children. He suggests that the amount of the educational voucher should be equivalent to the cost of educating pupils in the public school System, and that parents could pay for additional services they wanted.

Under Friedman's plan, private for-profit and not-for-profit schools would be eligible to accept vouchers:

> The voucher plan embodies exactly the same principle as the GI bills that provide for educational benefits to military veterans. The veteran gets a voucher good only for educational expense and he is completely free to choose the school at which he uses it, provided that it satisfies certain standards. [Friedman more recently notes that] vouchers are essentially a refund to parents of the taxes they are required to pay to support the educational system. Parents who choose to send their child to a private school, whether parochial or not, are required to pay twice for the schooling of their child, once through the taxes they pay, a second time directly. If they spare the government the expense of schooling their child, they should receive a refund.[11]

Friedman also states that "it is far from clear that there is any justification for the compulsory attendance laws themselves."[12] Although this concept is not essential to the voucher plan, it would result in a small savings to the government when parents elect not to have their children attend school.

Myron Lieberman[13] analyzes Friedman's voucher plan and the spectrum of privatization and educational choice. Lieberman's balanced analysis endorses vouchers for private or public schools and allows the school bureaucracy to contract out educational services.

Chubb and Moe[14] describe how politics and bureaucracy have caused The System of education to become second rate. They have analyzed data demonstrating that government is the problem. Chubb and Moe studied the attempts of education reform in the 1980s and documented the successes and failures of such attempts. They show that innovative reforms (school-based management, teacher professionalism and empowerment, and choice) have been used to improve education.

They note that choice has been associated with the voucher system but that:

in recent years, however, choice has come to be viewed very differently, even by many in the educational establishment. This new movement puts choice to use as part of a larger set of strategies for reform *within* the public sector. . . . Choice is being embraced . . . as a powerful means of transforming the structure and performance of public education—while keeping the public schools public. [They argue that the changes do] not go far enough. The demand side has essentially been freed up by giving parents and students choice. But the supply side—the set of alternatives from which they choose—remains firmly under the control of all the usual democratic institutions. Schools do not emerge in response to what parents and students want.[15]

Knowing that it is being attacked, The System has devised a bogus choice plan. Although it is presented as a valid way of changing The System, most of the changes are cosmetic in that the members of the iron triangle remain intact with all their prerogatives, controls, and jobs. The students would have only a limited choice of existing public school—those within the school district or nearby districts.

Chubb and Moe conclude that choice alone is the panacea to the education problem:

Choice is not like the other reforms and should not be combined with them as part of a reformist strategy for improving America's public schools. Choice is a self-contained reform with its own rationale and justification. It has the capacity *all by itself* to bring about the kind of transformation that, for years, reforms have been seeking to engineer in myriad other ways. . . . Taken seriously, choice is not a system-preserving reform. It is a revolutionary reform that introduces a new system of public education. [16]

They point out that the best way to achieve significant reform is for the individual states:

to design institutions around fully decentralized authority and then to install them through constitutional amendment. The legal foundation of the new system would then be very difficult to change or violate once put in place. And, because state constitutions are the ultimate authorities in state government, they have the power to constrain what future legislatures and governors (and the political groups that pressure them) can do in controlling the schools. [17]

They propose a New System with the following properties:

1.   The state would set the minimal criteria defining what constitutes a public school under The New System. Any applicant that meets the minimal criteria would "then be chartered as a public school and granted the right to accept students and to receive money." The school district governments would continue running only their present public schools and would not have any authority over other schools within their district that are chartered by the state.

2.   The state would set up a Choice Office in each district that maintains the records and "the level of funding—the 'scholarship' amounts—associated with each child." The schools would be compensated directly by the Choice Office based on the specific number of children that they enroll. Money from all government sources (federal, state, and district) would go to the Choice Office and then to the schools. At no point would the money go to parents or students. The parents would not be permitted to supplement the scholarship amounts with personal funds, because that could produce too many disparities and inequalities within The New System. The district could add more funds on to a scholarship for students with special educational needs.

3.   Each student would be free to attend any public school in the state. The state would provide transportation for students if the government funds are available. A Parent Information Center

would be part of each local Choice Office; its staff would be available to consult with parents about choosing the best school for their children. The school would be the sole judge of the children it admits "subject only to nondiscrimination requirements." The public school will establish its own scholarship fee requirements and will be free to expel students or deny them readmission.

4.   Each public school would be "granted sole authority to determine its governing structure." However, the schools would be subordinate units within an educational district government. No state-mandated requirements would exist for anything except for minimal state certification of teachers. State-wide tenure laws would be eliminated but district-wide tenure may be retained. Teachers would continue to have a right to join unions and engage in collective bargaining only for the school in which they are employed. The state would hold the schools accountable for meeting procedural requirements and will provide the public with optional standardized test scores. The state would not hold the schools accountable for their students' performance. This account-ability would be provided by the student and the parents who can exercise their choice of schools.

Chubb and Moe have been very creative in proposing that their New System should be created by the states and that choice should be the sole criteria used to control the performance of the schools that become part of The New System.

However, their imaginative New System still permits the iron triangle its pound of flesh. The New System requires that the state instead of the potential customers of such schools mandate minimal criteria for each school. Why should the state mandate teacher certification requirements? Wouldn't the principal and/or the governing board of the school be sufficiently accountable to satisfy their potential customers? Why should the state's criteria be considered the best, or even optimum or necessary?

In The New System, the state would also set limitations on how religious schools would have to separate their sectarian functions from their educational functions. In other words, the Book of Ruth could not be used as a lesson in English, spelling, values, and grammar. Why should the state mandate such limitations when the potential customers could in their choice of schools? The answer that Chubb and Moe would give would be that the state then could not be accused of promoting a religion, and thus payments to such schools would be constitutional.

In The New System, the state would set up choice offices to ensure that the schools are being run correctly and that the funding and recording accountability is acceptable. However, the choice offices could become a large state bureaucracy unless the state initially privatized these offices and mandated that their services be used.

In The New System, government funds would go to the choice offices directly, which then would disperse them to the public schools. This charade would permit the state to claim that it was not funding the establishment of religion. Instead, the state could mandate that the choice offices disperse the scholarship funds as vouchers directly to the parents, who then would transfer them to the schools. Thus the state would not be a participant in a legal charade since the funds would be given to and controlled by the parents.

In Chubb and Moe's New System, the government would restrict parents from adding to the scholarship funds. This would limit the new schools to the funds available from the school district. Therefore, if a school wanted to establish a uniquely superior school—with small classes, outstanding and highly paid teachers, facilities very conducive to learning, optional physical education, first-rate books and supplies, and a tuition of $10,000 per year per student—it would be permitted to do so. Assuming that a sufficient number of parents and children chose such a school, it would be considered a proper school. However, such a school would take more of its share of available funds, thereby reducing funds for the other schools. Therefore, The New System would have to mandate that the scholarship funds be equal for each regular student in the school district.

Consequently, these expensive but unique and superior schools would not be permitted under The New System. Chubb and Moe justify disallowing parents to supplement the standard scholarship funds by saying that they would "threaten to produce too many disparities and inequalities within the public schools, and many citizens would regard them as unfair and burdensome."[18] The New System would be a semi-socialist System limited to government funding. Obviously, Chubb and Moe are not completely free of The System, although The New System would be a significantly modified version of The System.

Virgil Blum has documented the legal precedents for an unregulated school voucher System.[19] He notes that the federal and state governments have subsidized children and students rather than schools and institutions, that is, they have subsidized demand rather than supply.

The direct subsidy principle, incorporating the principle of freedom of choice, was adopted, in one form or another, in the Servicemen's Readjustment Act of 1944, The Veteran's Readjustment Act of 1952, The War Orphan's Educative Assistance Act of 1956, and the educational provisions of the Legislation Reorganization Act of 1946 for the education of the pageboys of Congress.

The beneficiaries of these expenditures . . . are the individual students; consequently, the constitutional question of separation of church and state cannot be properly raised. . . . A state may, for example, give text books to children attending church-related schools. "The schools," said the Court, "are not the beneficiaries of these appropriations. They obtain nothing from them, nor are they relieved of a single obligation, because of them. The school children and the state alone are the beneficiaries." A state may also subsidize parents to help them transport their children to the school of their choice, even though the school be church-related. When such grants are made to parents, declared the Court, "The State contributes no money to the schools. It does not support them. Its legislation, as applied does no more harm than provide

a general program to help parents get their children, regardless of their religion, safely and expeditiously to and from accredited schools."
Blum suggests that besides using educational vouchers or certificates, tax credits for school expenses could be given to parents to subsidize children's education.

Charles Handy[20] has creatively proposed how public schools could be changed significantly. He notes that public schools treat students as their products and not as their customers or workers. He asks what organization would require its workers to work in one week for ten different bosses and in three or four different work groups, require them to move and work at a temporary work station or desk, forbid them to ask their colleagues for help, expect them to carry all relevant facts in their heads, require them to work in thirty-five minute periods, and prohibit any social interactions except at official break times.

Handy points out that the quality of output in the public schools is very poor, with a large percentage of substandard products (children) being shipped (graduated) each year. He states "that education needs to be re-invented. . . . The changes needed require some upside-down thinking, initiatives by government, and determination by organizations." He suggests turning the school into an organization with a central basic core activity and contracting out or using part-time people for all other activities. In this way, schools would allegedly become more flexible and accommodating to parents and children, who would be able to choose "not so much between schools as within schools, between the variety that was on offer." The schools would not need to operate on average-grouping basis, and the week's activities would be flexible enough to cover most curricula:

> The upside-down school would make study more like work, based on real problems to be solved or real tasks to be done, in groups of mixed ages and different types of ability, all of them useful.

Handy's creativeness is laudable but misdirected because he fails to understand the crux of the problem—The System. He proposes many reforms, but The System is modified and not fundamentally changed. The iron triangle still remains in control, but maybe some real innovation could take place in some schools and the children could receive a better education. He does not understand that first The System must be destroyed by applying a change function.

A change function that would completely destroy The System would be one that combines Friedman's voucher approach with parts of the Chubb and Moe approach. The proposed educational change function follows:

Title: An Amendment to the State Constitution for the Educational Voucher System

1.   The state shall determine the total amount of available state funds to be used solely for scholarship fund vouchers for each kindergarten through twelfth grade pupil in the state, using the state revenue estimates for the forthcoming year, including federal subsidies if they do not conflict with any part of this Amendment.
2.   An equalized scholarship fund education voucher shall be made available to the parents or legal guardian of each child. The educational voucher shall be used solely to buy educational services from any school that provides the educational services that the parents and the child are willing to purchase. Any private school, present public school, and new school will be eligible for the educational voucher program if it meets the following requirements: The school shall (1) offer at least a core curriculum of English, mathematics, geography, and American history; (2) promulgate student achievement data as measured by standard state tests; and (3) disclose teacher and staff credentials to the parents of prospective students. No other government source of funds shall be supplied to any school. Parents may supplement the said educational voucher with private funds to purchase enhanced educational services from the schools of their choice.
3.   The local, privatized choice offices shall distribute and monitor the use of the educational vouchers generated by the state

and monitor and promulgate the financial, educational, and administrative information that the schools generate.

4. Existing public schools shall be privatized within three years of the initiation of this program. Any existing school revenue bonds and mortgages shall be sold to the entity that becomes the owner of the schools. No government body or agency shall own or invest in any school under this program.

5. In the initial three-year period of this amendment, the state may supplement funding to the existing public schools that become privatized.

6. Other than the provisions of this Amendment, the state shall not mandate any other requirements, and all other previous state mandates regarding education shall be rescinded. (This means that the state's compulsory education laws and age restrictions for working laws would be invalid. Also, all teacher certification requirements, teacher salary and tenure laws, and state pension for teachers and educators laws shall be invalid. Thus all of the educational services mandated by the state shall be privatized. All teachers would become members of private companies or institutions and thus participate in their private pension plans. Religious and other specialized schools would be eligible to be part of this System.)

This proposed amendment to the states' constitutions will completely isolate the management of the schools from interference by the states' politicians, bureaucrats, and mandated special interests. It changes The System radically since the iron triangle no longer supports and protects it. In its place, thousands of different Systems, one for every school, will be created and controlled by the parents, children, teachers, principals, and private owners of the schools.

The System in each school will have to respond to its customers. Failure to satisfy them will destroy The System for that school automatically. All schools eventually will become improved because competition will cause the marginal ones to either improve their performance and maintain their viability by attracting students (and their vouchers) or close their schools due to a lack of student patronage. Thus the threat of real competition for a student's support will eventually result in all children attending an improved school even if the parent or student were indifferent to its quality and output.

A similar state constitutional amendment should be established for higher education. By ratifying such an amendment, the state would privatize all of its colleges, which would have to attract the educational vouchers of students to survive.

Change Function for the Health Care System

We have seen in Chapter 4 that The System of health care in the United States is continuously undergoing cosmetic changes. These changes, however, do not eliminate any of the three major problems of The System: increasing costs; increasing restrictions and limitations on patients, physicians, and other health care providers; and subtle but increasing forms of rationing health care, especially for the poor and elderly.

Politicians and other iron triangle members have been proposing various changes to The System, claiming that such changes would solve its major problems. The loudest proposals are for a national health care System, and most of those voices suggest implementing a Canadian style health care system in the United States.

Any national health care plan would escalate the total costs of health care probably at least 20 percent per year. Restrictions and rationing would increase proportionately such that the problem of health care would be worse for most people. The only ones who could benefit would be the alleged 15 percent who are not covered adequately or at all by health care insurance.

Butler and Haislmaier[21] have proposed a comprehensive set

of market-based reforms that they believe will end the:

frustration and cure the ills of America's health care system. [Their] key elements of a consumer-oriented, market-based, comprehensive American health system would include [the following]:[22]

1.   Every resident of the United States must, by law, be enrolled in an adequate health care plan to cover major health care costs. . . .

2.   For working Americans, obtaining health care protection must be a family responsibility [and not the responsibility of another party, such as an employer or the government]. . . .

3.   The government's proper role is to monitor the health market, subsidize needy individuals to allow them to obtain sufficient services and encourage competition.

Medicare and Medicaid would be provided but modified.

According to Butler and Haislmaier, the following ten steps would have to happen to accomplish these policies:

1.   Eliminate the tax exclusion of employer-provided health insurance and treat these benefits as the rest of a worker's cash income is treated.

2.   Expand tax deductions or tax credits in the personal income tax code for health insurance purchased directly by workers for themselves and their families.

3.   [Make tax credits refundable;] if a family's income tax liability was less than the value of the credit, the family would receive money back from the government.

4.   Abolish Medicare taxes and premiums on the elderly.

5.   Readjust Medicare coinsurance and deductibles to give better protection from the cost of major illnesses; require the elderly to pay more out-of-pocket costs for routine medical services.

6.   Restructure Medicaid by removing the long-term assistance from the program and providing it through a separate program for the elderly poor.

7.   Promote the purchase of long-term care insurance for retirees by providing tax relief for such expenses and allowing retirement funds to purchase long-term insurance.

8.   Introduce Medicare vouchers that would be used to purchase private health insurance coverage or other plans, or used to pay hospitals and physicians directly.

9.   Permit health care savings accounts that would accumulate tax-free investment returns until retirement.

10. Eliminate restrictions and regulations by the government on the states regarding health care programs.

They believe that the above three elements and ten steps, plus other minor steps, would change The System radically. These changes would establish a national health care System for the United States that would be different from the Canadian, English, Swedish, and other national health care programs because the consumer (patient) would be purchasing the services directly.

If Congress made all the changes necessary to implement such a program, the present System would be improved significantly. However, it is very doubtful that the three major problems would be eliminated. Although The System would be changed radically in many areas, the overall change still would be cosmetic because the long-term problems probably would remain.

There is a good possibility, however, that some form of this proposed change function will be passed by Congress. If so, it will take about five years to show that it was merely a cosmetic change and not a fundamental one. Of course, this assumes that the Supreme Court would rule that this proposed new unconstitutional law is constitutional.

A second, potentially more attractive change function is the "Medisave" approach to providing health care services. Goodman and Musgrave[23] propose to reduce the costs of health care in the United States by changing the incentive of people to use third-party health insurance, that is, insurance paid for by an employer or the federal government. They want to replace the third party's direct expenses for health care with a program that allows an individual to deposit funds each year in an IRA-like account called Medisave. The third party would be permitted by the federal government:

to allow employers and employees to choose higher-deductible policies and place the untaxed premium savings in Medisave accounts. For employees, there would be no change in the amount reserved for health care benefits or in the total tax subsidy* for employee benefits. Yet the change would encourage prudence, eliminate waste, and give employees greater control over their health care dollars.

They also propose similar tax incentives for self-insured programs. They note that a Medisave program would lower the cost of health insurance, restore the doctor-patient relationship, create competitive advantages in the marketplace, expand health insurance options during retirement, and provide for the portability of health care funds for those who change jobs.

A third new approach being touted is managed competition. Managed competition is a government controlled and regulated System of health care imposed upon all employers, individuals, doctors, hospitals, insurance companies, and health maintenance organizations. Under this approach, most employers would be required to provide a standard package of benefits to their employees by using government-mandated health insurance purchasing networks. All doctors, hospitals, insurance companies, and health care providers would compete for such contracts. To make it even more onerous to businesses, the government would limit the tax deduction that businesses could take for employee benefits. Unemployed people would be permitted to purchase standard packages through a network financed by the government from general tax revenues. The alleged benefit of managed competition would be the generation of large networks of insurance companies and health care providers that would compete for the employers' and individuals' health care funds. This mandatory program would increase costs for businesses. Marginal businesses would have to increase productivity accordingly or cut costs elsewhere. In many instances, jobs would be lost or not created because of these managed competition costs.

---

* The System uses the term "tax subsidy" instead of tax "deduction" because it wants everyone to think that it is the federal government's money that is being dispensed and not the individual's.

However, it is conceivable that Congress (and The System) eventually will pass a single payer (the federal government) program for everyone in the United States, which will be similar to the Canadian "free" health care program. The claim by the government will be that the administrative cost savings will pay for the additional people insured by the new universal health care programs. The claim will also be that because of an ample supply of physicians, hospitals, and other health care facilities, rationing will not occur. This proposed health care program for everyone without rationing would be unique in the history of economics —where something given "free" to people would not cause excessive use of the product or service that consequently then drives up the costs and eventually causes rationing.

Former Health and Human Services Secretary Louis Sullivan stated in 1991 that the government would "not propose another grand, sweeping, speculative scheme." He said that he wanted instead "a public debate to focus on some immediate, practical options that address our most urgent health care concerns."[24] Some of these options were:

– Making health insurance more affordable to small businesses.
– Easing barriers to "high quality, cost effective managed and coordinated care."
– Researching the effectiveness of various medical procedures to encourage the use of the most cost-effective ones.
– Altering the tax code to "increase consumer awareness of the true cost of health care and distribute current tax subsidies more equally. . . ."
– Increasing the availability of primary care to the neediest people.
– Reducing the administrative costs of health care.

Sullivan was against establishing a Canadian type of health care System or a mandatory employer health care benefit program. Such approaches, he said, would be inflationary, "smother competition," and lead to "rationing and waiting lists." [He said that experimentation in reforming the health care System] "should be left to the states. Local solutions for local problems should be our working philosophy, as should learning from local mistakes in order to avoid harm to the nation as a whole."

If such a Canadian style health care program were passed, it would take at least five to ten years for financial chaos and health care rationing to become disasters. Therefore, a change function eventually would be required to eliminate the present or revised System and also to minimize or optimize the three major problems that The System currently has.

The root cause of the problems is the federal and state governments mandatory laws that affect the health care of individuals and thus preempt individual and private initiatives in this area. The Constitution does not give the federal government the right to provide or regulate health care to individuals or to restrict or regulate private contracts between individuals and health care providers. These rights are reserved for the people and states according to the Ninth and Tenth Amendments. Thus the government does not have the right to establish or promote social programs by using taxation and regulations.

Therefore, my proposed change function would require the government to get out of the health care business by eliminating the Department of Health and Human Services' budget and regulations as being unconstitutional, reducing the U.S. budget accordingly, and proportionally reducing the proposed flat tax rate. It should be noted that the basic Social Security program is partially funded by a federal payroll tax on peoples' incomes. This results in the establishment of a pseudo trust program that is not self-sustaining. The program also has constitutional problems.

The government also should eliminate the Food and Drug Administration's mandatory imposition of drug certification requirements on the pharmaceutical companies. These regulations result in some drugs being certified at a cost of over $200 million and others being banned in the United States but used in other countries. The net result of the mandatory regulations is the establishment of government-imposed semi-monopolies that restrict competition and thus increase costs to the consumer. The FDA's services, if any, should be strictly advisory and available free to the public, medical profession, health care industry, and state legislatures.

However, if all of the federal health care laws and regulations were repealed or declared unconstitutional, it would take a long time to phase out all of the programs. In fairness to people already in these programs, the government would have to eliminate the programs gradually. Those people presently on Social Security would be taxed on those benefits in excess of their original contributions plus 7 percent per year interest. The future cost of living adjustments (COLA) would be indexed to the complete 100 percent of the consumer price index. Income tax caps adjusted for inflation would be placed on all benefits based on annual adjusted gross incomes over $60,000 for a family or $30,000 for an individual. All present Social Security reductions of benefits due to additional income earned or received by retirees would be abolished so that retirees could work and contribute to generating wealth in the country. All Medicare entitlements would be based on an initial deduction according to a percentage of the annual benefits possible, plus copayments of 10 percent or higher based on annual adjusted gross income for annual benefits received.

However, those individuals not being supported by federal welfare programs would have to modify their short-term and retirement plans accordingly. Those people not receiving Social Security benefits would be required to withdraw their previous Social Security payments plus 7 percent interest per year and allowed to place them in a self-directed medical IRA and a regular IRA. The medical IRA would be tax deductible forever, and the regular IRA would be tax deductible and would not be subject to income taxes if used for retirement purposes. No new Social Security or government health care programs would be initiated. Thus the marketplace for private health care insurance would expand explosively and competitive forces would reduce the cost per person of health care in the United States. The elimination of government subsidies to doctors and health care facilities also would force them to become more efficient and competitive.

If the government was forced out of the health business and those related taxes remained with the taxpayers in the form of a lower income tax rate, then individuals and families would have the funds and incentive to purchase health care services that best meet their personal circumstances and not some bureaucrat's idea of mandatory requirements. For example, in 1993 a family of four could buy an insurance policy for about $1,500 a year that would provide for all physician and medical fees (assuming a semi-private hospital room if required) with a deductible of $3,000. The tax deductibility of insurance costs for businesses and nonprofit organizations would be allowed and would be counted as income to a member of such institutions. However, health care expenses would be 100 percent income tax deductible for individuals.

However, because the general public does not understand the root causes of our national health care problems, and because the members of the iron triangle and The System want to keep it that way, there is no chance that this proposed change function could be implemented or even seriously considered in the next five years.

The System reasserted itself in 1996 (a presidential election year) by passing another health care law that would increase the government's control over the country's health care. The government mandated that private insurance companies which offer group insurance plans must cover employees with preexisting medical conditions within 12 months of when they start a job. The government also mandated that health insurance companies make available health insurance for people moving from group to individual plans. In addition, the government set up a four-year demonstration project for tax-deductible medical savings accounts (M.S.A.'s) for small businesses, the self-employed, and the uninsured. The number of such policies will be limited to about

750,000 in any one year, compared to the total number of policies (90 million) presently in effect. The first two mandates above will increase the total cost of insurance for all policies. The demonstration project is so small that it will probably not result in a strong affirmation of M.S.A.'s.

Instead, costs will continue to escalate, and the federal budget deficits and taxes will respond accordingly. At the same time, the quality of medical care will start to deteriorate and rationing of health care will become more prevalent. By the year 2002, it will be clear that fundamental changes to The System of health care will have to be made because of the adverse financial effect on all other activities in the United States.

In the next century, we will have to make fundamental, structural changes in how the federal government works. We will have to return to the limited government that existed for the first 150 years according to the Constitution. Then each individual's freedoms and opportunities will be expanded, and the quality of life for everyone improved significantly. This will happen because of the resultant reduction in the excessive taxation and regulations that are now being selectively imposed on the vast majority of people in the United States. However, The System most likely would say, "Don't count on it."

Change Function for the Illicit Drug System

The United States has had an illicit drug problem for over seventy-five years, during which many attempts have been made to eliminate the problem. However, The System has not changed significantly and is much stronger today than it was fifty years ago.

It is clear that a second-order change (a change function) is required to destroy The System, since all of the first-order changes have served to perpetuate The System. Three kinds of change functions are possible in this case. The first change function destroys the supply side of The System, and the second one destroys the demand side. The third one eliminates the illicit drug problem by redefining it in new terms.

Destroy the Supply Side of The System

The supply side of the drug trade consists of the farmers or manufacturers, processing centers, distribution network, salesmen (pushers), and money launderers. The federal and state governments have concentrated most of their efforts on trying to eliminate each of these process steps. It is obvious that their attempts to eliminate or reduce any of these steps significantly have been unsuccessful.

The government has enlisted the help of those foreign nations that are the major sources of illicit drugs flowing into the United States. Although most countries are cooperative, they are very ineffective in stamping out such trade, mainly because the local populations depend on that trade for their livelihood or because corrupt politicians and businessmen profit from supporting these activities. The foreign governments also have difficulty in destroying the processing centers, because they are relatively small, easy to hide, and easy to rebuild.

The distribution network is very large, potentially very profitable, and dangerous. The United States has a very large and active force trying to interdict this illegal trade, but the scope of the trade is sufficient to overwhelm the enforcement groups. The pushers interact with the terminals of the distribution networks. Most pushers act like self-employed salesmen, who in effect sell drugs "door-to-door" in their territory.

The sale of illicit drugs results in the transfer of cash from the buyer back up the distribution network to the persons who finance, plan, and manage the basic operations. The major problem such criminals have is the large amount of cash they have that is difficult to use, hide, or distribute. All economic transactions that entail $10,000 or more in cash must be reported to the U. S. Department of Revenue. Thus drug traffickers must create schemes to launder their illegally obtained cash, such as using foreign banks.

The government and most other foreign governments have not been successful in eliminating or significantly reducing any steps of the drug traffic process. The application of these enforcement tools has resulted in cosmetic changes. Second-order changes have been used in only a few, isolated instances.

In Malaysia, for example, anyone caught with drugs is either jailed or hanged. A mandatory death sentence is imposed for any drug trafficker. A drug trafficker is someone who possesses at least one-half ounce of heroin or morphine, seven ounces of marijuana or hashish, or thirty-three ounces of raw or prepared opium. Someone caught with less amounts can receive a prison term ranging from several months to life.[25]

The imposition of mandatory death or prison sentences for those caught with illicit drugs is a second-order change and a solution to the drug problem in the United States. However, most politicians are probably not willing to propose or vote for such punishment, especially since many highly vocal special interest groups, including the press, could be opposed to such actions.

Destroy the Demand Side of The System

The demand side of the drug trade consists of consumers who use illicit drugs for personal pleasure. At present, multiple cosmetic solutions are being tried at all levels of society. Elementary and high school students are urged to say "no" to drugs. The government's "war on drugs" is supported by most people in the entertainment, sports, or media industries, in addition to business and health care organizations. Laws that prohibit the use of illicit drugs are enforced sporadically.

However, all of these attempts are cosmetic, since basically nothing has changed in decades of demand side solutions. Therefore, a second-order change is required to prevent someone from demanding (buying) illicit drugs. Since present laws and admonitions are cosmetic, more of the same will only perpetuate The System.

A proposed change function that would tend to deter one from demanding illicit drugs would be a new law imposing mandatory death or prison sentences for those caught buying or using illicit drugs. Such a law also would make it a felony to give birth to a baby with a drug addiction. This proposed change function, however, would be fought by the same groups that would oppose a similar solution to the supply side of the problem.

Redefine the Problem

The third change function changes the illicit drug problem into a licit drug problem. Hard drugs would be decriminalized, which would make drugs legal to possess and use. The theory is that once hard drugs were made legal, legitimate companies would supply drugs that could be purchased over the counter at any drug store. The availability of low cost drugs would eliminate the present black market in drugs. Therefore, crime related to the trafficking of drugs would be almost eliminated, and the police, courts, and prisons could concentrate on other problems.[26-27]

The basic premise of the legalization approach to changing The System is that it is too costly to continue to fight the nation's drug war considering the relatively poor results to date. William Bennett,[28] former director of the Office of National Drug Policy, responded to Milton Friedman's op-ed article on legalizing drugs by noting that:

the potential costs of legalizing drugs would be so large as to make it a public policy disaster. [He stated that in the past] wherever drugs have been cheaper and more easily obtained, drug use–and addiction–has skyrocketed. In opium and cocaine producing countries, addiction is rampant among the peasants involved in drug production.

Bennett projected the additional costs of legalization: lost productivity, rising health insurance costs, increased hospital drug overdose emergencies, increased drug-caused accidents, premature deaths, continual criminal activities by drug addicts, easier access to drugs for children and pregnant mothers, and the reduction of morality in the nation.

This change function would shift the problem from law enforcement to health care and moral degeneracy. The total dollar costs probably would eventually be higher than the dollar costs associated with today's attempts at solutions.

Today's cosmetic approaches will continue until the public demands that Congress apply the above proposed supply side and demand side change functions. The drug problem is actually a moral and political problem. Thus The System will remain the same until a change function is demanded by the people and the federal and state governments respond accordingly.

Change Function for the Post Office System

Chapter 4 describes The System that has controlled the U.S. Postal Service for over 200 years. During this time, The System changed superficially to alleviate the demands made by Congress and the public. However, The System basically never changed. It always supported the iron triangle members and maintained its monopolistic status. Like all government-owned monopolies, it never had to be efficient and self-supporting or satisfy completely the customers' requirements.

The Constitution does not require that mail service be a government monopoly or even a monopoly. Congress, however, has enacted laws that establish the government as the monopolizer of first-class mail delivery.

The change function that would solve the problem of poor, inefficient, costly, and untimely mail service is for Congress to repeal the private express statutes. The author's proposed change function for changing The System that controls the U.S. Postal Service (USPS) is that Congress shall enact a law that:

1.   Repeals all statutes that give the USPS exclusive rights to any of its operations or responsibilities.
2.   Permits private companies to supply any postal services that they desire.
3.   Privatize the USPS by selling it to private parties or splitting it into geographical areas and then privatizing the mail services in each area. The government will not prevent organizations from hiring personnel at competitive wages.
4.   Eliminate subsidies to organizations delivering the mail.

By privatizing the USPS, the government could have private taxpaying organizations delivering the mail in different areas of the country. If five-year awards were made, competition would remain intense, and the overall service would improve yearly.

Change Function for The Supreme Court

Since the Supreme Court and its powers were established by the Constitution, an amendment to it would be required to change The System that presently controls the Supreme Court. The change function that would solve the problem of justices rewriting the Constitution requires introducing a means of placing and keeping on the Court justices who believe in the rule of law. This can be done by ratifying another new amendment:

The Third Proposed New Amendment: [Amendment No. 30]

**Title: Requirements, Terms, and Conditions
for Supreme Court Justices.**

Section 1. This Amendment supplements and includes paragraphs (4), (5), and (6) of the (proposed) 28th Amendment.
Section 2. The President shall nominate to the Supreme Court only U.S. citizens who affirm under oath that the Constitution is

the supreme law of the land; that it supersedes any and all laws enacted by Congress or any conditions imposed by Treaty; that the Constitution and all laws shall be construed according to the common sense of the terms and the intention of the enacting parties; and that he or she will apply the law of the land, ignoring all other matters.

Section 3. Supreme Court Justices who fail to abide by such an oath shall be impeached in accordance with Article I of the Constitution. To determine whether Supreme Court Justices abide by their oath, an analysis shall be made by the House of Representatives which shall determine if each Justice has held office during Good Behavior as identified under common law. Good Behavior also shall include the strict fidelity to an understanding of the limitations place on the Federal Government as found in the Ninth and Tenth Amendments. Any contrary opinion shall be a cause of misbehavior by such a Justice and subject to the Representatives for their consideration of impeachment.

Section 4. At least two justices shall not be lawyers by profession. New nominees by the President shall meet this requirement until two justices have been appointed to the Court in accordance with this Amendment and with Article II, Section 2, of the Constitution.

This proposed amendment would cause all new Supreme Court justices to abide by the Constitution in accordance with its original intent. This would result in the Supreme Court not legislating laws and emphasize the importance of Congress in passing new and rescinding poor laws.

It is important that nonlawyers be on the Supreme Court for the Court to receive a broader, varied analysis of its cases. A nonlawyer would evaluate a case from a fundamental constitutional viewpoint. A nonlawyer also could have a better understanding of scientific, technical, financial, medical, or social aspects of legal controversies. In addition, nonlawyers are needed on the Court to prevent lawyers from being the sole judges of other lawyers' actions or opinions. This action would eliminate the government's imposed monopoly for lawyers on the Court.

In 1957, David Lawrence,[29] editor of *U.S. News and World Report*, suggested what could be called a change function for the Supreme Court; unfortunately it was never attempted. He points out that:

> the words "life tenure" do not appear anywhere in the Constitution and that the Constitution states that the Judges, both of the Supreme and inferior Courts, shall hold their Offices during good behavior. Since Supreme Court Justices may hold office only "during good behavior" and since obviously The Court itself cannot be the judge of its own "behavior," it follows logically that The President and The Senate, acting together, have the Constitutional power to determine first how "good behavior" shall be defined. [He suggests that] Congress could require by statute that every justice come before the Senate periodically—perhaps every six years ~ for reconfirmation. [The law would] provide that a two-thirds vote be required for an adverse judgment—withdrawal of consent by the Senate.

Lawrence notes that it is up to Congress to define the term "good behavior" and it would be part of "the system of 'checks and balances' which the American people have written into their Constitution." He summarizes the situation, which still exists today as follows:

> It is time for the people of the United States, through their elected representatives, to stop judicial usurpation and to prevent the growth of judicial despotism. It is time to bring well-meaning but misguided Justices to a realization that they cannot and must not expect to function in contempt of The Constitution itself and still remain in office.

This change function could work if Congress voted for it since it would not require a constitutional amendment. However, the chance of getting Congress to do its job is less than the chance of getting two-thirds of the states to call for a constitutional convention and then getting three-fourths of the states to ratify an amendment to the Constitution.

FOREIGN INSTITUTIONS

Change Function for the Republics
of the Former Soviet Union

It is clear from the discussion in Chapter 4 that The System in the Soviet Union must be changed drastically. In a March 1989 interview with David Evanier,[30] who was a Russian human rights activist in the 1960s, Boris Shragin discusses Gorbachev's approach to obtaining improvements in the Soviet Union.

> There is no question that Gorbachev does want to improve things, but at the same time he wants to increase his own personal power and to keep in tact the system . . . as it is and as it was created. There are moments in history when a politician appears who wants to save the system by making some liberal gestures. But as a matter of fact, his historical role is to push the system into deeper and deeper crisis. Because his attempts to renovate things are halfway measures.

Since the dissolution of the USSR, the Soviet Union has broken up into 15 independent republics and a weakened central government. However, some of the republics have established a confederation that is able to deal with certain specific areas on a joint basis. The powers of the new confederation, which is called the Commonwealth of Independent States (C.I.S.), are mainly limited to the central ministries of defense, foreign affairs, railroads, and atomic energy. At this writing, most of the republics are tending toward retaining their political independence from each other; some, however, are choosing to become more dependent on Russia.

To change The System in the C.I.S. and the republics, multiple change functions that encompass judicial, financial, and economic issues must be created and applied to each republic simultaneously, or within a close time frame. This is because they form a unified scheme whereby the governments of the C.I.S. and its republics are drastically transformed and the lives of most people are improved. My proposed change functions, which would solve the problem of establishing a lasting, republican form of government, would limit the government and optimize individual choice and opportunity. The change function consists of 12 parts:

1.   A written constitutional rule of law must be established and followed. The burden of proof must be placed on the accuser and not the defendant. The courts and the police must rigorously apply the law in an unbiased fashion. The KGB replacement, the military, the Communist party, and their officials and members shall not have any control over initiating, maintaining, or changing the laws, the judicial System, the courts, and the police. Members of the *nomenklatura* shall have no special rights or privileges but only those rights and privileges guaranteed to all citizens of the country.

2.   The establishment of private property as an inherent, inviolable natural right of individuals must be written into the constitution. The government shall not be permitted to restrict the ownership or use of personal property, including but not limited to money and credit, gold, land, housing, natural resources, patents, and literary rights. The government may not take private property without prior approval by the courts, and remuneration approved by and given to the owners of the property.

3.   The sanctity of private contracts must be maintained and enforced by the law and the courts. The government shall not be allowed to regulate, control, tax, or modify such private agreements.

4.   The generation of profits through legal business activities shall be considered ethical and desirable since the generation of profits confirms that customers are being satisfied and there is an apparent need for allocating resources to those areas experiencing profits.

5.   The money supply must be based on a fixed gold standard, with unhampered convertibility to other monies permitted. Gold and gold-based money issued by the central bank or treasury or privately owned banks shall be legal-tender.

6. Privately owned banks shall be permitted to issue credit, checking accounts, mortgages, and trade securities and perform other financial transactions. The government shall not restrict the establishment and operation of private banking Systems and privately owned stock markets.

7. The government shall not restrict the establishment of a free market where goods and services are traded, purchased and sold. Prices shall be free to change depending on the law of supply and demand. The government shall not restrict an individual's right to import or export goods and services, except military equipment, illegal drugs, unhealthy foodstuffs, stolen property, and other illegal items.

8. The government shall not limit the freedom of citizens to communicate, change jobs, travel and relocate, have free speech and a free press, and change their political leaders by periodic secret ballot elections. It shall be unconstitutional for the government to control prices, wages, interest rates, and rents and to impose fees or limitations on such transactions.

9. The government shall not have an unbalanced annual budget. Government debt shall be amortized and paid off annually during the next forty years.

10. The government shall tax individuals only on their compensation. There shall be a single tax rate with only a single deduction for each individual in the family and no other deductions or credits. The government shall tax businesses only on the value added by the businesses. The tax rate shall be identical to the individual tax rate. The maximum annual tax rate for individuals or businesses shall be 10 percent.

11. The central government shall provide only the basic services required for law and order, including the courts, the issue of legal tender, the maintenance of a defense establishment, the establishment and maintenance of interconfederation agreements and environmental regulations, and the right to make treaties in conjunction with the confederation.

12. The government shall not own any means of producing or generating services. All production and services, except those required for Section 11 above, shall be privately owned. All means of production, as well as all land and housing owned or controlled by the government shall be privatized. The government shall not subsidize private companies or consumers.

These twelve parts of the change function have a common theme: the limitation of the government and the optimization of opportunities and choices for individuals. The maxim to be followed is Thomas Jefferson's:

> A wise and frugal Government, which shall restrain men from injuring one another, shall leave them otherwise free to regulate their own pursuits of industry and improvement, and shall not take from the mouth of labor the bread that it has earned. This is the sum of good government. . . .[31]

This change function is necessary to destroy the Communist party's and the nomenklatura's privileges that have led to subjugating the rest of the people in the Soviet Union and to control and limit the government's potential for using its power for the benefits of the iron triangle. It may be considered an economic and financial bill of rights that will lead to a tremendous growth in the personal liberty, freedoms, and well-being of all people in the C.I.S., except those who have been plundering the welfare of the people.

Limiting the government's annual revenue to 10 percent of the country's total income is very liberal since the government will have very few expenses other than the justice and financial departments and the military. Because most government services will be privatized, the government's costs will be minimized or at least reduced in size and scope. In 1990 the military spending was about 35-45 percent of the government's yearly budget. This figure could be reduced to below 10 percent assuming that it would provide a sufficient defense force to deal with potential aggressors.

Changing The System to one that automatically promotes individual rights and freedoms will cause a complete revision in the enormous waste and inefficiencies being generated presently each day by The System. The funding of the Communist party apparatus, including the KGB replacement, will be eliminated. Billions of rubles will be saved by eliminating government-sponsored monopolies or replacing them with private corporations. With private ownership a resurgence of work in productive, useful areas will generate new wealth that will be shared by almost everyone throughout the country.

Russian President Boris Yeltsin has already introduced aspects of the twelve change function steps. As an independent republic, Russia has taken control of its valuable natural resources and repudiated the role of the C.I.S.'s central banking authorities. Yeltsin has initiated repatriating profits for foreign businesses, controlling C.I.S. gold reserves, printing and issuing Russian money, setting its own foreign exchange rates, establishing a new Russian central bank to establish hard currency reserves, removing bureaucratic obstacles to foreign trade, and freeing prices on all but a few staples.

However, piecemeal economic reforms without reforming the rule of law, contracts, private property, currency, and other areas will only muddle the economic situation and prevent real changes from occurring. As Yeltsin compromises with The System, it grows stronger and slows the possibility for fundamental, long-term change. Unless Yeltsin abandons his incremental approach to change and implements a change function that grants full freedom to individuals, the Russian people will be resigned to one or two decades of a second or third world existence.

The Change Function for Japan

The System that controls Japan is run jointly by the components of the iron triangle: politicians from the Liberal Democratic Party

(LDP) or a group of coalition parties, the bureaucracies of the government ministries, and the many special interest groups, chief of which are large businesses and their conglomerates, the press, the educational industry, and The System of justice (law, police, and gangsters). The present iron triangle members do not want to change The System since they need it to maintain or better their welfare.

Karel van Wolferen[32] asks : "Shall The System last forever?" and "Can The System change?" He answers yes to the latter question, stating that "there is no good theoretical reason why the Japanese should forever be held under political tutelage."

He suggests abolishing Tokyo University and instituting law courses in a large number of universities because many lawyers have to be trained:

> to give the individual Japanese the means to protect themselves against the arbitrariness of the administrators. . . . Control over the judiciary and over access to the bar would have to be taken away from the secretariat of the Supreme Court. . . . The schools and the media would have to work to foster individual political awareness and a sense of individual responsibility while de-emphasizing the importance of membership in companies and other organizations.
>
> Any essential change for the better would also require the emergence of political parties not dependent on the pork-barrel and intent on truly representing the interest of the middle class factory workers. . . . The wonderful alternative of turning The System into a genuine modern constitutional state, and Japanese subjects into citizens, would require realignments of power akin to those of a genuine revolution.

A change function is required in order to change The System in a fundamental manner. Van Wolferen suggests that there are two undesirable ways such a change could occur. One is that nationalist extremists bent on saving the nation could obtain sufficient power to eliminate the balancing forces that maintain The System. The other possibility is a confrontation with a hostile world apparently brought on by Japan's aggressive economic trade policies.

The weakest and smallest element of the iron triangle is the LDP. Completely corrupted, it enjoys financial and political support from its two partners within The System because it uses the legislative process to support their financial and political growth. Therefore, the LDP is the best vehicle through which to initiate fundamental change in The System.

A new political party that replaces the LDP is needed to destroy this key link in The System's chain of operations. However, The System would use all of its resources to attack a threat to its existence, including intimidation, blackmail, loss of jobs, financial and tax pressures, and even violence against the leaders and supporters of such a new party. Therefore, to form a viable opposition party to the LDP, one would need a large base of potential activists with a common and broad reform agenda.

The large base in Poland is Solidarity, the shipbuilding union and its allies, the anticommunists and Roman Catholic Church. In the ex-U.S.S.R., the large base is the vast majority of people who are economically and spiritually suppressed by The System, which was controlled by the Communist party.

In Japan, reformers from the LDP have succeeded in forming a Japan New Party and a coalition government with six other smaller parties. However, any coalition government will be unstable because of its inherent conflicting interests and should be considered a temporary solution that operates until a new majority party is created.

To change The System, a change function is proposed that entails the creation of a new political party that would have to have at least the following planks:

1. Nondiscriminative enforcement of the Constitution and the rule of law.
2. Strict accountability and criminal penalties for government bureaucrats who break the law.
3. A new federal tax code based upon a single tax rate for individuals and businesses.

4.   Broadening of the educational System and elimination of the caste System of promotion into the top universities and the government.

5.   The elimination of restrictions on competition, including the breakup of government-supported monopolies.

6.   A fixed single term for all members of the legislature and the prime minister.

7.   A maximum twelve-year term for judges who would serve during good behavior and receive salaries set initially by the legislature and that may be increased but never decreased during their term of office.

The formation, growth, and eventual success of the new party could take ten or more years, depending on the internal and external events affecting the Japanese people. However, two impulses could energize the formation of the new party. One impulse could be the United States and other countries erecting a severe trade barrier to Japanese products and services. Although this action on the part of the United States could be self-defeating, especially in the areas of semiconductors and robotics, it would be devastating for Japan. In 1993, Japan had a yearly trade surplus of manufactured goods with the United States of about $59 billion. Continued loss of the U.S. market would impact the entire Japanese economy and The System. The newly generated economic problem could strengthen the new opposition party by giving it the opportunity to point out the root causes of the problem and The System that is responsible for the problem. However, it is unlikely that the United States would erect such a barrier since it would also hurt the U.S. exports to Japan. More likely, the United States would continue to try to have Japan lower its trade barriers and remove the artificial restrictions erected by The System on a case-by-case basis.

The second impulse could be the United Nations generating a boycott of Japanese products because of Japan's trade barriers to worldwide imports. Their trade surplus of manufactured goods worldwide was approximately $130 billion in 1993. Although the possibility of this type of action is remote, if it were proposed by the United Nations, The System might accommodate the formation of a new party, with the expectation that it would assimilate the new party in the near future.

It is more likely that The System will continue its dominance for many years and that possibly something in the future will cause a political revolution to change The System.

Change Function for Peru

The legal institutions of Peru no longer respond to the very complex and changing social conditions in the country. Unrest, unlawful and corrupt government, suppressed opportunities for the majority of the people, large black market activities, overcrowding, increased diseases, inflation, and other problems have created an atmosphere where real change must occur.

The election of President Alberto Fujimori in April 1990 may have been the first step in a change function that will make fundamental changes in The System that controls Peru. Fujimori has initiated substantial changes that could affect Peru's long-term economy if they are implemented and not countermanded by the bureaucracy. These changes include reducing the 7,650 percent inflation in 1990; reducing the barriers to trade and capital flows, such as eliminating a 10 percent tax on imports and reducing the value-added tax; reforming the state's and its institutions' regulations; eliminating the state monopoly in reinsurance and the privileges of the state insurance company; liberalizing foreign investment laws and laws regarding the labor market; reducing the state payroll by 30,000 bureaucrats; privatizing 23 state-owned companies, such as the telephone company; eliminating the central bank financing of the treasury; and agreeing with the World Bank that Peru would provide insurance for foreign investments. However, these changes must be considered cosmetic at this time because the basic root cause of the general malaise that affects Peru still is the legal System that supports an elite minority at the expense of the majority.

By June 1991, the annual inflation rate was about 70 percent, a 100-times improvement over the previous year. However, the basic cause of inflation—the printing of money by the government to finance its oligarchic control of The System—still remains in place.

Hernando de Soto stated the obvious in *The Other Path*:

It is now clear that the central problem is not whether formal institutions should or should not incorporate the informals for humanitarian reasons, but whether they will manage to do so in time to avoid the violent destruction of representative democracy. . . . Mercantilism has almost always ended in violence and there is no reason to think it will be any different in Peru, especially if the authorities persist in remaining inflexible.[33]

The following are elements of a change function that de Soto believes must be applied to Peru:[34]

1.   Integrate the formal and informal organizations into a single economic and legal System that outlaws discrimination. This means a new System that ensures firm property rights, reliable transactions, secure activities, facilitative legal instruments, and the elimination of obstructive legal norms.

2.   Replace in as many areas as possible the state with informal and private organizations.

3.   Simplify the "functioning of legal institutions so that the duplicative and unnecessary parts of laws can be reduced or eliminated." This means eliminating barriers that raise the costs of entering and remaining in the formal activity. Institute "debureaucratization" by replacing the rules that specify how to fill certain requirements with rules that state the ends to be achieved. Enact sunset provisions that automatically void laws unless reenacted by the government.

4.   Decentralize by "transferring legislative and administrative responsibilities from the central government to local and regional governments and bodies." This means giving local governments the authority to legislate on all matters that can be handled at the regional level.

5.   [Deregulate by] increasing the responsibilities and opportunities of private individuals and reducing those of the state. . . . Replace the state's regulatory control of the economy by control expressed in judicial decisions. [Grant] access to the market to all citizens and [extend] facilitating legal instruments to all, [Increase] the portion of available resources so that the state can do what private individuals cannot do well. [Delegate] to informal organizations the responsibilities they can best meet.

6.   "Reform and expand the judiciary, arbitration, the system of justices of the peace, and in general, all institutions which permit order without the immobility, corruption, and inefficiency that accompany direct state intervention in economic life."

7.   Justify future laws by establishing their necessity and determining their cost/benefit ratios. Such laws, along with their need and justification, first must be disclosed to the public by being published. The same conditions must apply to the laws drafted by the executive branch agencies.

In addition to the reforms suggested by de Soto, one other major reform element should be initiated. The makeup of Congress should be changed to one of representation by districts and not of at-large representatives. In this way, local interests would be supported by each elected representative and the power exercised by the national party would be reduced.

The change function described above assumes that Peru's present democratic process would allow significant change to create a New System. However, experience indicates that The System will do everything it can to modify or prevent its demise. Incremental changes with governments and large institutions usually become cosmetic, and The System remains basically the same. Often it is only when conditions reach a boiling point that sharp, rapid fundamental changes can be imposed on The System.

Peru's president, elected in 1990 for a five-year term, tried initially to institute such fundamental changes by two means: first, through his party in the legislature and second, by preempting executive control of the executive agencies and their laws and regulations. However, the increased violence caused by Maoist Shining Path guerrillas, narcoterrorists, and other criminal bands, along with the inaction of Congress and the corruption of the legal System, led President Fujimori to utilize a third approach. In April 1992, he closed the Congress, suspended the constitution, and directed the military to maintain law and order while he restructured the government. He began a successful counter-terrorism program with the help of the army, and obtained voter approval of a new constitution. In 1995 he was reelected to a second five-year term with 64% of the legal votes cast. At that time a congress also sympathetic to his policies was elected. Through a complete modernization and structural reform program, the government has liberalized markets, privatized most state owned companies, simplified and reduced all import tariffs, eliminated export subsidies, liberalized private sector wages and prices, allowed free access to other currencies, and allowed competition from abroad.

It appears that President Fujimori has initiated a change function along the lines suggested above. It remains to be seen if The System will be replaced with a New System.

The Change Function for Canada

William Gairdner[35] proposes that The System that presently controls Canada be destroyed and replaced by one that democratizes Canada. Without eliminating any of their valuable political institutions, Canadians must depoliticize Canada, modify

Canadian political institutions, and impose financial restraints on government.

He states that the Canadian people should demand that popular democracy become entrenched in the Canadian "parliamentary system once and for all so that politicians will be forced truly to do *our* will, instead of we doing theirs." He proposes to copy, almost exactly, The System of government in Switzerland!

The change function that he proposes completely devolves the power of the parliaments of Canada and institutes popular democracy in which the people take active control of their provinces and the country. Each province, like the Swiss cantons, would become:

> self-governing and look after *everything* for their residents, except for certain matters dealt with by seven federal departments. [Each province would have] its own laws, courts, constitution, parliament, medical systems, schools, welfare and other government services, distinctness, culture, and, of course, language(s). [Thus] all important political, economic, social, and cultural matters [would] be dealt with *at the political level closest to the people.*

In Switzerland, with its twenty-three self-governing cantons, only seven basic functions that serve the common good are run on the federal level. By law, no more federal ministries can be created without the specific permission of the people. Thus the Canadian government would have to shrink from a cabinet composed of thirty-nine members to one composed of seven national ministries: Justice and Police, Transport and Energy, National Defense, Interior, Finance, Economic Affairs, and Foreign Affairs.

Limiting the federal government to seven ministries could eliminate about 100,000 civil servants from the federal payrolls. Since the provinces could expand their governments, the costs saved by reducing the federal government would be partially offset by additional costs of the provinces. However, the provinces would control such costs better, and the costly duplication of federal and provincial ministries could be eliminated.

The central government would become "*utterly dependent on the will of the people by removing its power to tax them directly.*" The central government would receive money from each province based on the constitutional agreements that were initially approved when The New System was established. This might be based on a fixed, equal percentage of each province's domestic product.

The people would control the provincial governments through entrenched people power. [The people of a province could] *vote on everything*. By law, all federal and [provincial legislation would] be submitted to a public referendum for direct approval by the people (called an "obligatory referendum").

Thus the present situation in Canada, where the politicians in Parliament ignore the fact that 80 percent of the people want less government spending, could not exist under The New System. The public could vote on about five issues at a time an average of four times per year. By gathering 50,000 signatures, the people could change legislation (called an "optional referendum") or even force the government to put issues to a referendum (called a "popular initiative"), requiring 100,000 signatures.

Under The New System, government by party would be greatly diminished or entirely averted. There could not be a national election to choose the political party that would rule the government, and the office of prime minister would be eliminated. Instead, each of the seven federal ministers mentioned above serves on the seven seat cabinet, and each takes a turn—for one year only—as chairman. Thus, there is nothing to race for. The cabinet is expected, as a team, to manage the government, with no false sense of glory attached to that task. Popularity, in short, is not an issue. But competence is. . . .

A key feature of The New System is that each province would end "up *competing* with all the others to provide the highest-quality government services at the lowest cost. . . . In effect, this system all but privatizes the supply of government services."

Taxes would not be hidden under The New System, as many are under the present System. "About 25 percent of the average Canadian's taxes are hidden in the prices of things" Canadians buy. Income taxes would not be deducted from wages but would be paid once a year. Income tax rates would be indexed for inflation or, preferably, a flat tax rate should be used for individuals and businesses. A "truth in billing" requirement would cause the government to identify the exact amount of one's taxes to be used to pay the government debt.

Gairdner proposes that the present Canadian constitution be kept until a constitutional convention changes the constitution. The convention would be composed of representatives of ordinary Canadians and not politicians. The proposed new constitution would be subject to approval by the people in a direct referendum.

Gairdner believes that the new constitution should have the following features:

- Principles to ensure that the liberty of the people is guaranteed as their inherent right.
- The Common Law as the basis for the Canadian legal System.
- The Swiss type confederation of provinces as the type of government.
- Elimination of all the "distinct society" clauses in Canada "on the grounds that each province could be naturally distinct and allowed to grow, each in its own way, with complete freedom of movement, languages, culture, etc., between provinces." Any socialist-style equalization requirements would be unconstitutional.
- A sanction that each government, like every citizen, is subject to the rule of law, including that reverse discrimination measures, e.g., affirmative action, would be unconstitutional.
- A Bill of Rights similar to the present Charter without the "notwithstanding clause" (section 33) of the Charter.
- The principle that the people have the right to alter their own Constitution by referendum, thus protecting them from unwise judges and ensuring that their will is always sovereign.
- Withdrawal of the federal government's right to tax directly. Its funds should be voted for and supplied by the provinces.

- All levels of government set aside regular amounts to settle their debts and submit to balanced budget legislation if required by the people or face a referendum for expulsion.
- Crown corporations sold within a certain time.
- All political bodies, including the Senate, elected directly by the citizens.

The above items comprise the change function proposed by Gairdner. Other items that might be incorporated into the proposed change function are:

- Fixed term limits for all elected officials and judges.
- A limit on the percentage of taxes that the governments can levy on each individual's income.
- A single comprehensive budget account for each government, with no off-budget funds permitted.
- Gold coin and bullion shall be legal tender that also may be used to satisfy contracts between parties.

It appears that the only legal way to initiate this proposed change function is to have the citizens elect people to the provincial and the central governments who pledge to pass a law initiating the constitutional amendment process.

SUMMARY

Change functions must be applied over relatively short periods to be effective, especially in governments or large organizations because they are usually loosely managed and The System is quite strong and resilient. The System will resist change wherever possible using different tactics to fit the local situations. If the change function is not broad or comprehensive enough, The System will react to the change function's inadequacies and fight it on its own grounds. Ideally, change functions should destroy The System once the change function is applied. However, it takes time to apply a change function in large institutions, and the longer it takes the harder it is to effect the change.

This chapter has proposed over a dozen change functions for various institutions. The change functions for Russia, Japan, Peru, and Canada all require fundamental changes in the way their respective governments perform. These countries could easily take longer than three years to institute the proposed change functions. The longer it takes to implement the change function the larger and more critical the problem becomes. If the change function is applied in a relatively rapid fashion, however, The System will not be able to sabotage it. Change functions must be applied such that the vast majority of people accept them and their potential for significant, fruitful, long-term benefits. However, short-term expedient actions may be required to alleviate the interior problems that the change function cannot yet overcome.

Each change function proposed for The Systems described in this chapter is the author's best idea for a force function that will automatically destroy The System and replace it with a new one. Undoubtedly there are alternate potential change functions that others could propose that will also destroy The System. The question is, what kind of New System would be created? It is obvious that the key to creating a change function is based on the objectives and goals that one wishes the New System to meet.

CHAPTER 8

Maintaining Renewal

Create in me a clean heart, O God;
and renew a right spirit within me.
—David[1]

This chapter reveals the measures that top management must take to create and maintain an outstanding organization. Maintaining excellence requires constantly renewing policies, procedures, and practices. Revitalizing an organization begins with revitalizing top management. Without such enlightenment, The System will prevail and significant and positive long-term change will be minimized. The revitalized top manager will understand the nine axioms that are applicable to replacing The System with a New System. The importance of the decision-making process, teamwork, and leadership is emphasized in this chapter. The change function is stressed as the vehicle for leadership and teamwork. The concepts of benchmarking, prevention, and time-based management are discussed as key elements in the process of renewal.

INTRODUCTION

Earlier chapters establish the background for the development of The System and explain and discuss the need for changing The System. This chapter suggests that top management must make certain that continuous improvement occurs throughout the organization in order to change The System successfully. Organizations are in a continuous state of change and either growing or decaying—there is no quiescent middle state. Growth occurs because top management has caused it to happen:

> The spirit of an organization is created from the top. If an organization is great in spirit, it is because the spirit of its top people is great. If it decays, it does so because the top rots; as the proverb has it, "Trees die from the top."[2]

Maintaining renewal means maintaining change, and maintaining change requires enlightened management. In destroying The System by introducing a new change function, top management in manufacturing or service organizations must ensure that total quality management and time-based management are implemented and continuously supported.

Satisfying the customer is the highest priority that the members of most manufacturing or service organizations have or should have. The change function must be able to address the future requirements of an organization's potential customers. The New System must be geared to continuously improving the quality of the product or service, reducing the cost and the price of the product or service, and anticipating the response to customers' long-term requirements. Successfully implementing the change function will require employee or member involvement in every improvement process.

This chapter outlines the steps that top management must take for an organization to attain and maintain world class status. Top management must create an innovative organization in which The System can change drastically. To accomplish this renewal, top management must be revitalized. Nine axioms that must be utilized for such a renewal are provided.

Leadership and teamwork are required if top management is to institute and maintain a successful renewal of the organization. The decision-making process is reviewed in detail. A recommended approach to improving management leadership is given. The vehicle for the application of leadership and teamwork is the implementation of a change function to the organization.

The renewal process includes benchmarking, the prevention process, and time-based management tools. The need for a management revolution is discussed, because managers often fail to overcome The System.

CHANGING LIFE CYCLES OF ORGANIZATIONS

The Classic Life Cycle

As L.M. Miller[3] shows, corporate life can be divided into seven stages, each characterized by a specific leadership style. The growth period of an organization involves three stages: that of the Prophet, the Barbarian, and the Builder and Explorer. During this period, The System is created and grows according to the constraints bounded by management's policies and procedures.

After the growth period comes a period of consolidation. This occurs with the stage of the Administrator, during which growth slows and the status quo becomes the rule. The organization's five-year plans are intensified and subsequently generally ignored, and the monthly budget reviews are expanded with increased documentation requirements. The System becomes entrenched as the de facto management of the organization.

The consolidation period eventually turns into the period of decay. This period is typified by the stages of the Bureaucrat and the Aristocrat. Growth becomes contraction, which leads to reduced profits or losses. In this period, cosmetic changes are implemented with the usual long-term results. The System is maintained, and the old remedies are recycled through the organization. The organization gradually declines until it is too late to resuscitate it unless real change is instituted.

Revitalization of Top Management

Real change is attempted when top management finds a leader, the Synergist, who understands that The System must be destroyed and that new fundamental and structural changes must be introduced and employed throughout the organization. Adapting Miller, the leader assumes that the following axioms apply if The System is to be changed:

1. **Vision:** The leader's main function is to create, instill, and maintain a sense of purpose and a unifying, challenging, and rewarding spirit in the organization.

2. **Customer Satisfaction:** The primary purpose of an organization is the complete satisfaction of its customers, which is accomplished by creating real wealth that results in profits.

3. **Innovation:** Real wealth is created by people inventing or discovering new or improved products, services, or means of production.

4. **Decisive Action:** Action that is promptly and decisively applied and executed leads to both short-term and long-term improvements, which are confirmed by meaningful measurements.

5. **Teamwork:** Leaders must synergize the diverse talents and traits of all members of the organization. The number of decisions at which a consensus is arrived by joint participation should be maximized. This means that most decisions should be made at the level where control is exercised.

6. **New Culture:** A new culture (beliefs and attitudes) must evolve that fosters creativity, innovation, and an aggressive and unrelenting commitment to satisfying the customers. This must result in a change of behavior in most people.

7. **Expertise Utilized:** Specialized knowledge and skills must be encouraged and integrated into the organization through organizational goals and team objectives.

8. **Self-control:** Administrative and bureaucratic controls must be replaced by commitment, awareness, technical knowledge, and

self-control of the individual in each job. The objective of every process should be a continuous improvement in quality while reducing the process cycle time. In fact, reducing the process time usually improves the quality of the process.

9. **Decentralization:** Decisions should be made by those in the process closest to the customer.

The indispensable requirement for the success of leaders is their vision of the future of the organization. Hickman and Silva[4] define vision as:

> *a mental journey from the known to the unknown, creating the future from a montage of current facts, hopes, dreams, dangers, and opportunities.* . . . . Clear vision results from a profound understanding of an organization and its environment.

Hickman and Silva outline the steps that a chief executive officer (CEO) should take to be successful according to Warren Bennis:

> The successful CEO:
> - Develops a compelling vision of firm's future.
> - Translates the vision into a reality by concentrating on the keys to success.
> - Remains deeply involved at the very heart of things, spurring the actions necessary to carry out the vision.
> - Motivates employees to embrace the vision.
> - Constantly articulates the vision so that it permeates all organizational levels and functions, taking the organization where it has never been before.[5]

Vision and a strategy of continuous improvement can lead to excellence if The System is destroyed and replaced with a new dynamic System. The initiator of real change, the leader, must cause The System to be permanently changed and a New System created that is responsive to everyone in the organization.

Peter Senge[6] suggests that Systems thinking is the key to developing a learning organization, which is:

> an organization that is continually expanding its capacity to create its future. . . . . Systems thinking is the discipline for seeing wholes. It is a

framework for seeing interrelationships rather than things, for seeing patterns of change rather than static "snapshots."

Senge believes that five basic technologies or disciplines are critical to the development of a learning organization: personal mastery, mental models, building shared vision, team learning, and Systems thinking. Systems thinking is the discipline that integrates the other disciplines using a conceptual framework of the whole System and not just part of The System. Senge emphasizes the need to understand the whole System, rather than the sum of all its parts. Systems thinking helps in understanding the basic concept of The System and how it works in an organization, and how to be able to change it.

Mikhail Gorbachev failed in his attempt to institute change in the Soviet Union because he failed to understand that The System that ran the Soviet Union had to be completely destroyed before real change could flourish. Boris Yeltsin, however, apparently understands that The System has to be destroyed and is attempting to institute a change function to replace it with a New System controlled by the people. He has applied the first axiom by creating the self-governing Republic of Russia. Yeltsin's main problem is instituting the other eight axioms over a short time frame while maintaining order and the welfare of the people in that country. Without employing most of the change function proposed in Chapter 7, the ensuing period will be one of relative chaos, inflation, inefficiencies, and continued lawlessness.

Because Yeltsin's change function is not yet completely formulated, The System will try to maintain whatever control it still has. The System in the form of unreconstructed communists will try to prevent the elements of the change function from being established throughout the country. If The System is successful in blocking many of the economic and legal reforms that Yeltsin is trying to implement, it will be changed only marginally and not fundamentally. If Yeltsin's completed change function does not automatically establish lawful incentives and processes that enable people to improve their own welfare, then the developing System will be almost as unwelcome as The System it replaced.

In the U.S. Congress, Miller's axioms also must be applied if it is to be changed into an effective and efficient guardian of the country's future. The proposed change function, i.e., the 28th Amendment, will automatically cause the axioms to be employed. However, they would be applied quicker and more effectively if the 29th Amendment was also passed. In this case, the Synergist (or top management) is the people of the United States.

Businesses and nonprofit institutions should exist solely to serve their customers. Therefore, they must be tasked with supplying outstanding products and services to their customers and satisfying also their employees, suppliers, and owners. Such organizations must continually provide the highest standards of products and services if they are to remain successful in the future.

Becoming a World Class Organization

The ultimate stage in the life cycle of an organization is heralded by the Synergist; during this stage an organization becomes world class. The term *world class manufacturing* (WCM) originated in describing the changes that manufacturers make to enrich, advance, and reinvent their products and services for customers.

The goals of world class manufacturing are:

continual improvement in quality, cost, lead time, customer service and . . . improved flexibility. [The challenge for management is to speed up] the pace of improvement. . . . WCM mandates simplification and direct action: Do it, judge it, measure it, diagnose it, fix it, manage it on the factory floor.[7]

World class manufacturing requires the following objectives: reduced inventory (just-in-time suppliers), small lot size (short setup and changeover times), total quality control (doing it right the first time), total preventive maintenance (planned downtime), flexible production lines (short cycle and lead times), a high value-added ratio (the ratio of value-added time to total cycle time) and reduced deviation and variability (zero defects and a high capability index[*]).

An organization's goals for world class service are the same as those for manufacturing. Service organizations employ about 85 percent of the U.S. work force. Drucker[8] notes that in contrast to manufacturing workers' productivity improvements, service workers' productivity has not increased significantly. He points out that capital and technology are factors of production but in knowledge and service work they are tools that may not replace labor and thus increase productivity. He suggests the following factors must be considered in order to increase productivity of knowledge and service workers: defining the task, concentrating work on the task, defining performance requirements, forming a partnership in productivity improvement between management and those who hold the jobs, and building continuous learning and teaching into the job of every employee and team. Drucker states:

> To raise the productivity of service work, we cannot rely on government or on politics altogether. It is the task of managers and executives in businesses and nonprofit organizations. It is, in fact, the first social responsibility of management in the knowledgement society.

It is also an important fiscal responsibility of management in a free enterprise System.

World class service requires similar internal operating objectives. For example, a hospital should have being a world class service organization as one of its goals. It should have as a minimum the following internal operating objectives: reduced inventory for noncritical supplies; optimum inventory for treatment-related drugs and supplies; short setup and changeover times; total quality control, including statistical process control for all major processes; total preventive maintenance; short cycle times

---

* The capability index is the ratio of the allowed tolerance spread to six times the standard deviation.

for treating patients; reduced deviation and variability of processes; and measures for controlling costs and effectiveness.

A world class hospital would have a System that organizes work on different service or production principles than a regular hospital. Patient care would be given on a unique product production basis. Medical services would be supplied on a flexible mass production basis. Plant services, such as steam, ice, electricity, water, and gases, would be supplied on a process production basis.[9] Each work area would have specific internal operating objectives that it monitors and controls. Like most complex organizations, The System that controls most hospitals manifests itself in unique ways in the various groups that comprise the typical hospital. However, The System is generally the same for all areas regarding management control, personnel practices and procedures, and general administrative controls and requirements. As in most organizations, The System controls most hospitals and seeks to maintain its status quo.

LEADERSHIP AND TEAMWORK

The Decision-Making Process

Instituting and maintaining renewal of an organization requires leadership by the top management. Leaders must transact business with people and communicate with them about ideas, values, objectives, and directions for taking action. This implies that the leader of the organization has decided on a course of action that the organization's management and people are to carry out.

The decisions that are made before initiating such actions are key to effective action. Heirs and Pehrson[10] point out that individuals go through a four-stage thinking process when considering a problem, question, situation, or action. They contend that organizations go through a similar four-stage thinking process before making decisions.

When any decision must be taken by an individual, the act of thinking follows a process of asking and answering a question. This process is not conscious or deliberate; it is an instinctive and natural pattern. . . . There are . . . four clearly definable stages in the question-and-answer *thought* process of decision-making.

According to Heirs and Pehrson, they are: the question, alternatives, consequences, and judgment/decision stages.

The question stage is a stimulus to the mind in the form of a question or problem and occurs in either the conscious or subconscious level of the mind. Only when the answer to the question is already in the brain can it be recalled by the action of the stimulus. When it is not already in the brain, the mind must think speculatively or creatively to answer the question. Heirs and Pehrson state that because:

the mind's decision-oriented thinking System *begins* with the stimulus of a question, [it is important] to recognize the critical importance of correctly defining the initial question to the final outcome of the thinking process—the decision.[11]

Thus the question to be answered must be correctly and exactly structured for the mind's activity to be directed and focused on the specific question and not on a diffused or spurious concept. If the root cause of a problem is not understood, the solution could be incorrect, inefficient, or ineffective.

In the alternatives stage, the mind analyzes, assembles, and creates information to develop alternate answers to a question. The alternatives may be founded in standard practices or uniquely formulated by the subconscious mind.

In the consequences stage, the mind predicts the potential consequences by assuming that one of the alternatives would be accepted as the solution or answer to the question. In addition to analytical solutions, the mind is potentially capable of creating new solutions.

In the judgment/decision stage, the mind analyzes and ranks the alternates and chooses the one that optimally satisfies the original question or problem. The mind in all four stages continuously asks and answers questions in order to analyze and compare the alternates, consequences, and decisions.

A leader must apply the above four stages before taking action on questions or problems that the organization faces. However, according to Heirs and Pehrson:

> The quality of the decisions taken by the leaders of our most important organizations today depends first on the quality of thinking within the organizations and second on their ability to carry out effectively the decisions made. [It is even more important] to improve the effectiveness of an organization's thinking efforts—in other words, to improve the effectiveness of the mind of the organization.[12]

An organization must perform its thinking and decision-making functions in an effective manner to meet its goals and objectives. Its members must utilize the above four-stage thought process for considering how their work, actions, and potential decisions affect others in the organization. In Senge's terms, Systems thinking must take place throughout the organization.

From both the organization's and the individual's performance capability viewpoints, top management must ensure that the decision-making process is effective. Thus top management must ensure that tasks requiring reflective thinking (such as long-range planning, research and development, marketing, developing strategies, engineering, manufacturing, human resources, and operations planning) are performed with greater exactness and comprehensiveness. As part of the organization's overall improvement program, everyone should be exposed to the principles of effective decision making. In companies where quality improvement programs have been initiated, many of the "efforts underestimate or ignore the need for improving the critical thinking skills of factory workers, overemphasizing the technical aspects of manufacturing and quality assurance."[13] Thinking skills are required for effective problem solving, and problem solving at the local level is the most effective way to ensure improvement and renewal.

Russo and Schoemaker[14] have analyzed the mistakes that decision makers commit. They identify "the ten most dangerous decision traps" as follows:

1. Plunging In
2. Frame Blindness
3. Lack of Frame Control
4. Overconfidence in Your Judgment
5. Shortsighted Shortcuts
6. Shooting From the Hip
7. Group Failure
8. Fooling Yourself About Feedback
9. Not Keeping Track
10. Failure to Audit Your Decision Process

They point out that it is critically important to understand the process of deciding how to decide the issue at hand. They note that the formal decision-making process can be organized into four main parts.

1. Framing
2. Gathering intelligence, which could lead to reframing
3. Coming to a conclusion
4. Learning (or failing to learn) from feedback

Each part of the process is necessary in reaching the optimum decision upon which action is based.

The correct framing of the question is the key to effective decision making.

In framing, good decision makers think about the viewpoint from which they and others will look at the issue and decide which aspects they consider important and which they do not.

Frame blindness occurs when one sets out to solve the wrong problem because the mental framework that was chosen was incomplete, incorrect, or both.

The way people frame a problem greatly influences the solution they ultimately choose. And the frames that people or organizations routinely use for their problems control how they will react to almost everything they encounter.

Thus the usual approach is to look for fault in a person or group of persons instead of The System.

Russo and Schoemaker state that:

perhaps the most important skill in decision-making is to recognize when an issue needs to be reframed. If you continually use an inappropriate frame—that is, if you continue to simplify in ways that blind you to what is most significant about the problem—you will eventually cast yourself and your organization into deep problems.

It is clear that reframing is most important if one is to change The System. Reframing requires understanding the present frame and its sources, generating alternate frames, and selecting the most appropriate frame. If no single frame exists, one must look at the problem through several concurrent frames to find a robust solution. In other words, a second-order change function must be found that results in a long-term, unassailable solution.

Management Must Lead

Drucker[15] explains that a manager has two tasks:

The first is the creation of a true whole that is larger than the sum of its parts, a productive entity that turns out more than the sum of the resources put into it. . . . The second specific task of the manager is to harmonize in every decision and action the requirements of immediate and long-range future. He cannot sacrifice either without endangering the enterprise.

Both tasks require reflective thinking and decision making by top management, and management's understanding how the organization (The System) actually works.

The first task can be achieved whether or not The System is in control of the organization. If The System is in control, the output probably is neither optimized nor responding to the challenges of the economic and other environments that affect the organization. If top management is in control of The System, then it is also in control of the organization, which means that it and the organization's members are jointly controlling The System.

The second task requires that The System be controlled jointly by top management and the other people in the organization. If it is not controlled jointly, then The System will be in control and top management will be hard pressed to harmonize short-range requirements and long-range opportunities because The System is maintaining the status quo. The System knows from experience that management usually only attempts cosmetic changes that are almost always tolerable for The System's survival.

Top management must lead by taking the following steps: (1) motivating the rest of the organization and communicating a vision of the goals and future of the organization, (2) establishing stretched objectives, (3) organizing the work responsibilities, (4) developing the members of the organization, including themselves, and (5) most importantly, setting an example of integrity and consistency for the entire organization. Top management also must understand how important the role of The System is and be able to analyze its degree of control over the organization.

Assuming that top management understands the importance of The System, then the leader must decide whether The System needs to be changed. If the leader decides that The System must be changed, he or she must initiate the renewal process by first introducing the concept of a change function to a broad spectrum of management.

It is clear that the renewal process can be effective and timely only if the people who are affected by changing The System help management change or destroy it and then help establish a New System that both control. The decision-making process must be understood throughout the organization if The System is to be destroyed and replaced by The New System. Top management must ensure that all members of the organization understand the need to create a New System and also feel secure that The New System will benefit them in the long run.

Vehicles for Leadership and Teamwork

The renewal process requires applying a change function to the organization that is controlled by The System. Implementing the change function requires that (1) top management promulgate its new vision of the organization's future, (2) top management be committed to the change function and be persistent and consistent in the implementation process, (3) top management's objectives be effectively communicated and accepted by the rest of the people in the organization, (4) management and the rest of the people in the organization receive training regarding Systems thinking, process evaluation and improvement, quality and cycle time evaluation and improvement, and problem solving and decision making, and (5) everyone be involved in the process of continuous improvement.

Through employing the change function, top management must create a climate that encourages initiative and creativity in everyone throughout the organization. Individuals must realize that self-control of their work is necessary for successfully changing and renewing each process in The New System.

The structure of the organization should be critically analyzed by top management as part of the renewal process. The number of management layers should be reduced if it would improve the ability of people to implement fundamental changes to The System.

Teams may increase the ability of the organization to institute process improvements and to improve output efficiencies and effectiveness. Corrective action teams, quality improvement teams, design and manufacturing teams, manufacturing cells, project teams, process teams, manufacturing and supplier teams, customer service teams, and marketing teams are examples of vehicles that can facilitate the renewal process.

An ongoing training program also most be initiated to develop the potential of individuals in an environment of continuous change, innovation, and renewal. Everyone must become aware of the concepts of variation in a process and the use of statistical process control. Problem solving, decision making, group dynamics, and Shewhart control charts are areas that usually require training.

Key to the process of continual renewal is the elimination of people's fear of management and its programs. People must believe that the renewal process is good for the organization and also good for them in both the short and long run. Management by objectives and self-control and constant innovation and improvements require a climate where prudent risk taking is expected and where failures must occur if successes are to be created and nurtured. Failed designs, experiments, and theories must be expected and at least applauded. People must become comfortable with The New System and believe that it will be controlled by them and not vice-versa.

NEVER-ENDING IMPROVEMENT

The renewal process involves never-ending improvement and should include benchmarking, prevention, and time-based management. The renewal process, also known as business reengineering, requires rethinking workflow, policies, and procedures.

Benchmarking

Webster's Ninth New Collegiate Dictionary defines a benchmark as "a point of reference from which measurements may be made," or "something that serves as a standard by which others may be measured." Top managers who wish to improve their organization's performance can use either an arbitrary standard as an objective to be met or a known performance level that has been accomplished by others. Benchmarking is the process of determining and understanding the practices of others who have accomplished superior results; it entails understanding a process and its capabilities and resultants.

"Benchmarking is the continuous process of measuring products, services, and practices against the toughest competitors or those companies recognized as industry leaders."[16] Benchmarking has to be done on a continuous basis to ensure that the thrust for constant improvement is meaningful. While a tendency always exists for an individual or a group to become satisfied with achieving a desired improvement, there is no room for complacency in most industries today. Only those organizations that practice benchmarking in determining the potential technical capabilities of their processes will be able to achieve and maintain world class status.

Benchmarking is a search for the best practices of industries that perform the same process. An organization does not necessarily want to benchmark a competitor if its practices are not superior and of a world class nature. A hardware manufacturer may wish to benchmark a retail clothing store's shipping practices that are considered outstanding. Benchmarking is essential if an organization's goal is to be the "best of the best" in its industry.

Benchmarking is leadership at its best, since it is a proactive way to affect constant renewal. Benchmarking requires participation by everyone involved in the process. It enables each individual to exercise self-control over the process and ensures that real, meaningful objectives meet the customers' satisfaction, including quality, delivery, and cost. Benchmarking helps to establish a climate of constant change and continuous employee and management control over The System. Benchmarking efforts eventually are ingrained in the organization and performed at all levels by people who are affected by the process. Management will not need to require benchmarking because it will become institutionalized and part of The New System.

Prevention — A Process

Prevention is very important in the renewal process because it is the key to total quality management. Prevention may be defined as being prepared, meeting or satisfying something in advance, keeping something from happening or existing, interposing an obstacle, or establishing an early warning System to detect potential problems.

Preventing or eliminating potential problems or errors is clearly top management's responsibility. Crosby[17] notes that the purpose of quality management:

> is to set up a system and a management discipline that prevents defects from happening in the company's performance cycle. To accomplish this, [one has] to act now on situations which may cause problems some time from now. Act now for reward later.

Everyone in the organization must subscribe to the concept of prevention and believe that the best and only way to perform a task is to do it right the first time. Most tasks, however, especially repetitive ones, are under the control of The System, and thus the person performing correctly the task under The System's control cannot be responsible for the output of the process. As discussed in Chapter 6, only management can change a process that is controlled by The System. If unwanted outputs are generated, management must modify the process steps or procedures so that the standard deviations of the output variables are significantly reduced and result in an acceptable process output.

Prevention should start in the development stage of a product, which could be hardware, software, or a service. The product should be designed to meet all of its objectives, including the reliability requirements of the customers. In addition to designing quality into the product, the mechanical design should be fool-proof (*poka-yoke* as the Japanese call it) and allow assembly or use of the product (or its elements) only in the exact manner for which it was intended. (The most common example of a foolproof design is the round manhole covers for sewers, etc. It is impossible for the round cover to fall into the hole.)

Preventive maintenance should be ongoing in the overall process of renewal. Good preventive maintenance should be applied on a continuous basis by a person who is intimately involved with the process. The operator of the process is almost always better informed about how the process is working and the equipment is functioning. This practice is used by world class organizations and called total preventive maintenance.[18]

Total preventive maintenance is more than the tender loving care by operators of machines or apparatus that are used in a process. It also includes a higher level of preventive maintenance from experts on a daily shift basis. The Japanese, for example, use a maximum of two working shifts per day, with maintenance shifts in between. With scheduled maintenance between shifts, the machines are always available because breakdowns and poor quality caused by machine malfunctions are eliminated. Buffer (inventory) stocks, and the space and handling of such stocks also are eliminated.

The key to total preventive maintenance is empowering all the people in an organization. People must exercise self control over their work (a process) and understand that a fundamental change is required to improve The System that controls their process. *Each person*, therefore, must understand statistical process control to determine when or if The System needs to be changed.

Time-Based Management

Time-based management can be summarized best by the advice Benjamin Franklin once gave to a businessman: "Remember that time is money."[19] Thomas et al.[20] demonstrate that a company's strategy for long-term success must be based on continually reducing the time it takes to supply goods and services to customers.

They note that by creating short cycle times, one concurrently generates a high number of "Cycles of Learning," which are:

the opportunities to improve performance that occur when the lessons of experience are systematically exploited. The rate of change in cost, quality, and productivity are driven far more by the intelligent use of

Cycles of Learning than by the cumulative volume of historical and present production.

Thomas et al. found that the impact of the concept of a short cycle time on a person is culture dependent and that a (second order) change in The System is required.

The culture changes effected included a change in mindset, requiring people to think in terms of radical change instead of incremental changes, to consider how to make the giant leap from weeks of time to hours, not how to make incremental reduction to fewer weeks. [They point out that] it is important to recognize that competitiveness through Total Cycle Time and the resulting responsiveness to customers' needs cannot be legislated, edicted, or bought. It can only be managed by leadership that knows what it is doing.

They highlight the fact that the total quality of an operation or process will automatically improve as its total cycle time decreases. Reducing total cycle time requires less rework, and less rework requires preventing errors, mistakes, and defects.

Time-based manufacturing entails minimizing production lot sizes, maximizing flexibility of the mix of products, and minimizing both the cycle time and lead time to design, develop, produce, and ship a product. Successful time-based manufacturing is the key to competitive advantage, and therefore a successful change function for most manufacturers or service organizations must include time-based management.

People Make It Happen

Renewal can occur when most of the people in an organization are working with a change function to change The System. Renewal efforts fail when: (1) a supposed change function is really a cosmetic change that management has instituted, (2) the change function is attempted but the climate in the organization has not changed because top management has not demonstrated its dedication to the process of ongoing, persistent change and, consequently, most people are going through the motions of participating in the new process, (3) there are inadequate communications with management leading to a poor understanding by most people of how such proposed changes will affect them personally in the future, (4) there is inadequate training, learning, and understanding on the part of middle managers and the other people in the organization, and (5) fear pervades the organization because top management has mismanaged so greatly that the organization's long-term survival is at stake, resulting in reducing or the threat of reducing a significant number of employees.

Probably thousands of improvement programs in the past few years failed or are failing because top management does not understand the commitment, dedication, and persistence required on its part in the renewal process. A "business as usual" approach or an insincere attitude by top management fails to convince most people that it is serious about the renewal process and is always detected by the other people in the organization. Thus people continue to pay lip service to changing The System knowing that top management is not going to cause a fundamental change.

However, whenever management introduces an acceptable change function, the other people in the organization have responded by demanding their self-control over The New System. The major Japanese companies have been very effective in promoting employee participation. For example, Toyota is implementing 5,000 new suggestions from its employees each day.[21]

NEEDED: A MANAGEMENT REVOLUTION

To change The System and maintain renewal in a New System, top management must change its thinking, its ways, and its goals and objectives because *Systems never fail, only System managers do.* The System always performs the way it was established and allowed to grow into becoming the de facto manager of the organization. The System may give poor results, be inefficient and ineffective, be very costly, and ignore competition but is always doing what it was established to do. One often hears or reads that

"The System does not work" or "The System is broken." These comments reflect the subconscious notion that The System is managing the organization and is out of control. The System always works according to the laws of The System and only "works" for the members of its iron triangle. The System's output and response to customers is exactly what top management has ordained and sustained and not what top management has propagandized.

There must be a revolution in the way that top management performs its stewardship of an organization. If people are to be empowered to make change, top management also must change. Top management must understand and implement, where applicable, the programs that Tom Peters proposes in *Thriving on Chaos—Handbook for a Management Revolution*.[22] The thrust of his book is that flexibility and rapid change are required by companies and nonprofit organizations if they are to survive and eventually become and remain world class organizations.

Peters prescribes forty-five programs, which he calls prescriptions, for management to follow if it wants to be successful in the future. Ten prescriptions are for creating total customer responsiveness by the organization. Another ten prescriptions are for pursuing fast-paced innovation. Ten more are for achieving flexibility by empowering people, and ten are for learning to excel with and to promote continuous change. The last five prescriptions are management tools or policies that are required if the other forty prescriptions are to be effective.

The central theme of this book is that The System exists and only top management can institute significant changes to The System. Peter's book could serve as the basic handbook for top management on ways to cause The System to change in a significant manner. In fact, employing most of Peter's prescriptions would be a change function that would fundamentally change The System.

In Peter's[23] recent book, the concept of change is replaced by the concept of abandonment or revolution. The organization must be completely decentralized, to the point that front line individuals are in complete charge of their work. Peters proposes to destroy The System and replace it with a New System in which everyone is energized.

A New System should result in the formation of a unique world class organization. R.H. Hayes, et al.[24] note that world class companies "tend to grow faster and be more profitable than their competitors." They point out that such companies also have other superior, unique attributes: they have very skilled and effective employees, they serve as consultants to their customers and potential customers, they are very responsive in a timely manner to the market's needs, and they incorporate their product designs with their special manufacturing process techniques which erects a high barrier for their competitors to reverse engineer their products.

SUMMARY

Significant improvements in an organization's future performance are possible if top management understands the need for drastic change to The System, and also has a vision that can unify everyone in the organization. Nine axioms are shown to apply to the process of renewal.

The organization must strive to become a world class manufacturer or service provider. Drucker shows the steps needed in order for a service organization to improve its service to its customers.

Improved leadership and teamwork are necessary if renewal of an organization is to be maintained continuously. The chapter shows the importance of the decision-making process in the formulation of the future thrust of the organization. It is shown that when considering either a problem, question, situation, or an action, the four-stage thinking process—the question, alternatives, consequences, and judgment/decision—should be applied. Heirs et al. point out that it is important to improve the effectiveness of the thinking effort of the organization as a whole—in other words, the thinking efforts of everyone trapped in The System's hegemony.

The chapter identifies the ten most dangerous traps that decision makers can fall into. The decision-making process is shown to have four parts: training, evaluation and reframing, conclusions, and feedback. It emphasizes the tools needed for the continuous renewal necessary in an organization. Three key processes are identified: benchmarking, prevention, and time-based management.

Finally, the chapter explains that a management renewal is also required. The following aphorism summarizes the situation: Systems never fail, only System managers do.

CHAPTER 9

Summary and Conclusions

The reform should be thorough, radical and complete.
—Rutherford B. Hayes[1]

This chapter explains the most important concepts related to change: The System exists and is in control; change functions are necessary; vision and objectives are prerequisites for creating a change function; and people empowerment, innovation, and flexibility are key ideas that must he integrated into the change concept. The chapter addresses social-based Systems in contrast to the process-based Systems discussed in Chapter 5. The chapter suggests that individuals have their own unique System through which they live and interact with other people. People, like top management, can either control The System or let it control them. S. R. Covey's approach to self-analysis and self-control is suggested as the change function for the individual. After applying a successful change function, a New System is created. The New System has attributes and laws that replace those of The System. These new attributes and laws indicate that The New System is drastically different from The System and is now in partnership with top management and the other people in the organization. The chapter also discusses seven reasons why certain change functions fail.

303

INTRODUCTION

The Popular Perception of The System

Stories containing negative comments about The System fill the media. One of the biggest ideological battles of the 1990s, as reported in *The Wall Street Journal*, is "a fight over the future and the ailing American health-care system."[2] A letter to the editor of the *Sarasota Herald-Tribune* states, "There is no doubt that payment for medical care is the biggest problem that Americans have to face today, and some other system has to evolve from the mishmash of Medicaid, Medicare and private insurance."[3]

The Wall Street Journal says: "They know the system and they know how to use it. . . . People who run school systems are very protective of their turf. . . ."[4] George F. Will explains that:

by now much research refutes the idea that variations in school expenditures correlate directly with school performance. And abundant experience suggests that private schools, operating without the sclerotic bureaucracies that burden Chicago's and other cities' schools, and spending less per pupil than public systems spend, often do better. They do better partly because parents are energized by the opportunity to shop for educational choices.[5]

"The bill's fate shows once again how impossible it is to promote reform inside a system dominated not by parents or individual teachers, but by unions and bureaucracy."[6] "We presently evaluate student and system performance largely through measures that tell us how many students are above or below average. . . ."[7] (Note that this last statement shows a lack of understanding of simple statistics—by definition, there is always one half of a population of anything that is below average.)

A guest editorial by the Times-Union of Albany, New York reads as follows:

The far more important matter is how it was possible for a CIA officer with top secret clearance to have peddled such sensitive information for so long without being found out. The defect with the CIA lies not in a personality but in the system.[8]

"Only 38 percent of all Clarke County bookings resulted in convictions—strong evidence of a system gone amok," as told by Neal R. Pierce[9] in a story about jail crowding.

G. Melloan reports in *The Wall Street Journal* story about Russian mistrust in their money: "Since property rights were denigrated in communist education and propaganda, cheating and theft were pervasive throughout the system."[10]

The implication in these and most other statements about The System is that it is not working or working correctly. Such statements are incorrect because The System usually works the way management initially intended. It always is in good working order except on those rare occasions when it runs out of statistical control because some element or process of The System deteriorates, malfunctions, or is incorrectly operated.

For example, the health care System in the United States works exactly the way it has been set up by the iron triangle members. Each group of iron triangle members continues to try to optimize its benefits and prerogatives and is pitted against the other groups only with regard to the portion of the influence and money that they share. The customers, who are the patients, know that they and their insurers are paying exorbitant prices for the medical services and supplies that they receive, which is the result of the governments' health care and tax policies. The trend is that The System will be changed cosmetically and there will be more of the same—more control by government, higher prices, a lengthening of waiting times for medical care, and rationing of medical care and services.

Most people do not realize The System usually is under autopilot and controlling itself. They are not aware that the top management of an organization is not in operational control of The System and thus attribute poor performance to The System instead of top management. As discussed earlier, The System cannot change itself; only top management is capable of making such a change. Therefore, the public comments about The System not working should be directed to top management, which is not addressing how to change The System but is optimizing the short term performance of the organization.

The Most Important Concepts

The following concepts are important in understanding how to make basic and fundamental changes in various operations:

- The System exists and is usually in control.
- Only a change function (a second-order change) can cause basic and fundamental change to occur in The System.
- A vision and stretch objectives are required before a useful change function is created.
- Management by objectives and self-control empowers people.
- Innovation and flexibility are necessary to become and remain a world class organization.

The System may be defined as an entity that conceptually controls and manages an organization. The members of an organization think and act as though The System is the absentee owner. The members believe that The System is invariant to real change because top management's past attempts to introduce such changes into The System have never been successful. The members believe that The System may not be perfect but can be relied on whenever top management exerts its prerogatives.

The following test should be used to determine if there is a System problem: If repeated attempts to correct an undesired situation or problem are unsuccessful over a long period, then a System problem exists and not a people behavior problem.

The above test should be applied whenever a problem or difficulty arises in an organization, whether it be a school, business, post office, motor vehicle registry office, or town meeting. Experience shows that the problem usually is due to a process that is under the control of The System and not under the control of a person. For example, if an experienced person behind a store counter has difficulty making the correct change, then a System problem exists because The System was such that the sales clerk was not required to be proficient in making change. The surly postal clerk is a product of The System that was initially established by the Government to maintain bureaucratic control over the postal system. The surly postal clerk would disappear if the postal service were privatized. Not only is it very easy but it is human nature to blame someone for a problem. However, both the Bible[11] and Abraham Lincoln[12] point out the correct way: "Judge not, that ye be not judged." Instead of assigning blame, we should assume that The System is in control of the situation and that it will be up to top management to make any necessary changes.

In Chapter 6 it was shown that a change function is required to change The System in a permanent, significant way. Slater[13] points out that the usual:

piecemeal problem-solving model, as a primary management methodology, is flawed. Apparent savings are not making it to the bottom line. . . . [and the] fundamental model for quantum jumps in performance must be promoted by a "starting over" mentality.

Using the concept of "imagineering," he suggests that one first set aside (but not totally abandon) negative problem solving activities and focus on what the operation or process would look like if it were running the way it should. The System's variables must be identified and analyzed, and if found wanting, The System must be revised to eliminate the undesired conditions or problems. Slater correctly states that "before people can work effectively in a System, there has to be an effective System for them to work in." He quotes K. Ishikawa:[14]

Our belief is that the process, which is a collection of cause factors, must be controlled to obtain better products and effects. This approach anticipates problems and prevents them before they occur, and we shall call it "vanguard control." In contrast, if a person worries about performance. . . . after the fact, that method is called "rear guard control."

Management by objectives and self-control is a management technique that automatically empowers employees or members of an organization. Self-control[15] means that people have the ability to control the portion of the process for which they are responsible. People who are empowered measure and analyze the results of their work. If the process on which they work is under statistical process control, empowered people can identify a new problem before it becomes a major problem. Empowered people usually are capable of determining how to change The System to improve the output of the process. Empowered people usually are able to identify problems elsewhere, willing and able to assist others in solving their problems, and comfortable in working with others in a team or manufacturing cell.

Empowered people are innovative and capable of creating new ways to perform a process more efficiently. They create new or improved versions of products or services that the organization provides, are not afraid to experiment with new ideas, and are willing to accept failure if a new approach is unacceptable.

Empowered people are flexible and use their flexibility to solve problems, help other people, and work in operations or situations that are unfamiliar to them. Flexible people are continuously growing in capability and able to meet stretch objectives. They consider stretch objectives a challenge and a means to improve their work output and self-esteem, and the organization's performance.

Classes and Types of Systems

There are two classes of Systems: Social-based and process-based. The process-based System was discussed in Chapter 5. It was noted that each unique process is either in statistical control of its own system or out of control because of external causes. There are three types of social-based Systems: personal, organizational, and institutional.

Organizational and institutional Systems have similar general characteristics. Both types incorporate multiple groups of people, with each group having its own subsystem that is part of the overall System. The major difference between organizational and institutional Systems is the type of top management that controls The System.

The typical organizational System has a well-defined management structure that usually is pyramidal, with top management being one person or a small group of people. The typical institutional System usually has a much more complex management structure or seems to have no overall management. The illegal drug System is an institutional System whose top management consists of the heads of states involved, owners of the major illegal drug organizations, and heads of the distribution and warehousing organizations. Each of these entities has its own system, and these systems form one large institutional System.

Thus organizational and institutional Systems are similar in nature and differ only in details and complexities. The third type of social-based System, which has not yet been discussed, is that of the individual.

THE INDIVIDUAL'S PERSONAL SYSTEM

Each individual has a System that encompasses how one operates when alone and when interacting with others. A person's System is formed during youth, and is in a continuous state of change that usually is marginal. The System that people develop allows them to perform various routine operations without having to replace and reprogram their detailed activities. The System forms habits that save time, allows people to do several things at once without consciously thinking about them, and facilitates predictions of future performance. When their personal System controls their actions, people usually are performing some type of activity that does not require their special scrutiny. During these frequent periods of System control, people usually are not aware of trends or problems indicating that the System is no longer under control. Therefore a routine activity or process could eventually lead to a problem that would attract the individual's attention. For example, a person driving a car ignores a warning light or gauge because he or she does not recognize its signal. Only when the car develops a serious problem that adversely affects the driving does the individual become aware of the problem.

People use their System to make life easier. However, The System always tries to maintain the status quo and thus does not recognize or respond to external stimuli that are potentially threatening to The System. For example, a driver who routinely rolls through stop signs eventually will receive a traffic violation ticket or be involved in an accident (maybe with another driver with a similar tendency).

People may get trapped within their own System because the habits become too strong to overcome easily or The System becomes a comfortable way to live and does not require much thinking and changing of their ways. Thus the changes people attempt are all usually cosmetic and do not threaten The System. Alcoholism, like an allergy, is an example of a System problem that is very difficult to change. Because drinking an alcoholic beverage satisfies the individual's short-term need, the usual cosmetic attempts at long-term abstinence most often fail. A second-order change function is needed to prevent The System from regaining control over the individual's behavior. The iron triangle members in the personal System are the external stimuli, the conscious mind, and the subconscious mind.

However, a person can decide that his or her System must be changed and that significant, fundamental changes are desired and required. Therefore an individual would have to follow the same steps that a top manager follows to change The System.

The person first would have to understand that his or her System exists and has to be changed significantly. The person then must be determined to make such a permanent change and have access to the resources required to accomplish the System change. After first determining what action to take, the person would have to take action in a timely fashion. Then the person would have to control the new process in such a way that The System could not adversely affect it; The New System would have to be nurtured continuously. The results of The New System would have to be analyzed, and when possible the process would have to be shown to be under statistical process control. Examples are: a person gets married, a person quits his or her job to attend college, a man joins a military service organization as a career change, a secretary quits smoking, and an alcoholic joins Alcoholics Anonymous.

People must understand that without self-control, The System will attempt to maintain its existence and prevent significant changes from occurring. Individuals must control their personal System in order to develop their talents fully. They must recognize that their personal System will interact with other personal, organizational, and institutional Systems. They should be aware that there could be a clash of values with other Systems and that special actions could be required to optimize these situations.

Covey,[16] in his brilliant and unique book, *The 7 Habits of Highly Effective People*, describes what special actions individuals should take if they are to develop their potential. He discusses the need for a holistic, integrated, "principle-centered, character-based, 'inside-out' approach to personal and interpersonal effectiveness."

He notes that the *Character Ethic* as compared with the *Personality Ethic* is the foundation for the basic principles of effective learning. He proposes seven habits that should be mastered if one is to change from being dependent or independent to interdependent. He explains that there is an optimum path for the development of change leading to a person's optimized well-being.

Covey states that a paradigm shift is required to enable one to change in a significant, positive manner. He states that perceptions are formed by the way one looks through the lens through which one sees the world. He notes that it is most important to look *at* the lens because "the lens itself shapes how we interpret the world." He points out that:

> Marilyn Ferguson observed, "No one can persuade another to change. Each of us guards a gate to change that can only be opened from the inside. We cannot open the gate of another, either by argument or by emotional appeal."

Covey presents a second-order change for the individual. If the individual applies such a change function, The System will be changed for the individual.

PEOPLE, MANAGEMENT, AND THE SYSTEM

People usually are not to blame for The System's shortcomings in an organization. The System is initially established because top management uses, albeit unintentionally, McGregor's Theory X type of management. Top management generally has been short-term, financial, and stock market oriented rather than long-term, productivity, and customer oriented.

Short-term financial performance is always important because the organization has to stay in business in the short-term to survive in the long-term. However, any organization that wishes to grow in the future must be intensely customer oriented, and innovative and flexible enough to satisfy its customers' changing requirements. The organization must introduce a change function that entails total quality management and time-based management, and that empowers the entire membership of the organization.

To implement fundamental changes, however, people must be able to adjust to the proposed changes and become involved in the change process in such a way that they make it part of their personal System. People must be able to dismantle The System and replace it with The New System that they and management control and monitor on a daily basis.

Management and others must be reorganized such that individuals and teams have complete responsibility for the tasks assigned to them. In addition, they must have the self-control ability to monitor and improve the processes that result in the output of the organization.

Each process in The System has to be critically reviewed and evaluated with respect to world class objectives and benchmark criteria. A process that does not meet these requirements must be analyzed and continuously improved until it is shown to be under control. The System that controls each process must be replaced with an improved System that gives the required improved output in a controlled fashion.

While reorganization and process changes are occurring, the organization's output must improve on a continuing basis. The financial improvements will be marginal at best in the beginning of the renewal process but will be cumulative exponentially over time.

FAILURE OF APPLIED CHANGE FUNCTIONS

The System sometimes remains in control in spite of the application of a change function. There are at least seven reasons why this process fails.

1.   A change function can fail because it appears to be a second-order change but it is really a first-order change. Upon examination most change functions proposed by members of the iron triangles are basically first-order changes. The proposed changes may result in marginal improvements to The System or the customers of The System, but they are not significant, trenchant,

and monumental changes that have long-term impact on The System and the customers.

2. A second-order change function usually should be applied to the solution of the problem and not to the alleged cause of the problem, because the cause generally is not known. The solution to the problem can be difficult to determine because there can be more than one cause, which can vary in intensity and can vary based on external circumstances. Therefore, a change function that is applied to correct a specific problem can be ineffective because the root cause or causes of the problem were not correctly addressed. A particular change function also might not be broad enough to address all of the problems.

3. A change function can fail to achieve its initial potential if new information becomes available that negates its application. This could happen if the organization's original goal or objectives, or the internal or external environments are changed significantly. It also could occur if key personnel, including top management, become dissociated with the application of the change function and those who are in charge of its implementation are inadequately informed of its significance or are nonbelievers.

4. A change function can fail because it is not focused and is applied only partially, temporarily, or sporadically to the processes for which it was created. Sometimes the application of the change function is poor, and The System reasserts itself such that the change function is never fully imposed on it. The System and its iron triangle proponents then use the improper application of the change function as an excuse to claim that the change function cannot work and therefore should be abandoned and replaced by The System's own cosmetic change agency. (That is what The System of education in the United States has done over the past forty years.)

5. A change function can fail because of inadequate or improper performance by those in charge of the process to which the change function has been applied. This could happen because of poor communication from top management or poor training and understanding on the part of the process operators and managers. Although the change function was the correct instrument to be used, the operators and managers were not adequately incorporated into the overall change process in a timely fashion. The optimum application of a change function should include and empower all of the people involved in the process. If this does not happen up front when the formation and application of the change function are being discussed and analyzed, then the people who are supposed to contribute to the development of the required process changes will not be wholly immersed in the process and also will be working within The System at least some of the time. People need time to understand, assimilate, and perform under The New System. If management tries to accelerate the change process such that it overwhelms the learning capacities of the people involved, the implementation of the change function can fail or at least be delayed until the people grow into their new environment.

6. A change function can fail because those who are supposed to apply it to The System lack the motivation to make such change. This lack of motivation can be eliminated by peer pressure, management or even by self-control if there is sufficient reason to change.

7. A change function can fail if the government interferes with the process. For example, the National Labor Relations Board ruled in December 1992 that an Indiana company's quality improvement labor and management teams "constitute a 'labor organization' and violate the National Labor Relations Act provision against setting up company-run unions."[17] Thus The

Systems of government—federal, state, and local—can override The Systems of individual companies and people.

The key to changing The System is first to develop an understanding of the causes of the problems that The System generates or enhances. Creating the proper change function then becomes the major critical task. It is imperative to choose and implement a change function that will cause The System problems to be eliminated even if the root causes are not identified. Therefore, top management must choose the right change function and be committed to implementing it.

Under Secretary of the Navy, Dan Howard[18] states that:

TQM [Total Quality Management] is a top-down approach to doing business. . . . When TQM fails, chances are it wasn't applied correctly, leadership wasn't steadfast in its efforts or was unable to live with the changes required to implement it. Leadership's commitment doesn't ensure success, but its lack of commitment will certainly guarantee failure.

GENERAL CHARACTERISTICS
OF THE NEW SYSTEM

Chapter 2 describes the attributes and laws of The System, many of which will not exist under The New System.

The attributes of The New System for an organization are the following:

1. **Pervasive**: It encompasses and empowers everyone in the organization to improve the operations on a continuous basis.

2. **Self-Consistent**: It demands a persistent focus on the customers' requirements. It requires flexibility and innovation such that each process is always in a state of controlled change in order to better the performance objectives.

3.   **Learnable**:   Most people can master The New System within a year of its introduction into the organization. This implies that everyone will be trained and educated in the concept of empowerment by self-control, and recognize that The New System will be beneficial to them in the future.

4.   **A Maximizer**:   The New System maximizes its efforts to meet the long-term goals of the organization and the members' control over it. The New System's norms are consistent with the organization's objectives and goals.

5.   **Self-Sufficient**:   The New System maintains itself by its constant climate of change in which everyone is always trying to improve the organization's performance. Its thrust is always toward satisfying its customers and thus optimizing its long-term profitability or viability.

6.   **Responsible**:   The New System is controlled by management and others in the organization. It responds positively to the new environment of continued change and reinforces the empowerment of everyone and the growth of the organization.

7.   **Not Sovereign**:   The New System is no longer the de facto management of the organization but is the vehicle of both top management and others in the organization. Management of the organization is shared equally by top management and the empowered members of the organization.

8.   **Stable**:   The New System is stable in the environment of continuous innovation, flexibility, and service toward satisfying the organization's customers. It is in stable equilibrium with the constant thrust of change and the development, growth, and sale of products and services.

9.   **Methodical**:   The New System maintains the change function as its basic mode of operation. The New System helps both top management and the others in the organization to perform their

jobs, which are continually being stretched and expanded with the constant change of renewal.

10. **Mandatory**: The New System is even more mandatory than the previous one, since it would be very difficult for everyone not to participate in its new thrust of constant improvement. Those who are not actively engaged in The New System's mode of operation after two year's exposure will become a liability to the organization.

11. **Monolithic**: Only one overall System can exist within an organization. The New System will replace the old one throughout the organization, although subtle, local differences will occur in various parts of the organization.

12. **Flexible**: The New System can change itself to recognize real, fundamental changes that are introduced into the organization. Basic changes are absorbed throughout The New System, which modifies its actions accordingly.

Laws of The New System

1. **"Fix It Even If It's Not Broken" Rule: Improvements are always beneficial in the long run.** Every process will be improved on an ongoing basis to assure continued and improved customer satisfaction and to lower long-term costs of the process.

2. **Law of Management: Management by objectives and self-control will be the guiding principle for the organization.** Management levels will be minimized consistent with maximizing empowerment to the members of the organization.

3. **Law of Equality: Management, other members of the organization, and The New System all share in the overall management of the organization.** Top management assumes its

rightful place as a key team member of the organization and joint controller of The New System.

4. **Law of Visibility: The New System is very visible to top management and all members of the organization.** Top management recognizes that problems with The New System require their immediate attention so that change functions can be applied whenever applicable. People have no fear in interfacing with top management in the environment of The New System.

5. **Rule of Productivity: The key to organizational growth is continuous productivity improvement.** The New System will continually emphasize the goal of zero defects in all processes. Process throughput time will be minimized consistent with meeting all of the process requirement standards. The New System will emphasize continuous improvement in everyone's performance.

6. **Law of Priority: Implementation of the optimum change function is paramount.** The optimum change function will include the requirement for innovation, flexibility, and continuous improvement in all processes. The change function will cause a renewed persistence in satisfying customers.

7. **Hidden Factory Rule: Every organization will eliminate its hidden factory.** Management by objectives and self-control will result in the dissolution of the hidden factories because no one will benefit from their existence.

8. **Law of Persistent Change: The thrust for change will be consistent in meeting the ever-changing customer requirements.** Established technology will compete with new technology that is compatible with meeting the benchmark objectives, which improve and become more critical and harder to meet as time goes on. However, management by objectives and self-control will also result in optimizing new technologies.

9. **Law of Profits: Increasing the supply of improved, unique products and services increases profits.** By saving buyer time and money, such products and services become more attractive to a larger number of buyers.

10. **Law of Growth: Growth occurs because continuous productivity improvement results in new products and services.** Growth occurs concurrently with the application of management by objectives and self-control. Growth occurs since output per person increases and space requirements, inventory, and total cycle time decrease throughout the organization.

11. **Law of the Iron Triangle: The New System minimizes the influence of the groups that form the iron triangle.** The New System is motivated by the customers it serves and not by the iron triangle members. The New System reduces third-party effects and maximizes the welfare of its customers, organization members, and owners.

These new laws indicate that The New System is different from The System in most aspects. The New System is a partner with top management and the people of the organization. The System is no longer the key management force in the organization. Although The New System is the creation of top management, it is integrated with management and the others such that all three entities provide the total management function for the organization. As a result of creating The New System and all that it entails, top management once again resumes the leadership position that is required in every organization.

SUMMARY

The media tend to give the impression that things go wrong *because* of The System. This chapter reiterates the fact that The

System most of the time performs exactly the way in which it has been established and maintained by top management.

The concept of vanguard control practiced by world class organizations is highlighted. Empowerment (management by objectives and self-control) for all members of the organization is stressed.

The social-based class of Systems is compared to the process-based Systems reviewed in Chapter 5. The three types of social-based Systems (organizational, institutional, and personal) are discussed in detail.

Individuals develop a personal System that allows them to perform routine operations without having to reconstruct and rethink their detailed activities. People can get ensnared within their own System because their habits become too strong to overcome easily. Their personal System becomes an easy way of life, but sometimes could have undesirable consequences. To change one's personal System, one needs to follow the same steps that are required to change The System of an organization:

1. Understand that The System exists.
2. Have a vision of a New System, with new (personal) goals.
3. Find a change function that will destroy the old and establish a New System.
4. Apply the change function in a timely fashion.
5. Measure and monitor the results of the changes.
6. Maintain renewal of personal empowerment.

Seven reasons are given for the failure of an applied change function to change The System.

The general characteristics of The New System are described in detail.

CONCLUSIONS

This book has attempted to establish the concepts that The System is for all intents and purposes a real entity that controls and manages organizations. The System develops from formal and informal policies and procedures; these evolve into practices that top management and middle management no longer control. The System gains control of the organization because top management becomes preoccupied with short-term results and the maintenance and enhancement of their salaries and prerogatives. Top management usually attempts to manage the organization by decreeing cosmetic changes or declaring new policies that are to be implemented by others in the organization.

Since The System is in control in most organizations, cosmetic changes imposed on The System and its sympathizers (those other than top managers) are accepted for what they are—short-term, top management changes. Although the cosmetic changes have a short-term effect on the organization, they are counterproductive eventually because such changes by top management are discounted by the others in the organization who understand that The System will not be changed.

Unfortunately, most top managements of organizations do not understand that The System exists and controls and limits the performance of the organization.

A small percentage of top managements recognizes the need for drastic change in their organization's performance. Some of these managers may sense the need for a drastic change, but many do not understand the need for a change function that will force the implementation of the desired change throughout the organization. Many top managers have attempted to implement change functions but have failed because the approach was halfheartedly understood and accepted by the others in the organization. Most of these managers never have understood the degree of control that The System has on the organization and therefore have underestimated what it takes to destroy The System and replace it with a New System.

Top management must understand the concept of a change function in order to make significant, long-term changes to their organization. After becoming knowledgeable about the concept, the most difficult part is to create, develop, or find a change function that will automatically cause the desired changes to occur. Top management then must ensure that all of the change function elements are accepted, understood, and applied by everyone in the organization.

Implementation of a change function should result in basic, fundamental changes and structural changes in the organization. Choosing the correct change function that will result in the desired performance of the organization is usually not a trivial exercise.

For example, choosing a change function to be applied to the U.S. Congress is very difficult because the choice depends on the desired results. Many people, including a large segment of the public sector that makes up the iron triangle, do not want The System that runs Congress changed in any significant way. However, most people, including the author, would like to have a Congress that is dedicated to improving the well-being of the *entire* country instead of its members' personal welfare and the rest of the iron triangle's welfare. Only a single, unrenewable term of office has the simplicity and the potential to cause the desired changes in Congress. All other suggested change functions appear to be very complicated, require sanctions or punishments, or would be only partially effective.

Only by changing The System with an appropriate change function can an organization be significantly changed. The top managements of most organizations will eventually recognize that their organizations are in trouble and that they will have to make meaningful changes. The test for top management is to understand the concepts of The System and a change function, and to use these concepts to improve the performance of the organization.

The one type of institution that is very different from the others is the government of a political body, such as a town, county, province, state, or country. If the political body of a country has serious persistent problems, then the people of that country will have to initiate and implement fundamental changes to The System that controls their country.

The people of Japan and Russia recently attempted to change The Systems that control their respective counties. However, it is not premature to speculate that the changes to date are mainly cosmetic. On the other hand, the new president of Peru is attempting to change The System that controls Peru by introducing a change function that completely revises the country's constitution, and legislative and judiciary Systems. The suggested changes to the U.S. Congress and the country that the 105th Congress has proposed will not be sufficient to destroy The System. In all of these and many other political bodies, The System has to be destroyed and replaced by The New System that is responsive to and controlled by the people and the governmental bodies that represent the people.

This book has attempted to set forth the proposition that The System is in de facto control of almost every organization. A drastic change function (second-order change) must be applied to destroy The System and replace it with a New System. This book has attempted to establish that top management in most cases has abdicated its leadership function in running the organization and that The System manages and leads the organization. The book concludes that only top management is able to change The System and therefore must either initiate such changes or be replaced with a more enlightened System-wise management.

When The System has been changed, the following aphorism can be used:

The System is dead. Long live The System.

"Well, so much for working for change within the system"

©1994. Reprinted courtesy of Bunny Hoest & Parade Magazine

PERMISSION ACKNOWLEDGMENTS

Excerpts from copyrighted materials have been reprinted with special permission:

Americam Management Association: Quoted, with permission of the publisher, from *THE HUMAN NATURE OF ORGANIZATIONS* by J. Douglas Brown, © 1973 AMACOM, a division of the American Management Association. All rights reserved. Quoted, with permission of the publisher, from *PRODUCTIVITY: The Human Side* by Robert R. Blake & Jane Srygley Mouton, © 1981 Robert R. Blake & Jane Srygley Mouton. Published by AMACOM, a division of the American Management Association. All rights reserved.

HarperCollins Publishers: Excerpts from *THE OTHER PATH* by HERNANDO DE SOTO. Copyright © 1989 by Hernando de Soto. Reprinted by permission of HarperCollins Publishers, Inc. Excerpts from *MANAGEMENT: TASKS, RESPONSIBILITIES, PRACTICES* by Peter F. Drucker. Copyright © 1973, 1974 by Peter F. Drucker.

Heirs Associates International S.A.: Excerpts from *The Mind of the Organization* by Ben Heirs and Gordon Pehrson, published by Harper and Row Publishers. ©1982, permission granted to reprint by Ben Heirs.

Hillsdale College: Excerpts from James L. Payne's essay, "Why Congress Can't Kick the Tax and Spend Habit," May 1991 *Imprimis*. Reprinted by permission from *Imprimis*, the monthly journal of Hillsdale College.

King Features Syndicate ● North America Syndicate: 10/28/86 release of HAGAR THE HORRIBLE: ©1986. Reprinted with special permission of King Features Syndicate.

McGraw-Hill, Inc.: Excerpts from *THE HUMAN SIDE OF ENTERPRISE*, by Douglas McGregor, © 1960, published by and reproduced with permission of McGraw-Hill, Inc.

MIT, Center for Advanced Engineering Study: Reprinted from *Out of the Crisis* by W. Edwards Deming by permission of MIT and The W. Edwards Deming Institute. Published by MIT, Center for Advanced Engineering Study, Cambridge, MA 02139. Copyright 1986 by W. Edwards Deming.

National Review, Inc.: Excerpts from "Morals, Markets, and Freedom" by Henry Hyde in *National Review*, November 5, 1990. Copyright ©1990 by National Review, Inc. Reprinted by permission.

W.W. Norton & Co., Inc.: Excerpts from *CHANGE Principles of Problem Formation and Problem Resolution*,by P. Watzlawick, J. Weakland and R. Fisch. Copyright ©1974 by W.W.Norton & Co., Inc.

Random House, Inc., Alfred A. Knopf, Inc.: Specified excerpts from *BARBARIANS TO BUREAUCRATS* by Lawrence M. Miller. Reprinted by permission of Crown Publishers, Inc. Specified excerpts from *THE ENIGMA OF JAPANESE POWER* by Karel van Wolferen. Copyright © 1989 by Karel van Wolfern. Reprinted by permission of Alfred A. Knopf, Inc.

Simon & Schuster, Inc.: Reprinted with permission of Scribner, an imprint of Simon & Schuster, Inc., from *THE ORGANIZATION GUERILLA: Playing the Game to Win* by Allen Weiss.

Stoddart Publishing Co. Limited: Excerpts reprinted from *THE TROUBLE WITH CANADA* by William Gairdner. Stoddart Publishing Co. Limited, Don Mills, Ontario, Canada controls the copyright to this title.

The Institute of Electrical and Electonics Engineers, Inc.: Excerpts from "A System Gone Awry" by Donald Christiansen, *IEEE Spectrum*, March 1987. Copyright ©1987 IEEE.

WM HOEST ENTERPRISES, INC.: Hoest cartoon: © 1994; Reprinted courtesy of Bunny Hoest and Parade Magazine.

APPENDIX
UNCONSTITUTIONAL
SUPREME COURT DECISIONS

The System has generated many laws which previously would have been deemed unconstitutional. Out of the hundreds of examples available, only a couple of egregious ones are noted below.

1)**Lochner v. New York** (198 U.S. 45,25S.Ct.539, 49L.Ed.937(1905). Lochner was convicted of violating a state statute which limited employers to requiring bakers to work no more than 10 hours a day or 60 hours a week. The Supreme Court struck down the state law because "the statute necessarily interferes with the right of contract between employer and employee . . ." The Court justified its rejection of the N.Y. State Law as follows: "The general right to make a contract in relation to his business is part of the liberty of the individual protected by the Fourteenth Amendment of the federal Constitution. Under that provision no state can deprive any person of life, liberty, or property without due process. The right to purchase or to sell labor is part of the liberty protected by this Amendment . . ."

The Supreme Court's majority based their decision on the concept that the fourteenth Amendment's wording; "nor shall any State deprive any person of life, liberty, or property, without due process of law;" meant that States could not limit the liberty of any to contract out his or her labor. Justice Oliver Wendell Holmes dissented. He noted that in the past:

various decisions of this Court that state constitutions and state laws may regulate life in many ways which we as legislators might think as injudicious or if you like as tyrannical as this, and which equally with this interfere with the liberty to contract . . . I think the word 'liberty' in the Fourteenth Amendment is perverted when it is held to prevent the natural outcome of a dominant opinion, unless it can be said that a rational and fair man necessarily would admit that the statute proposed would infringe fundamental principles as they have been understood by the traditions of our people and our law. It does not need research to show that no such sweeping condemnation can be passed upon the statute before us.

The majority of the Supreme Court Justices thus expanded the scope of the Fourteenth Amendment to, in effect, include transferring the U. S. Constitution's Bill of Rights to the States' constitutions. Justice Harlan, in dissent, wrote:

Responsibility, therefore, rests upon the legislators, not upon the courts. No evils arising from such legislation could be more far reaching than those that might come to our system of government if the judiciary, abandoning the sphere assigned to it by the fundamental law, should enter the domain of legislation, and upon grounds merely of justice or reason or wisdom annul statutes that had received sanction of the people's representatives . . . The public interest imperatively demand—that legislative enactments should be recognized and enforced by the courts as embodying the will of the people, unless they are plainly and palpably beyond all question in violation of the fundamental law of the Constitution.

2) **Griswold v. Connecticut** (381 U.S. 479,1965). Estelle Griswold, Executive Director of the Planned Parenthood League of Connecticut and Dr. Buxton, a licensed physician and professor at the Yale Medical School gave birth control information to a patient, and were subsequently fined $100 as an accessory to aiding a person in committing the offense of using contraceptives, which was against an old (1879) Connecticut statute. This episode was originally planned by Yale law professors as a means of eventually having the statute declared unconstitutional. It was an attempt to enlist the active Supreme Court on one side of a cultural issue that was initially enacted into law by the representatives of the people, and kept there by all subsequent legislatures. The case against the law was supported by The American Civil Liberties Union, The Catholic Council on Civil Liberties, and the Planned Parenthood Federation of America, Inc.

Justice William O. Douglas wrote the majority opinion which declared the Connecticut statute unconstitutional. He reviewed other previous cases which were related to individual rights that were not guaranteed by the Constitution's Bill of Rights, and noted:

The foregoing cases suggest that specific guarantees in the Bill of Rights have penumbras, formed by emanations from those guarantees that help give them life and substance . . . Various guarantees create zones of privacy . . . [He cited the First, Third, Fourth, Fifth and Ninth Amendments as examples of zones of privacy. He justified his dissent based on the privacy of the marriage relationship:] We deal with a right of privacy older than our political parties, older than our school system. . . .

Justice Goldberg, joined by the Chief Justice Warren and Justice Brennan also concurred with the reversal, noting the relevance of the Ninth Amendment to the decision. Goldberg stated that because of the Fourteenth Amendment's Due Process Clause, it protects personal rights and liberties "from impairment by the States."

Justice Black, joined by Justice Stewart, dissented:

I do not to any extent whatever base my view that this Connecticut law is constitutional on a belief that the law is wise or that its policy is a good one . . . I feel contrained to add that the law is every bit as offensive to me as it is to my brethren of the majority . . . The Court talks about a constitutional "right of privacy" as though there is some constitutional provision or provisions forbidding any law ever to be passed which might abridge the 'privacy' of individuals. But there is not. There are, of course, guarantees in certain specific Constitutional provisions which are designed in part to protec t privacy at certain times and places with respect to certain activities. Such for example, is the Fourth Amendment . . . I have expressed the view many times that First Amendment freedoms, for example, have suffered from a failure of the courts to stick to the simple language of the First Amendment in construing it, instead of invoking multitudes of words substantial for those the Framers used . . .

I like my privacy as well as the next one, but I am nevertheless compelled to admit that the government has a right to invade it unless prohibited by some specific constitutional provision. For these reasons I cannot agree with the Court's judgment and the reasons it gives for holding this Connecticut law unconstitutional.

Black also disagreed with the arguments put forth by the majority using the Due Process Clause and the Ninth Amendment:

I think that if properly constructed neither the Due Process Clause nor the Ninth Amendment, nor both together, could under any circumstances be a proper basis for invalidating the Connecticut law. I discuss the due process and Ninth Amendment arguments together because on analysis they turn out to be the same thing—merely using different words to claim for this Court and the federal judiciary power to invalidate any legislative act which the judges find irrational, unreasonable or offensive . . . Surely it has to be admitted that no provision of the Court specifically gives such blanket power to courts to exercise such a supervisory veto over the wisdom and value of legislative policies and to hold unconstitutional those laws which they believe unwise or dangerous . . . The use by federal courts of such a formula or doctrine or whatnot to veto federal or state laws simply takes away from Congress and States the power to make laws based on their own judgment of fairness and wisdom and transfers that power to this Court for ultimate determination—a power which was specifically denied to federal courts by the convention that framed The Constitution.

Justice Stewart added:

If, as I should surely hope, the law before us does not reflect the standards of the people of Connecticut, the people of Connecticut can freely exercise this true Ninth and Tenth Amendment rights to persuade their elected representatives to repeal it. That is the constitutional way to take this law off the books.

3) **Johnson v. Transportation Agency, Santa Clara County** (480 U.S. 616-677, 1987). Paul E. Johnson, sued his employer, the Transportation Agency of the Santa Clara County, California, for violating Title VII of the Civil Rights Act of 1964 by its refusal to promote him to the position of road dispatcher for which he was qualifed because of his merits. The agency had announced a job vacancy, and nine of the twelve employee applicants were found to be qualified, and seven were eligible for selection since the seven received scores above the minimum requirement. Johnson was recommended for the promotion but a female employee (Diane Joyce) who also received a qualifying but lower score, complained to the county's Affirmative Action Office about not receiving the promotion. That office contacted the Agency's Affirmative Action

Coordinator who then recommended promoting her in place of Johnson, and subsequently the Agency's Director gave her the job instead of Johnson.

The U. S. District Court for the Northern District of California "found that Johnson was more qualified for the dispatcher position than Joyce, and that the sex of Joyce was the 'determining factor' in her selection." The Court of Appeals for the Ninth Circuit reversed the decision based on the Agency's Affirmative Action Plan was only an objective and was not dispositive. The Supreme Court then decided to evaluate the Court of Appeals decision.

Justice William J. Brennan, Jr., delivered the opinion of the Court:

We therefore hold that the Agency approximately took into account as one factor the sex of Diane Joyce in determining that she should be promoted to the road dispatcher position. The decision to do so was made pursuant to an affirmative action plan that represents a moderate, flexible, case-by-case approval to effecting a gradual improvement in the representation of minorities and women in the Agency's workforce . . . Accordingly, the judgment of the Court of Appeals is Affirmed.

Justice Antonio Scalia dissented, with the Chief Justice William Rehnquist joining him in the dissent. Justice Byron White also dissented. Justice Scalia used the actual law as the justification for his dissent: "With a clarity which, had it not proven so unavailing, one might well recommend as a model of statutory draftsmanship, Title VII of the Civil Rights Act of 1964 declares:

It shall be an unlawful employment practice for an employer — (1) to fail or refuse to hire or to discharge any individual, or otherwise to discriminate against any individual with respect to his compensation, terms, conditions, or privileges of employment, because of such individual's race, color, religion, sex, or national origin; or (2) to limit, segregate, or classify his employees or applicants for employment in any way which would deprive or tend to deprive any individual of employment opportunities or otherwise adversely affect his status as an employee, because of such individual's race, color, religion, sex, or national origin.

The court today completes the process of converting this from a guarantee that race or sex will not be the basis for employment determinations, to a guarantee that it often will. Ever so subtly, . . . we effectively replace the goal of a discrimination-free society with the quite incompatible goal of proportionate representation by race and by sex in the workplace. . . . The most significant proposition of law established by today's decision is that racial or sexual discrimination is permitted under Title VII when it is intended to overcome the effect, not of the employer's own discrimination, but of societal attitudes that have limited the entry of certain races, or of a particular sex, into certain jobs."

REFERENCES

CHAPTER 1 and INTRODUCTION

(1) Tom Peters, *Thriving on Chaos*, Alfred A. Knopf, Inc., New York (1987), p. 580.

(2) Nicolo Machiavelli, *The Prince*, The New American Library, N.Y. (1952), p. 49.

(3) Douglas McGregor, *The Professional Manager*, McGraw Hill Book Co., New York (1967), pp. 35-36, 116-118, 123-124.

(4) Warren G. Bennis and Philip E. Slater, *The Temporary Society*, Harper and Row, Publishers, New York (1968), pp. 114-117.

(5) *The Bible*, King James Version, Exodus, 18th Chapter.

(6) Peter F. Drucker, *Management: Tasks, Responsibilities, Practices*, Harper and Row, New York (1973), pp. 21-23.

(7) Warren G. Bennis, "The Coming Death of Bureaucracy," *Think*, published by IBM, (1966); also p. 11, Cleland and King, see following reference.

(8) David I. Cleland and William R. King, *Systems, Organizations, Analysis, Management*, McGraw Hill Book Co., New York (1969), pp. 1-2.

(9) Douglas McGregor, *The Human Side of Enterprise*, McGraw Hill, New York (1960), pp. 3-4, 38-40.

(10) Thomas J. Peters and Robert H. Waterman, Jr., *In Search of Excellence*, Harper and Row, New York (1982), p. 58.

(11) Robert R. Blake, Jane S. Mouton, *Productivity: The Human Side*, AMACON, New York (1981), pp. 17, 19-21.

(12) J. Douglas Brown, *The Human Nature of Organizations*, AMACOM, New York (1973), pp. 1, 4-5, 136-138.

(13) Ben Heirs and Gordon Pehrson, *The Mind of the Organization*, Harper and Row Pub., New York (1982), pp. 1, 4-5, 11-20, xi.

(14) James J. Cribbin, Leadership, *Strategies for Organizational Effectiveness*, AMACOM, New York (1981), p. 52.

(15) L. M. Miller, *Barbarians to Bureaucrats*, Clarkson W. Potter, Inc., New York (1989), pp. 1-2, 216-222, 165, 8.

(16) Allen Weiss, *The Organization Guerrilla*, Antheneum, New York (1975), pp. 13-14.

(17) George C. Homans, "Social Behavior as Exchange," *American Journal of Sociology*, Vol. 62 (May 1958), pp. 597-606; also reprinted: D.R. Hampton, C. E. Summer, R. A. Webber, *Organization Behavior and the Positive of Management*, Scott, Foresom & Co., Glenville, IL (1968), pp. 40-51.

(18) Robert R. Blake and Jane Srygley Mouton, *Productivity The Human Side*, AMACOM, New York (1981), Chap. 2.

(19) Chris Argyris, *Personality and Organization*, Harper & Row, New York (1957); also D. R. Hampton, et al., Loc. cit., pp. 150, 281, 23.

(20) Stuart M. Klein and R. Richard Ritt, *Understanding Organizational Behavior*, 2nd edn., Kent Pub. Co., Boston, MA (1984), p. 377.

(21) D. R. Hampton, et al., Loc. cit., pp. 281-283.

(22) Ibid.

(23) Chester I. Barnard, *The Function of the Executive*, Harvard Univ. Press, Cambridge, MA (1938), pp. 115, 123.

(24)   Fred E. Katz, "Explaining Informal Work Groups in Complex Organizations," *Administrative Science Quarterly*, Vol. 10, No. 2 (Sept. 1965), pp. 204-221; also D. Cleland and W. King, Loc. cit., pp. 320-327.

(25)   J. Douglas Brown, Loc. cit., pp. 68-72.

(26)   Peter F. Drucker, Loc. cit., p. 504.

CHAPTER 2

(1)   *The Machiavellians Defenders of Freedom*, James Burnham, Books for Libraries Press, Freeport, NY (1943), p. 166, etc.; also Robert Michels, *Political Parties*, Hearst's International Library Co., New York (1915) [English translation by Eden and Ceder Paul].

(2)   Cyril Northcote Parkinson, *Parkinson: The Law*, Boston, MA, Houghton Mifflin Co. (1980), p. 199.

(3)   Peter M. Blau and W. Richard Scott, *Formal Organizations*, San Francisco, CA, Chandler Pub. Co. (1962), p. 6.

(4)   John Gall, *SYSTEMANTICS: How SYSTEMs Work and Especially How They Fail*, Pocket Books, New York (1975), pp. 9-134.

(5)   Tom Peters and Nancy Austin, *A Passion for Excellence*, Warner Books, Inc., New York (1985), p. 380.

(6)   Philip Crosby, *Quality is Free*, McGraw Hill Book Co., New York (Mentor Book Edition) (1979), p. 43.

(7)   Robert H. Hayes, Steven C. Wheelwright, and Kim B. Clark, *Dynamic Manufacturing*, The Free Press, New York (1988), p. 15.

(8)   Thomas J. Peters and Robert H. Waterman, Jr., Loc. cit., p. 267.

(9)   J. D. Batten, *Tough-Minded Management*, American Mgmt. Assoc., New York (1963), pp. 110-111; see also David L. Yunich, *How to Kill Progress*, The Economic Press (1958).

(10)   Laurence J. Peter, *The Peter Pyramid*, William Morrow & Co., Inc., New York (1986), pp. 76-77.

(11)   Charles B. Handy, *Understanding Organizations*, Facts on File Publications, New York (1976, 1981, 1985), p. 235.

(12)   George Box, "When Murphy Speaks — Listen," *Quality Progress*, ASQC, Milwaukee, WI, Vol. XX11, No. 10 (Oct. 1989), pp. 79-84.

(13)   Paul Dickson, *The Official Rules*, Dell Publishing Co., Inc., New York (1978), p. 104.

(14)   D. McGregor, Loc. cit., (1960) p. 33.

(15)   J. M. Juran, "Management's Corner," *Industrial Quality Control*, ASQC, Milwaukee, WI (Feb. 1955), p. 27.

(16)   A. V. Figenbaum, "Quality and Productivity," *Quality Progress*, ASQC, Milwaukee, WI (Nov. 1977), p. 21; also "Quality and Business Growth Today," *Quality Progress* (Nov. 1982); also "How to compete with quality," *Industry Week*, Penton Pub. Co., Stanford, CT (April 1984), p. 8.

(17)   Jeffrey O. Miller and Thomas E. Vollman, "The Hidden Factory," *Harvard Business Review*, Boston, MA, Vol. 63, No. 5 (Sept.-Oct. 1985), p. 142.

(18)   Wesley G. Matthei, "Hidden Factory," Letter to Editor, *Harvard Business Review*, Boston, MA, Vol. 63, No. 6, (Nov.-Dec. 1985), p. 239.

(19)   Arthur Block, *Murphy's Law and Other Reasons Why Things go Wrong!*, Price, Stern, Sloan Publishers, Inc., Los Angeles, CA (1978), p. 51.

(20)   Peter F. Drucker, *The Changing World of the Executive*, Random House, Inc., New York (1982/1985), p. 115.

(21)   Max Gammon, *Health and Security: Report on Public Provision for Medical Care in Great Britain*, St. Michael's Organization, London, England (Dec. 1976), p. 27; also quoted in Milton & Rose Friedman, *Free to Chose*, Harcourt, Brace, and Javanovich, Inc., New York (1979), p. 154.

(22)   Milton and Rose Friedman, *Tyranny of The Status Quo*, Harcourt, Brace, Jovanovich, Inc., Orlando, FL (1983), pp. 42, 165.

(23)   Philip Crosby, Loc. cit., p. 15.

(24)   T. Peters, Loc. cit., p. 99.

(25)   Patrick L. Townsend with Joan E. Gebhardt, *Commit to Quality*, J. Wiley and Sons, Inc., New York (1986), pp. 6, 127.

(26)   John Young, "Executives urge quality strategy," *Update*, American Electronics Assoc. (Nov. 1983), p. 1.

(27)   George Fisher, "Your business health is in your hands," *Update*, American Electronics Association, Santa Clara, CA (March 1987), p. 8.

(28)   William E. Conway, "The Right Way to Manage," *Quality Progress*, ASQC, Milwaukee, WI, Vol. XXI, No.1 (Jan. 1988), p. 14.

CHAPTER 3

(1)   John Bartlett, *Familiar Quotations*, 13th edn., Little, Brown and Co., Boston, MA (1955), p. 12, also Rogers: Student's History of Philosophy.

(2)   T. Peters and N. Austin, Loc. cit., p. 292.

(3)   Ibid., p. 293.

(4)   Milton and Rose Friedman, *Tyranny of the Status Quo*, Loc. cit., p. 48.

(5)   Tibor R. Machan, "What We Should Teach The Eastern Europeans," *The Freeman*, Vol. 40, No. 1, Irvington-on-Hudson, NY (Jan. 1990), p. 24.

(6)   Karel van Wolferen, *The Enigma of Japanese Power*, Alfred A. Knopf, New York (1989), pp. 3, 5.

(7)   Ibid., p. 43.

(8)   Ibid., pp. 48-49.

(9)   Ibid., p. 409.

(10)   Hernando de Soto, *The Other Path*, Harper and Row, Pub., New York (1989).

(11)   Mario Vargas Llosa, Ibid., pp. xiv-xv.

(12)   W. Edwards Deming, *Out of the Crisis*, MIT, Center for Advance Engineering Study, Cambridge, MA (1982, 1986), p. 1.

(13)   Ibid., pp. 314-318.

(14)   Donald Christiansen, "A SYSTEM gone awry," *IEEE Spectrum*, Vol. 24, No. 3 (March 1987), p. 23.

(15)   Myron Lieberman, *Privatization and Educational Choice*, St. Martin's Press, New York (1989).

334

(16)   Warren T. Brookes, "Public Education and the Global Failure of Socialism," *IMPRIMIS*, Hillsdale College, Hillsdale, MI, Vol. 19, No. 4 (April 1990).

(17)   Newt Gingrich, "The Life of the Party," *Policy Review*, Washington, DC, No. 51 (Winter 1990), p. 6.

(18)   Sven Rydenfelt, *A Pattern for Failure Socialist Economics in Crisis*, Harcourt, Brace, Jovanovich Publishers, San Diego, CA (1984), p. 36.

(19)   Lester R. Brown, "U.S. and Soviet Agriculture: The Shifting Balance of Power," *Worldwatch Paper* 51 (Oct. 1982), p. 12.

(20)   Henry Grunwald, "'The West's Challenge, as Communism Declines,'" *The Wall Street Journal*, New York (June 12, 1989).

(21)   Paul Craig Roberts, "Are America's Liberals to the Left of Gorbachev?," *Business Week*, New York (Sept. 7, 1987), p. 14.

(22)   Charles Peters and James Fallows (eds.), *THE SYSTEM The Five Branches of American Government*, Praeger Publishers, New York (1976), p. 4.

(23)   Jerome R. Waldie and Michael D. Green, "Congress and the Realities of Life on Capital Hill," Ibid., pp. 55-80.

(24)   Henry J. Hyde, "Morals, Markets, and Freedom," *National Review*, New York (Nov. 5, 1990), pp. 52-54.

(25)   Robert Rector, "America's Poverty Myth," *The Wall Street Journal*, New York (Sept. 3, 1992).

(26)   Most of the above examples were given by Ralph R. Roiland, "Plundering America for the Banks of the Potomac," *Human Events*, Vol. L, No. 5, Washington, DC (Nov. 10, 1990), p. 968.

(27)   Warren T. Brookes, "Dead Wrong Again," *National Review*, Vol. XLIII, New York (Oct. 7, 1991), p. 32.

(28)   Justice Leonard Hand, Commissioner of Internal Revenue vs. Newmen, 159 F.2d 848, 850-851 (2d Cir 1947).

(29)   Robert E. Hall and Alvin Rabushka, *Low Tax, Simple Tax, Flat Tax*, McGraw-Hill Book Co., New York (1983), p. 39.

(30)   M. Stanton Evans, "Government Now Absorbing 50 Per Cent of GNP," *Human Events* (Feb. 8, 1992), p. 8.

(31)   Lawrence A. Hunter, Donald R. Leavens, and Orawin T. Velz, "The Hoax on You," *Policy Review*, No. 51, Washington, DC (Winter 1990), p. 62.

(32)   *United States Constitution*, Article III, Section 1.

(33)   Robert G. McCloskey (ed.) *The Works of James Wilson*, Vol. 1, , Harvard University Press, Cambridge, MA (1967), p. 75.

(34)   Alexander Hamilton, *The Federalist*, Book II, Tudor Publishing Co., New York (1937), p. 101.

(35)   Daniel J. Popeo, "Privatizing the Judiciary," *The Freeman*, Vol. 38, No. 8, Irvington- on-Hudson, New York (Aug. 1988), pp. 300-301.

(36)   Doug Bandow, *The Politics of Plunder*, Transaction Publishers, New Brunswick, NJ (1990), pp. 267-274.

(37)   James McClellan, "A Lawyer Looks at Rex Lee," *Benchmark*, Washington, DC (March-April, 1984), p. 2.

(38)   Raoul Berger, *Government by Judiciary, The Transformation of the Fourteenth Amendment*, Harvard University Press, Cambridge, MA (1977), p. 304-307.

(39)   James McClellan, Loc. cit., p. 14.

(40)   Walter Berns, *Taking The Constitution Seriously*, Simon and Schuster, New York (1987), pp. 214, 206.

(41)   Roger Pilon, "Rethinking Judicial Restraint," *The Wall Street Journal*, New York (Feb. 1, 1991).

(42)   James T. Bennett and Thomas J. DiLorenzo, *Unfair Competition*, Hamilton Press, Lanham, MD (1989), Chap. 7, pp. 177-198.

(43)   Edward M. Brecker, et al, "Licit and Illicit Drugs," *Consumers Union*, Mount Vernon, NY (1972), p. 50.

(44)   D. Bandow, Loc. cit., pp. 382-385.

(45)   Cox New Service, "Administration Claims Gains in Drug War," *Sarasota Herald-American*, Sarasota, FL (Sept. 6, 1991).

(46)   Leroy L. Schwartz, "The Medical Costs of America's Social Ills," *The Wall Street Journal*, New York (June 24, 1991).

(47)   David Frum, "English Canadians Get Ready to Say Goodbye to Quebec," *The Wall Street Journal*, New York (April 5, 1991).

(48)   William D. Gairdner, *The Trouble With Canada*, Stoddart Publishing Co. Limited, Toronto, Canada (1990), p. 203.

(49)   Most of this section is from Hernando De Soto, Loc. cit.

(50)   Jeane Kirkpatrick, "Leading the revolution of Freedom in Peru," *Los Angeles Times Syndicate*, Los Angeles, CA (April 11, 1990).

(51)   Alvaro Vargas Llosa, "Peru: Another Link in the BCCI MoneyLaundering Chain?", *The Wall Street Journal*, New York (May 17, 1991).

(52)   Walter Palomino Villamonte, "The Case for Fujimori's Coup", *The Wall Street Journal*, New York (April 16, 1992).

(53)   Karel van Wolferen, Loc. cit., p. 2.

(54)   Robert Chapman Wood, "Micro Economics," *Policy Review*, The Heritage Foundation, No. 42, Washington, DC (Fall 1987), pp. 54-55.

(55)   Karen Lowry Miller, "Just-in-Time is Becoming Just a Pain," *Business Week*, McGraw Hill, New York (June 17, 1991), p. 100H.

(56)   News Item, "Work-Centered Lives in Japan," *The Wall Street Journal*, New York (Aug. 12, 1991).

(57)   Yumiko Ono, "Women's Movement in Corporate Japan Isn't Moving Very Fast," *The Wall Street Journal*, New York (June 6, 1991).

(58)   News Item, "Japanese Salaries Set a High," *The Wall Street Journal*, New York (Oct. 8, 1991).

(59)   Karel van Wolferen, Loc. cit., pp. 5-9.

(60)   W. Edwards Deming, *Out of the Crisis*, Loc. cit., pp. 97-148.

(61)   Ibid., pp. 24-26, 98.

(62)   Ibid., pp. 99-100.

(63)   Ibid., pp. 102-103.

(64)   Ibid., p. 121.

(65)   H. Thomas Johnson and Robert S. Kaplan, *Relevance Lost*, Harvard Business School Press, Boston, MA (1987, 1991), p. 1.

(66)   Ibid, pp. 256-258.

(67)   W. E. Deming, Loc. cit., pp. 59-61.

(68)   Donald Lambro, "Congress Didn't Lay a Glove on Deficit," *Human Events*, Vol. L, No. 49, Washington, DC (Dec. 8, 1990), p. 16.

(69)   Karel van Wolferan, Loc. cit., pp. 12, 375-407.

(70)   National Conference of Catholic Bishops, Washington, DC (Nov. 11, 1984).

(71)   Michael Novak, *The Spirit of Democratic Capitalism*, Simon and Schuster, New York (1982), p. 287.

336

(72) Stephen Knack, "Why We Don't Vote, or Say Thank You," *The Wall Street Journal*, New York (Dec. 31, 1990), p. 6.

(73) Thomas G. Gunn, *Manufacturing for Competitive Advantage*, Ballinger Pub. Co., Cambridge, MA (1987), pp. 1-2.

(74) Ibid., pp. 2-3.

(75) Kiyoshi Suzaki, *The New Manufacturing Challenge — Techniques for Continuous Improvement*, The Free Press, Div. of Macmillan, Inc., New York (1987).

(76) Thomas J. Peters and Robert H. Waterman, Jr., Loc. cit.; Tom Peters and Nancy Austin, Loc. cit.

(77) Warren T. Brookes, "Deindustrialization Never Materialized," *Human Events*, Washington, DC (March 9, 1991), p. 11.

CHAPTER 4

(1) Martin Van Buren, *Inquiry into the Origin and Course of Political Parties* (1867); see also, *The Bully Pulpit*, Elizabeth Frost (ed.), Facts on File Publication, New York (1988) p. 159.

(2) Milovan Djilas, *The New Class*, Frederick A. Praeger, Publisher, N.Y. (1957).

(3) Paul Craig Roberts and Karen LaFollette, *Meltdown Inside the Soviet Economy*, CATO Institute, Washington, DC, pp. 15-22.

(4) Ibid., p. 25.

(5) Djilas, Loc. cit., p. 67.

(6) Vladimir Bukovsky, "In Russia, Is It 1905 Again?," *The Wall St. Journal*, New York (Nov. 27, 1989).

(7) Roberts, et al., p. 10.

(8) Ibid., p. 8.

(9) Ibid., p. 137.

(10) K. van Wolferen, Loc. cit., pp.212-213.

(11) Ibid., pp. 5, 25.

(12) Gary M. Anderson, "Profits from Power: The Soviet Economy as a Mercantilist State," *The Freeman*, Vol. 38, The Foundation for Economic Education, Irvington-on-Hudson, New York (Dec. 1988), p. 483.

(13) K. van Wolferen, Loc. cit., pp. 44-45.

(14) Ibid., pp. 212-225.

(15) Ibid., pp. 55-80.

(16) Thomas Rohlen, *Japan's High Schools*, Univ. of California Press (1983), p. 209.

(17) K. van Wolferen, Loc. cit., pp. 82-83.

(18) Ibid., pp. 93-109, 136.

(19) Hernando de Soto, Loc. cit., pp. xiv-xv, 197.

(20) Ibid., pp. 5-6.

(21) Ibid., pp. 189-194.

(22) Winston S. Churchill, *A History of the English Speaking Peoples: The Great Democracies*, Vol. 4, Dodd, Mead and Co., New York (1958), pp. 104-106.

(23) *Encyclopedia Britannica — 1983 Book of the Year*, Encyclopedia Britannica, Inc., Chicago, IL (1983), pp. 225-226.

(24) William D. Gairdner, Loc. cit., pp. 63-65, 422.

(25)   Ibid., pp. 137-159.

(26)   Curtin Winsor Jr., "Change in Canada could signal problems for the elephant," *Bangor Daily News*, Bangor, ME (June 25, 1991).

(27)   W. D. Gairdner, Loc. cit., p. 390.

(28)   Ibid., pp. 410-414.

(29)   James L. Payne, "Why Congress Can't Kick The Tax and Spend Habit," *IMPRIMIS*, Hillsdale College, MI (May 1991).

(30)   James T. Bennett and Thomas J. DiLorenzo, *Destroying Democracy*, Cato Institute, Washington, DC (1985), pp. 386-387.

(31)   James L. Payne, Loc. cit.

(32)   Christopher Cox (Representative, U.S. Congress), "How Congress Adopted Transportation Boondoggle," *Human Events* (Dec. 14, 1991), pp. 5-6.

(33)   Randy Fitzgerald, "Pork and Gravy and Damn the Cost", *Reader's Digest*, Pleasantville, N.Y., October 1992, p.208.

(34)   John McCain, Senator, *Congressional Record*, Washington, D.C., November 9, 1989, p. S15345.

(35)   John Fiske, *Civil Government in the United States*, Houghton Mifflin and Co., Boston, MA (1891), p. 22.

(36)   John E. Chubb, Terry M. Moe, *Politics, Markets, and America's Schools*, The Brookings Institution, Washington, DC (1990), p. 3.

(37)   David B. Tyack, *The One Best SYSTEM: A History of American Urban Education*, Harvard Univ. Press, Cambridge, MA (1974).

(38)   Ellwood P. Cubberley, *Public School Administration: A Statement of the Fundamental Principles Underlying the Organization and Administration of Public Education*, Houghton Mifflin and Co., Boston, MA (1916).

(39)   Michael B. Katz, *Class, Bureaucracy and Schools: The Illusion of Educational Change in America*, Praeger (1971).

(40)   J. E. Chubb, et al., Loc. cit., p. 4.

(41)   Reginald G. Damerell, *Education's Smoking Gun: How Teachers Colleges Have Destroyed Education in America*, Freundlich Books, New York (1985), p. 71.

(42)   Ibid., p. 89.

(43)   James B. Koener, *The Miseducation of American Teachers*, p. 17, quoted by Reginald G. Damerell, Loc. cit., p. 125.

(44)   C. Emily Feistritzer, "Break the Teaching Monopoly," *The Wall Street Journal*, New York (June 29, 1990).

(45)   Warren T. Brookes, "Public Education and the Global Failure of Socialism", *IMPRIMIS*, Hillsdale College, Hillisdale, MI, April 1990, p. 1.

(46)   William Murchison, "Money in Education: Gets 'A' for Power, 'F' for Progress," *Human Events*, Washington, DC (April 21, 1990), p. 20.

(47)   William J. Bennett, "The Report Card on American Education 1993," American Legislative Exchange Council, Washington, D.C., (Sept.1993).

(48)   Reginald G. Damerell, Loc. cit., p. 190.

(49)   Stewart Dill McBride, "The literary Galbraith on the art of writing," *Christian Science Monitor* (Dec. 9, 1975), p. 7; also quoted in Reginald G. Damerell, Loc. cit., p. 261.

(50)   Bella Rosenberg, *American Education* (Summer 1989); also quoted by Robert W. Carr, "Markets Can't Fix Schools' Problems," *The Wall Street Journal*, New York (May 2, 1991).

338

(51)   Milton and Rose Freidman, *Free to Choose*, Harcourt Brace Jovanovich, New York (1980), pp. 175-183.

(52)   Martin Anderson, *Impostors in The Temple*, Simon & Schuster, NY,NY, 1992, p.15.

(53)   Dick Armey, "Socialism on Campus", *The Wall Street Journal*, NY, NY, August 19, 1992, p. A10.

(54)   Edmund F. Haislmaier, "Why America's Health Care Service is in Trouble," *Critical Issues: A National Health System for America*, Stuart M. Butter and E. F. Haislmaier (eds.), The Heritage Foundation, Washington, DC (1989), p. 5.

(55)   David T. Beito, "When Americans Took Care of Themselves," *The Wall Street Journal*, New York (May 28, 1991).

(56)   E. Haislmaier, Loc. cit., pp. 6-7.

(57)   Peter G. Peterson and Neil Howe, *On Borrowed Time*, Simon and Schuster, Inc., New York (1988), p. 194.

(58)   Dorothy Ganfield Fowler, *Unmailable — Congress and The Post Office*, The Univ. of Georgia Press, Athens, GA (1977), pp. 1-8, 9-14, 19.

(59)   Ernest L. Bogart and Donald L. Kemmerer, *Economic History of the American People*, Longmans, Green and Co., New York (1942), pp. 621-622.

(60)   D. G. Fowler, Loc. cit., pp. 187-188, 192-202.

(61)   Melvin D. Barger, "Free-Market Mail Is on the Horizon," *The Freeman*, Vol. 37, The Foundation for Economic Education, Irvington-on-Hudson, New York (1987), p. 286.

(62)   Robert J. Myers, *The Coming Collapse of The Post Office*, Prentice-Hall, Inc., Englewood Cliffs, NJ (1975), p. 29

(63)   James Bovard, "'On-Time' Delivery: The Great Mail Fraud," *The Wall Street Journal*, New York (Jan. 30, 1991), p. A10.

(64)   Richard L. Lesher, "Postal Service Stampedes Toward Another Rate Hike," *Human Events*, Washington, DC (May 19, 1990), p. 17.

(65)   Charles Warren, *Congress, The Constitution and The Supreme Court*, Little, Brown, and Company, Boston, MA (1935), p. 22.

(66)   Felix Morley, *Freedom and Federalism*, Henry Regency Company, Chicago (1959), p. 229.

(67)   Charles Warren, Loc. cit., pp. 22-39.

(68)   William H. Rehnquist, *The Supreme Court: How it Was, How it Is*, William Morrow and Co., Inc., New York (1987), pp. 219-234.

(69)   H. Thomas Johnson and Robert S. Kaplan, *Relevance Lost The Rise and Fall of Management Accounting*, Harvard Business School Press, Boston, MA (1991).

(70)   Irving L. Janis, *Victims of Group-Think* (1972); also Charles B. Handy, *Understanding Organizations*, 3rd edn., Facts on File Publications, New York (1985), pp. 169-170.

(71)   Frederick Herzberg, B. Mausner and B. Snyderman, *The Motivation to Work*, John Wiley, New York (1959).

(72)   *National Drug Control Strategy, Budget Summary*, Office of National Drug Control Policy, Executive Office of the President, Washington, DC (Jan. 1992), pp. 1-214.

(73)   Michael Hammer and James Champy, *Reengineering the Corporation*, HarperCollins, Publishers, N Y, (1993), pp. 149-199.

CHAPTER 5

(1)   Woodrow Wilson, Speech, Detroit, MI (July 10, 1916).

(2)   Leon Martel, *Mastering Change*, Simon and Schuster, New York (1986), p. 32.

(3)   Ibid., p. 180.

(4)   Walter A Shewhart, *Economic Control of Quality of Manufactured Product*, Van Nostrand, N.Y. (1931); Republished by ASQC, Milwaukee, WI (1980), p. 6.

(5)   L. Martel, Loc. cit., p. 251-300.

(6)   Kiyushi Suzaki, *The New Manufacturing Challenge*, The Free Press, Div. of MacMillen, Inc., New York (1987), pp. 146-179.

(7)   Eliyahu M. Goldratt and Jeff Cox, *The Goal, A Process of Ongoing Improvement*, Revised edn., North River Press, Inc., Croton-on-Hudson, NY (1986), p. 9.

(8)   A. V. Feigenbaum, *Total Quality Control*, McGraw Hill Book Company, Inc., New York (1961), p. 12.

(9)   Tom Inglesby, "An Interview with John Young," HP/Manufacturing Systems, Hitchcock Publishing Co., Carol Stream, IL (June 1991), p. 2.

(10)   George Stalk, Jr., "Time — The Next Source of Competitive Advantage," *Harvard Business Review* (July-Aug. 1988), pp. 41-51.

(11)   John J. Kendrick, "New IQS Performance-Based Model for Quality Management Shows What Works Best," *Quality*, Hitchcock Publishing Company, Carol Stream, IL (Nov. 1992), p.11.

(12)   William E. Conway, "The World Competition Secret," paper given at Annual Meeting of The Society of Automotive Engineers Quality and Productivity Conference, Dearborn, MI (Sept. 25, 1985); also *The Quality Secret: The Right Way to Manage*, Conway Quality, Inc., Nashua, NH (1992), pp. 167-190.

(13)   W.E. Conway, "The Right Way to Manage," *Quality Progress*, Vol. XXI, No. 1 (Jan. 1988), p. 15; also *The Quality Secret: The Right Way to Manage*, Conway Quality, Inc., Nashua, NH (1992), pp. 29-131.

(14)   D. McGregor, Loc. cit. (1960), p. 45.

(15)   Richard J. Schonberger, *World Class Manufacturing*,The Free Press, Division of McMillian, Inc., New York, (1986), p. 126.

(16)   Masaaki Imai, *KAIZEN*, McGraw Hill Publishing Company, New York, (1986), pp. 239-240.

(17)   Eliyahu M. Goldratt and Robert E. Fox, *The Race*, North River Press, Croton-on- Hudson, NY (1986).

(18)   Peter F. Drucker, *Management-Tasks, Responsibilities, Practices*, Harper and Row, Pub., New York (1973), p. 440.

(19)   W. Edwards Deming, *Out of the Crisis*, MIT Center for Advanced Engineering Study, Cambridge, MA (1982/1986), pp. 121-126.

(20)   H. Thomas Johnson and Robert S. Kaplan, *Relevance Lost: The Rise and Fall of Management Accounting*, Harvard Business School Press, Boston, MA (1991), pp. 227-251.

(21)   Stephen R. Covey, *The Seven Habits of Highly Effective People*, Simon and Schuster, New York (1990), p.42.

(22)   T. Peters, *Thriving on Chaos*, Harper & Row, New York (1987), p. 4.

CHAPTER 6

(1)   Henry Ford, *Forbes*, New York, (January 1, 1928).
(2)   John Naisbitt and Patricia Aburdene, *Re-inventing the Corporation*, Warner Books, Inc., New York (1985), p. 42.
(3)   W. E. Deming, Loc. cit., pp. 373-377.
(4)   C. Argyris, Loc. cit., pp. 140-145.
(5)   Victor A. Thompson, "Bureaucracy and Bureaupathology," *Organizational Behavior and Practice of Management*, David R. Hampton, Charles E. Summer, Ross A. Webber, Scott, Foresman and Co., Atlanta, GA (1968), p. 228; also from *Modern Organization*, Alfred A. Knopf, Inc., New York (1961).
(6)   Paul Watzlawick, John Weakland, and Richard Fisch, *Change — Principles of Problem Formation and Problem Resolution*, W. E. Norton & Co., N.Y. (1974).
(7)   Ibid., p. 2.
(8)   Ibid., pp. 2-5.
(9)   Ibid., p. 6.
(10)   Alfred North Whitehead and Bertrand Russell, *Principia Mathematica*, 2nd edn., abridged to *56, Cambridge University Press, Cambridge, London, England (1910-1962), p. 37.
(11)   P. Watzlawick, et al., Loc. cit., p. 6.
(12)   W. Ross Ashby, *An Introduction to Cybernetics*, Chapman and Hall, London, England (1956), p. 43; also quoted in Watzlawick, et al., Loc. cit., p. 9.
(13)   P. Watzlawick, et al., Loc. cit., pp. 9-10.
(14)   Ibid., pp. 10-12.
(15)   Herbert Butterfield, *The Origins of Modern Science*, London, England (1949), pp. 1-7; also rev. edn., The Free Press, New York (1965); quoted by: Thomas S. Kuhn, *The Structure of Scientific Revolution*, U. of Chicago Press, Chicago, IL, (1970), p. 85.
(16)   Arthur Koestler, *The Act of Creation*, ARKNA, Penguin Group, London, England (1964), pp. 35-38.
(17)   Ibid., p. 73.
(18)   Ibid., p. 651.
(19)   Ibid., pp. 659-660.
(20)   P. Watzlawick, et al., Loc. cit., pp. 81-83.
(21)   Ibid., pp. 83-85.
(22)   Ibid., pp. 90-91.
(23)   Ibid., p. 95.
(24)   Ibid., p. 110.
(25)   Max Black, *Models and Metaphores*, Cornell Universiry Press, Ithaca, NY (1962), pp. 236-237.
(26)   Ikujiro Nonaka, "The Knowledge-Creating Company," *Harvard Business Review* (Nov.- Dec. 1991), pp. 96-104.
(27)   *The Holy Bible*, King James Version, Thomas Nelson, Publishers, Nashville, TN, St. Luke 5:18-26.
(28)   Ibid., St. Mark 8:35; see also St. Luke 5:24.
(29)   "Exodus," *The Holy Bible*, King James Version, Thomas Nelson, Publishers, Nashville, TN, Chap. 14, Verses 21, 22.
(30)   A. Koestler, Loc. cit., pp. 121-144.

(31)   Eugen von Bohm-Bawerk, *Capital and Interest*, Vol. II, Libertarian Press, South Holland, IL (1959), pp. 127-183.

(32)   Murray N. Rothbard, "The Essential Ludwig von Mises," *Planning for Freedom*, 4th edn., Ludwig von Mises, Libertarian Press, South Holland, IL (1980), p. 235.

(33)   Ibid., p. 239.

(34)   Michael Beer, Russell A. Eisenstat, and Bert Spector, *The Critical Path to Corporate Renewal*, Harvard Business School Press, Cambridge, MA (1990), pp. 1-2.

(35)   Ibid., p. 29.

(36)   Ibid., pp. 45-61.

(37)   Peter F. Drucker, "Don't Change Corporate Culture — Use It!", *The Wall Street Journal*, New York (March 28, 1991).

(38)   Philip R. Thomas and Kenneth R. Martin, *Competitiveness Through Total Cycle Time*, McGraw-Hill Pub. Co., New York (1990).

(39)   T. Peters, Loc. cit., pp. 340-355.

(40)   Ibid., pp. 57-338.

(41)   Philip B. Crosby, *Quality Is Free*, NAL Penguin, Inc., New York (1979), p. 9.

(42)   Ibid., pp. 108-110.

(43)   Ibid., p. 169.

(44)   M. Beer, et al., Loc. cit., p. 210.

(45)   C. N. Parkinson, Loc. cit., p. 13.

(46)   Peters, Loc. cit., pp. 635-653.

(47)   Edgar H. Schein, "Management and Development as a Process of Influence," *Industrial Management Review*, M.I.T., Cambridge, MA (May 1961), pp. 59-77; also reprinted in Hampton, et al., Loc. cit., pp. 525-539.

(48)   J. Naisbitt, et al., p. 137.

(49)   Charles Handy, *The Age of Unreason*, Harvard Business School Press, Boston, MA (1989), pp. 5-6, 25.

(50)   Donald Schon, *Displacements of Concepts*, Tavistock Publications Limited, London, England (1963).

(51)   M. Beer, et al., Loc. cit., pp. 94-95.

(52)   Michael Beer, Russell A. Eisenstat, and Bert Spector, "Why Change Programs Don't Produce Change," *Harvard Business Review*, Cambridge, MA (Nov.-Dec. 1990), p. 161.

(53)   T. Peters, Loc. cit., pp. 452-465.

(54)   Ibid., pp. 604-607.

(55)   Ibid., p. 585.

(56)   George E. P. Box, Loc. cit., pp. 79-84.

(57)   Kaoru Ishikawa, *Guide to Quality Control*, Kraus International Pub., White Plains, NY, UNIPUB (1982).

(58)   George E. P. Box, Loc. cit., p. 82.

(59)   D. Schon, Loc. cit., pp. 97-98.

CHAPTER 7

(1) William Shakespeare, *Hamlet*, Act 1, Sec. 5, line 166 (1601).

(2) *Congressional Quarterly* (Feb. 24, 1990), p. 567.

(3) Henry Steele Commager (ed.), *Documents of American History*, 5th edn., Appleton— Century—Crofts, Inc., New York, p. 112.

(4) *The Constitution of The Commonwealth of Massachusetts*; Part the First, Article VIII, (June 16, 1780).

(5) Robert E. Hall and Alvin Rabushker, Loc. cit., pp. 119-122.

(6) Walter H. Drew, "Original Intent: An Appointed Senate," *The Wall Street Journal*, New York (Dec. 14, 1990), p. A19 (Letter).

(7) Jonah J. Goldberg, "To Reform Congress, Enlarge It", *The Wall Street Journal*, New York, (Nov. 5, 1992), p. A16.

(8) James L. Sundquist, *Constitutional Reform and Effective Government*, The Bookings Institution, Washington DC (1986), pp. 1-251.

(9) Lamar Alexander, Speech to the Governor's Summit on Education in Kansas (Nov. 1989). Quoted in *Human Events*, Washington, DC (June 22, 1991), p. 4.

(10) Milton Friedman, "The Role of Government in Education," in:, *Economics and the Public Interest*, Robert A. Solo (ed.), Rutgers Univ. Press, New Brunswick, NJ (1955); also, *Capitalism and Freedom*, Univ. of Chicago Press, Chicago, IL (1962), pp. 85-107.

(11) Milton Friedman, *Free to Choose*, Harcourt Brace Jovanovich, New York (1979), p. 161; and "Vouchers No Threat to Church-State Split," *The Wall Street Journal*, New York (letter) (Dec. 31, 1991).

(12) Ibid., p. 162.

(13) Myron Lieberman, Loc. cit.

(14) John E. Chubb and Terry M. Moe, Loc. cit.

(15) Ibid., pp. 206-212.

(16) Ibid., p. 217.

(17) Ibid., p. 309.

(18) Ibid., pp. 219-229.

(19) Virgil C. Blum, S.J., *Freedom of Choice in Education*, Macmillian, New York (1958), pp. 39-48; also in: G. R. LaNoue (ed.), *Educational Vouchers: Concepts and Contraversies*, Teachers College Press, New York (1972), pp. 21-28.

(20) Charles Handy, Loc. cit., pp. 211-236.

(21) Stuart M. Butler and Edmund F. Haislmaier, *Critical Issues: A National Health System for America*, The Heritage Foundation, Washington, DC (1989), pp. v-viii.

(22) Ibid., pp. 50-90.

(23) John C. Goodman and Gerald L. Musgrave, "How to Solve The Health Care Crisis," *Human Events*, Washington, DC (Feb. 22, 1992), pp. 10-12.

(24) Hilary Scott, "Secretary Sullivan Calls for Summit on Health Costs," *The Wall Street Journal*, New York (Sept. 24, 1991).

(25) Michael Schwarz, "Deadly Traffic," *New York Times Magazine*, New York (March 22, 1987), p. 54.

(26) Milton Friedman, "An Open Letter to Bill Bennett," *The Wall Street Journal*, New York (Sept. 7, 1989); also *Newsweek*, New York (May 1, 1972).

(27) Kurt Schmoke, "Should hard drugs be legalized?," *St. Petersburg Times*, St. Petersburg, FL (June 5, 1988), p. 1D.

(28)   William J. Bennett, "A Response to Milton Friedman," *The Wall Street Journal*, New York (Sept. 19, 1989).

(29)   David Lawrence, "'Good Behavior' of Judges — Who Defines It?," *U.S. News and World Report*, Washington, DC (Oct. 7, 1968), p. 114; originally published on July 5, 1957.

(30)   David Evanier, Boris Shragin, "Will The Soviet Union Survive Until 1994?", *National Review* (April 7, 1989), pp. 25-26.

(31)   Thomas Jefferson, "First Inaugural Address," Washington, DC (March 4, 1801).

(32)   Karel van Wolferen; Loc. cit., pp. 432-433.

(33)   Hernando de Soto, Loc. cit., pp. 233-235.

(34)   Ibid., pp. 244-258.

(35)   William Gairdner, Loc. cit., pp. 439-450.

CHAPTER 8

(1)   David, Psalm 51, V.10, *Holy Bible*, King James Version.

(2)   Peter F. Drucker, *The Practice of Management*, Harper and Row, Publishers, New York (1954), p. 158.

(3)   Lawrence M. Miller, Loc. cit., pp. 173-189.

(4)   Craig R. Hickman and Michael A. Silva, *Creating Excellance*, New American Library, New York (1984), pp. 151-153.

(5)   Ibid., p. 159; also Warren Bennis, *The Temporary Society*, Harper and Row, Inc., New York (1968).

(6)   Peter M. Senge, *The Fifth Discipline*, Doubleday Currency, New York, pp. 14, 68.

(7)   Richard J. Schonberger, *World Class Manufacturing*, The Free Press, New York (1986), pp. 1-16.

(8)   Peter F. Drucker, "The New Productivity Challenge", *Harvard Business Review*, Boston, MA (Nov.-Dec. 1991), pp. 69-79.

(9)   Peter F. Drucker, *Management — Tasks, Responsibilities, Practices*, Harper and Row, New York (1973), p. 215.

(10)   B. Heirs and G. Pehrson, Loc. cit., pp. 11-12.

(11)   Ibid., p. 12.

(12)   Ibid., p. 23.

(13)   Michel Robert, Bernard Racine, and Craig Bowers, "A Worker's Mind Is a Terrible Thing to Waste," *Quality Progress*, Milwaukee, WI (Oct. 1990), p. 59.

(14)   J. Edward Russo and Paul J. H. Schoemaker, *Decision Traps*, Simon & Schuster, Inc., New York (1989), pp. xvi-xviii, 2-63.

(15)   P. F. Drucker, Loc. cit., pp. 398-399.

(16)   David T. Kearns, quoted in: Robert Camp, "Benchmarking: The Search for Industry Best Practices That Lead to Superior Performance," *Quality Progress*, ASQC, Milwaukee, WI (Jan. 1989), p. 62; also book by same title (1989), p. 10.

(17)   P. Crosby, Loc. cit., p. 24.

(18)   Richard J. Schonberger, Loc. cit., pp. 68-72.

(19)   Benjamin Franklin, "Advice to a young Tradesman, written by an old One," (July 21, 1748), *Benjamin Franklin — A Biography in His Own Words*, Harper and Row, Pub., New York (1972), p. 81.

(20)   P. R. Thomas, et al., Loc. cit., pp. x-xii.

344

(21)   T. Peters, Loc. cit., p. 98.
(22)   Ibid.
(23)   T. Peters, *THE TOM PETERS SEMINAR*, Vintage Books, A Div. of Random House, Inc., New York, (1994).
(24)   Robert H. Hayes, Steven C. Wheelwright, and Kim B. Clark, *Dynamic Manufacturing*, The Free Press, Div. of MacMillan, Inc., N.Y., (1988), p. 23.

CHAPTER 9

(1)   Rutherford B. Hayes, "The Republican Campaign," *New York Times*, New York (July 1876); also, Inaugural Address (March 5, 1877).

(2)   Hilary Scott, "Roads to Reform Health Care Choices: A Bigger Federal Role Or a Market Approach?," *The Wall Street Journal*, New York (Jan. 15, 1992).

(3)   J. L. Fraser, "Doctor: Health Care Should Be 'Socialized'," Letter to The Editor, *Sarasota Herald-Tribune*, Sarasota, FL (Jan. 26, 1992).

(4)   Gary Putka, "Teaching Aides Some Schools Give Parents Crucial Roles in Educating Children," *The Wall Street Journal*, New York (Dec. 30, 1991).

(5)   George F. Will, "Fresh funds for failing systems," *Sarasota Herald-Tribune*, Sarasota, FL (May 8, 1994), p.3F.

(6)   "Education Dinosaurs," Editorial, *The Wall Street Journal*, N. Y. (Jan. 27, 1992).

(7)   Gov. Carroll A. Campbell, Jr. and Gov. Roy Romer, letter as reported in the article, "Panel Wants Independent Educational Organization," by the *Los Angeles Times* and *Sarasota Herald-Tribune*, Sarasota, FL (Jan. 25, 1992).

(8)   Guest Editorial, *Times-Union*, Albany, N.Y., "The spy who should have been been spied upon," *Sarasota Herald-Tribune*, Sarasota, FL (Mar. 4, 1994), p.13A.

(9)   Neal R. Peirce, "Jail Crowding Issue Is a Sham," *Sarasota Herald-Tribune*, Sarasota, FL (Jan. 25, 1992).

(10)   George Melloan, "How to Teach Russians to Trust Their Money," *The Wall Street Journal*, New York (Jan. 27, 1992).

(11)   *Holy Bible*, Book of Matthew 7:1, King James Version.

(12)   Abraham Lincoln, "Second Inaugural Address," (March 4, 1865) *A Compilation of the Messages and Papers of the Presidents*, Bureau of National Literature, Inc., New York (1897), p. 3478.

(13)   Roger H. Slater, "Integrated Process Management: A Quality Model," *Quality Progress*, ASQC, Milwaukee, WI (May 1991), pp. 75-80.

(14)   Karou Ishikawa, *What is Total Quality Control? The Japanese Way*, Prentice-Hall, Englewood Cliffs, NJ (1985), p. 64.

(15)   Peter F. Drucker, *The Practice of Management*, Harper and Row, Publisher, New York (1954), pp. 130-133.

(16)   S. R. Covey, Loc. cit., pp. 17-61.

(17)   Kevin G. Salwen, "NLRB Says Labor-Management Teams at Firm Violated Company- Union Rule," *The Wall Street Journal*, New York (Dec. 12, 1992).

(18)   Dan Howard, Letter to the Editor, *Newsweek*, New York (Sept. 28, 1992), p. 13.

INDEX

346

DISCOUNT SCHEDULE

1-2 books	no discount
3-9 books	- 20%
10-199 books	- 40%
200-499 books	- 50%
500 and up books	- 40%, - 25%

TERMS AND CONDITIONS

- TERMS. Our terms are net 30 days from date of invoice. A finance charge of 1.5% per month will be added to all overdue balances over 60 days. Discounts will be forfeited if accounts are not paid within 90 days of due date.

- PURCHASE ORDERS. Orders over $50.00 must be postpaid or send credit references from three trade organizations and one bank.

- STOP. STOP orders for 1-2 books earn a 20% discount, and for 3-9 books a 40% discount. Please add $2.00 per book for shipping.

- SHORTAGES. Shortages or non-receipt must be reported to us within 30 days of the order date.

- SHIPPING. Shipping charges are added to all orders. Books are shipped via the U.S. Postal Services "book rate." Shipping is FOB Sarasota.

ORDER FORM

- **Fax orders:** (941) 379-9009
- **Telephone orders:** Call toll free 1 (888) 225-2855
  State credit card name, number, bank name, & expiration date
- **On-line orders:** WGMATTHEI@aol.com
- **Postal orders:** NUSYSTEMS
  N.E. Plaza, P.O. Box 14040
  Sarasota, FL 34278

- Please send the following number of copies [_____] of
  [Mis]Managing The System to the address below:

Company name: _____

Name: _____

Address: _____

City: _____ State: ___ Zip: _____

Telephone #: (___) _____

- I understand that within two months of purchase I may
  return any books in new condition along with a copy of the
  original invoice, for a full refund of the purchased price –
  for any reason, no questions asked.

- **Price $19.95 ea.** For 3 or more, see discount schedule on
  the reverse side. Price subject to change without notice.
  All costs higher outside the United States.

- Sales tax: Please add 7% for books shipped to FL address.

- Shipping: First book: $3.00, $2.00 for each additional book.

- **Payment:**
  - ☐ cheque [U.S. bank only]
  - ☐ credit card: ☐ VISA, ☐ Master Card, ☐ AMEX, ☐ Discover
    ☐ Diners Club

Card Number:_____Expiration_____

Name on card:_____

Name of bank: _____

Call toll free and order now.